WITHDRAWN
From Toronto Public Library

NETWORK PROGRAMMING IN CA-CLIPPER 5.2

PLEASE NOTE—USE OF THE DISK(S) AND THE PROGRAMS INCLUDED ON THE DISK(S) PACKAGED WITH THIS BOOK AND THE PROGRAM LISTINGS INCLUDED IN THIS BOOK IS SUBJECT TO AN END-USER LICENSE AGREEMENT (THE "AGREEMENT") FOUND AT THE BACK OF THE BOOK. PLEASE READ THE AGREEMENT CAREFULLY BEFORE MAKING YOUR PURCHASE DECISION. PURCHASE OF THE BOOK AND USE OF THE DISKS, PROGRAMS, AND PROGRAM LISTINGS WILL CONSTITUTE ACCEPTANCE OF THE AGREEMENT.

Network Programming in CA-Clipper 5.2

Joseph D. Booth
Greg Lief

Ziff-Davis Press
Emeryville, California

Development Editor	Jeff Green
Copy Editor	Janna Clark
Technical Reviewer	Cecilia Smith
Project Coordinator	Kim Haglund
Proofreader	Vanessa Miller
Cover Design	Carrie English
Cover Illustration	Carrie English
Book Design	Gary Suen
Technical Illustration	Cherie Plumlee Computer Graphics & Illustration
Word Processing	Howard Blechman, Cat Haglund, and Allison Levin
Page Layout	Anna Marks and M.D. Barrera
Indexer	Mark Kmetzko

This book was produced on a Macintosh IIfx, with the following applications: FrameMaker®, Microsoft® Word, MacLink®Plus, Aldus® FreeHand™, Adobe Photoshop™, and Collage Plus™.

Ziff-Davis Press
5903 Christie Avenue
Emeryville, CA 94608

Copyright © 1993 by Ziff-Davis Press. All rights reserved.

Ziff-Davis Press and ZD Press, are trademarks of Ziff Communications Company.

All other product names and services identified throughout this book are trademarks or registered trademarks of their respective companies. They are used throughout this book in editorial fashion only and for the benefit of such companies. No such uses, or the use of any trade name, is intended to convey endorsement or other affiliation with the book.

No part of this publication may be reproduced in any form, or stored in a database or retrieval system, or transmitted or distributed in any form by any means, electronic, mechanical photocopying, recording, or otherwise, without the prior written permission of Ziff-Davis Press, except as permitted by the Copyright Act of 1976 and the End-User License Agreement at the back of this book and except that program listings may be entered, stored, and executed in a computer system.

EXCEPT FOR THE LIMITED WARRANTY COVERING THE PHYSICAL DISK(S) PACKAGED WITH THIS BOOK AS PROVIDED IN THE END-USER LICENSE AGREEMENT AT THE BACK OF THIS BOOK, THE INFORMATION AND MATERIAL CONTAINED IN THIS BOOK ARE PROVIDED "AS IS," WITHOUT WARRANTY OF ANY KIND, EXPRESS OR IMPLIED, INCLUDING WITHOUT LIMITATION ANY WARRANTY CONCERNING THE ACCURACY, ADEQUACY, OR COMPLETENESS OF SUCH INFORMATION OR MATERIAL OR THE RESULTS TO BE OBTAINED FROM USING SUCH INFORMATION OR MATERIAL. NEITHER ZIFF-DAVIS PRESS NOR THE AUTHOR SHALL BE RESPONSIBLE FOR ANY CLAIMS ATTRIBUTABLE TO ERRORS, OMISSIONS, OR OTHER INACCURACIES IN THE INFORMATION OR MATERIAL CONTAINED IN THIS BOOK, AND IN NO EVENT SHALL ZIFF-DAVIS PRESS OR THE AUTHOR BE LIABLE FOR DIRECT, INDIRECT, SPECIAL, INCIDENTAL, OR CONSEQUENTIAL DAMAGES ARISING OUT OF THE USE OF SUCH INFORMATION OR MATERIAL.

ISBN 1-56276-119-6
Manufactured in the United States of America

10 9 8 7 6 5 4 3 2 1

This book is dedicated to my two chldren, JJ and Kellie! I love you both!
—Joe

This book is for my son, Justin, with my love.
—Greg

Contents at a Glance

	Foreword	xvii
	Introduction	xxi
1	Introduction to Networks	1
2	How Clipper Operates on a Network	28
3	Establishing a Network Library	56
4	Opening Files	74
5	File and Record Locking	102
6	Browsing Network Data	124
7	Using Configuration Files	144
8	Semaphores	164
9	The Novell Bindery: A Usable Database	182
10	Printing on a Network	220
11	Sending Messages across the Network	246
12	System Information	264
13	EMAIL Program User Reference	290
14	EMAIL Program Source Code	302
A	Function Reference	327
B	Sources for Further Information about Clipper and NetWare	406
C	Using the Disk Accompanying This Book	411
	Index	417

TABLE OF CONTENTS

Foreword — xvii
Introduction — xxi

Chapter 1   Introduction to Networks — 1
What is a Network? — 1
   The Personal Computer and DOS — 2
Network Hardware — 5
   Network Cards — 6
   Cabling — 7
   The File Server — 8
Network Software — 9
   Network Operating System — 9
Networks and Memory — 10
   Loading into High Memory — 10
   Other Memory Programs — 12
   Linking for More Memory — 13
Programming on a Network — 18
   The Efficient Secretary — 18
   Network Programming Guidelines — 23
Summary — 27

Chapter 2   How Clipper Operates on a Network — 28
.DBF Files — 29
Clipper .NTX Files — 31
   Bit 4-1: New Lock Offset Bit — 32
   Bit 0-1: Conditional Index Bit — 32
FoxPro .IDX and .CDX Files — 33

dBASE .NDX and .MDX Files	35
Using Index Files on a Network	37
Is My Index File Corrupt?	41
Index File Locking	43
Buffers	44
Clipper Work Areas	44
DOS Buffers	45
Network Buffers	45
What Happens When Clipper Talks to DOS	46
Opening Files	46
Locking Files	47
Clipper Commands and Functions for Accessing Files	48
APPEND BLANK / DBAPPEND()	49
COMMIT / DBCOMMIT() / DBCOMMITALL()	50
DELETE / DBDELETE()	51
FLOCK()	51
NETERR()	52
NETNAME()	53
RECALL / DBRECALL()	53
RLOCK()	53
SKIP / DBSKIP()	54
UNLOCK / DBUNLOCK() / DBUNLOCKALL()	54
USE … SHARED | EXCLUSIVE / DBUSEAREA()	55
Summary	55

Chapter 3   Establishing a Network Library   **56**

Enhancing Clipper's LOCKS Program	57
Configuration Files	65
Communicating with NetWare	66
Novell Application Program Interface (API)	66

Using the FT_INT86() Function to Access DOS Interrupts	67
NETWARE()—A Function to Call Novell's API	69
XLATE—A Program for Translating Functions between NetWare and Clipper	71
Summary	73

Chapter 4 Opening Files — 74

Opening .DBF Files	75
Does the File Exist?	76
Is the File a DBF?	76
Does the File Need a Memo File as Well?	77
File Attributes	80
Shared vs. Exclusive Mode	82
Opening Index Files	86
Creating Index Files on a Network	87
Is It an Index File?	87
OPENEM()—A File Opening Program	90
FIXEM()—A Function to Repair Open Errors If Possible	94
Using Alternate Device Drivers	99
Opening Other Types of Files	99
Summary	101

Chapter 5 File and Record Locking — 102

Levels of Locking	104
Exclusive Use	104
File Locking	105
The FLOCK() Function	107
Record Locking	107
Semaphore Locking	108

Clipper's Locking Mechanism	110
DOS and Locking	110
.DBF Locking	111
Index File Locking	111
Designing a Locking Strategy	112
Two Locking Considerations	112
Temporary Files and Multiple-Record Updates	113
Single-Record Updates	114
Locking Problems	116
Locking Multiple Records	116
Locking Text and Memory Files	117
Lunch-Time Locking	117
Summary	123

Chapter 6 Browsing Network Data   124

TBROWSE—A Quick Review	125
The TBROWSE:REFRESHALL() Exported Method	127
TBROWSE and Networks	131
TBROWSE() Example 1—An Accounting Application	131
Making the Application Network Aware	135
All Together Now	136
TBROWSE() Example 2—Monitoring a Telephone Process	139
Summary	143

Chapter 7 Using Configuration Files   144

What are Configuration Files?	145
Why Use a Configuration File?	146
Active Versus Passive Configuration Files	146
Working with Passive Configuration Files	147

Working with Active Configuration Files	153
Reading the System File	153
Example Using the System File	153
Summary	163

Chapter 8 Semaphores — 164

Why Use Semaphores?	165
Creating Semaphores in Clipper	166
Creating a Semaphore .DBF File	166
Accessing the Semaphore .DBF File	168
A Simple Semaphore Example	171
Accessing NetWare's Semaphore Services	171
Opening a Semaphore	172
Examining a Semaphore	173
Closing a Semaphore	174
Using a Semaphore	175
Two Semaphore Examples	176
Limiting the Number of Users	177
A Different Approach to Record Locking	178
Summary	180

Chapter 9 The Novell Bindery: A Usable Database — 182

What Is the Bindery?	183
Why Use the Bindery?	183
How the Bindery Is Organized	184
Objects	185
Properties	191
Property Values	195
Bindery Object Types	197
Users	197
Groups	201

Print Queues	205
File Servers	206
Other Object Types	208
Updating the Bindery Files	209
Bindery Object Functions	209
Object Property Functions	212
Working with Set Properties	215
Technical Overview of the Bindery	216
Bindery Files	216
Bindery Record Formats	217
Summary	218

Chapter 10 Printing on a Network — 220

Accessing a Network Printer	221
Using CAPTURE	222
Setting Printer Flags	227
Print Queues	233
Determining the Available Print Queues	233
Where Is the Job Being Printed?	234
Getting a List of Jobs in a Print Queue	234
Changing a Job's Queue Position	235
Removing a Job from the Print Queue	236
DOS Printing	237
Checking If PRINT.EXE Is Installed	237
Adding a File to the Print Queue	238
Removing a File from the Print Queue	239
Canceling All Files in the Print Queue	240
All Together Now: Functions for Printer Management	240
Summary	245

Chapter 11 Sending Messages across the Network — 246

Communicating between Clipper Applications — 247
    The Message File Structure — 247
    Retrieving a Message from the Message File — 248
    Wait States — 249
    Placing a Message into the Message File — 252
NetWare Messaging — 254
    Broadcast Messages — 254
    Pipe Messages — 257
Summary — 262

Chapter 12 System Information — 264

Making Contact with a File Server — 265
    Connection Tables — 266
    Attaching to Other Servers — 269
    Detaching from a File Server — 272
    Logging In and Out — 273
Workstation Information — 275
    Server Hierarchy — 275
    Information about This Connection — 278
    Determining the Network Shell Version — 280
File-Server Information — 281
    Checking Console Privileges — 281
    Determining the Current Login Status — 282
    Retrieving the Server Date and Time — 283
    Retrieving Network Installation Information — 284
    Miscellaneous Server Information — 285

Console Operations	287
Downing the File Server	287
Clearing a Connection	287
Setting the Server Date and Time	288
Summary	288

Chapter 13 EMAIL Program User Reference — 290

What Is Electronic Mail?	291
EMAIL Program Components	292
Checking Your Mail	292
Sending Mail	292
Reading Your Mail	292
EMAIL and the Network	292
Directory Structure	293
The EMAIL Program	293
Reading Mail	293
Sending Mail	296
Erasing Mail	297
Configuring the Mail System	297
The Pack/Index Option	298
Using the Mail System	299
Summary	300

Chapter 14 EMAIL Program Source Code — 302

Databases	303
Program Source Code	304
Summary	324

Appendix A	Function Reference	327
Appendix B	Sources for Further Information about Clipper and NetWare	406
Appendix C	Using the Disk Accompanying This Book	411
Index		417

Foreword

CA-Clipper has long provided the power and flexibility serious developers demand. Each version has introduced new features and given developers more power. CA-Clipper 5.2 is no exception. Full documentation of the Application Programming Interface (API), the addition of several new replaceable database drivers (RDDs), and multiple-record locking are just a few examples. Greater demands are being made on developers and CA-Clipper provides them with an application-development system powerful enough to keep up.

As organizations look to downsize applications, local area networks are becoming increasingly important. More and more developers today find themselves concerned with the intricacies of complex problems such as contention management, transaction control, and referential integrity. Put simply, application complexity is increasing. It's no longer enough to be satisfied that two or three users on a network can work simultaneously. Larger networks require attention to obscure details like speed optimization of locking protocols. Moreover, these LAN-based applications are becoming more critical to the operation of entire enterprises. These more advanced and sophisticated applications are more difficult to program.

Much has been written about programming in CA-Clipper, but Joe Booth and Greg Lief are the first to focus on network programming. *Network Programming in CA-Clipper 5.2* covers this very important topic comprehensively. It begins by discussing the most fundamental concepts and takes the reader smoothly through advanced programming techniques. The definition of terms associated with network programming provides a solid base upon which sophisticated concepts are built. The authors' experience as programmers, writers, and trainers is brought to bear, and readers benefit by their clear explanations and well thought-out examples. If you are programming for networks now, or plan to soon, this is the book for you.

Larry Eiss
Product Manager, CA-Clipper

Acknowledgments

We'd like to thank the following people for all their help in getting this book to your hands. Ceci Smith, for tireless reading and rereading of chapters and code to make sure that everything is technically correct. Jeff Green, for taking the drafts from us, moving them all over the earth, adding more red ink than our government uses, and somehow getting them back into page proofs. Kim Haglund, for taking our drafts, pen marks, and comments and suggestions, and making a printed page out of them. Rob Hannah, for helping unravel the mysteries of why Clipper locks an index file! Larry Eiss, for somehow making time in his schedule of promoting Clipper to read this book and offer some fine-tunings. And last, but not least, we'd like to thank our wives for putting up with another few months of not seeing their husbands.

Introduction

Welcome to *Network Programming in CA-Clipper 5.2*. This book attempts to provide guidance to those souls who wish to write robust multiuser Clipper applications. If you are content to merely place the required locks at the proper spots in your program, then this book may not be for you. If, however, you wish to take advantage of all that the network has to offer, then read on.

This is not an introduction to CA-Clipper nor a networking primer. The reader is assumed to be comfortable with Clipper and to know some basic networking concepts. What this book offers is some guidance on programming on the network, and a variety of functions to access the network resources.

The book begins with some discussion of network theory and how Clipper communicates with the network operating system. We also discuss problems that you may encounter in a network environment that do not occur when only one person is using an application. Along the way, we present some usable code to handle file opening and offer suggestions on how to address some of the problems that can arise.

After the theory is explained, we provide some code that permits you to communicate directly with the NetWare operating system from within your Clipper application. Do you need to print on a network printer? Access NetWare's semaphores or its bindery files? Or how about send messages between stations? All the code needed is right here in the book!

The code in this book was written for Clipper 5.2, although it will run equally well under Clipper 5.01. You should find this book filled with enough material to build a solid relationship between your Clipper application and the Novell network on which it runs.

So fire up your PC, load the network shell, and dig in. Before you know it, you will have your application running as smoothly on the network as it does on your single-user PC.

How this book is organized

In Chapter 1, we cover the basics of what a network is and how a personal computer can communicate with it. We also discuss some basic rules to keep in mind when you are writing a network application. These guidelines show how to reduce some of the network programming problems that can occur when more than one program wants to share data.

In Chapter 2, we explain how Clipper operates on a network. What really happens when you lock a file and what does COMMIT do? These are some of the topics that are covered. We also discuss those commands that need special consideration when running on a network.

In Chapter 3, we start our own network function library. We add some data-driven control parameters to the standard LOCKS.PRG and also explore NetWare's Application Program Interface. Since NetWare is one of the most popular network operating systems, we set up the functions to communicate directly with NetWare in this chapter.

In Chapter 4, we discuss how to open files. As Clipper expands the number of .DBF formats it can work with, the potential for conflicts and corrupted files increases. We will expand the basic NET_USE() function to accept a few additional parameters and we will add some extra checks to the basic file-opening routine.

In Chapter 5, we explain when you should lock files and/or records. We also talk about a strategy for determining the most appropriate locking level to use and Clipper's new multiple-record locks. Finally, we address some locking problems and offer solutions to them.

Chapter 6 discusses the TBROWSE object. We briefly review how TBROWSE is set up and then discuss how to keep it in touch with the network. We include two examples showing the flexibility that TBROWSE can offer in a network environment.

Chapter 7 covers configuration files, sets of externally stored parameters that can be used to control how programs operate. Passive configuration files are useful for setting colors and lock timings, and active configuration files allow changes to the configuration file to take place immediately. As an example of active configuration, we include an appointment function that can be controlled by a master program.

Chapter 8 covers semaphores, which are signals between two programs. We show how you can set up semaphores by using .DBF files, as well as how you can directly access NetWare's semaphore system. We end the chapter by showing a couple sample uses for semaphores.

Chapter 9 discusses NetWare's bindery, a database that contains information about all network objects, including users, groups, printers, servers, and so on. You can use the functions in this chapter to extract data from the bindery and update the bindery files.

Chapter 10 covers how to print on the network printers. We discuss the CAPTURE process that permits any application to print on a network, and provide functions to allow you to control the CAPTURE from within your

Clipper program. We also cover DOS's print queue and how to access it. We wrap up the chapter with a general-purpose printing routine that handles the selection of where to print, and then starts and finishes the print job. This routine transparently handles printing sent to the screen, a file, any local printer, or any network printer.

Chapter 11 discusses how to send messages between workstations and/or the file console. There are three methods for communicating between two running programs or workstations: One method uses a .DBF file to hold messages, while the other two are specific to NetWare. All three are covered in this chapter.

Chapter 12 covers how to connect to a file server and access the large amount of information available from it. You'll learn, for example, how to determine the server's name when you want to restrict your program to running on a single network.

Chapter 13 presents a complete e-mail application as an example of network programming. It includes many of the functions discussed in the book, illustrating how they can be used in your applications. It is also a basic, functioning e-mail application you can add to your Clipper programs.

Chapter 14 is the actual source code for the e-mail application described in Chapter 13. The source code is explained to make sure each network aspect is clearly understood.

By the time you've finished reading this book, you should be eager to find a network and start programming away. The many functions presented can serve as a solid networking library that allows you to take advantage of all the network has to offer.

 ## ABOUT THE DISK ACCOMPANYING THIS BOOK

The disk bound to the inside of the book's back cover contains the source code to the e-mail application and a library of over 100 networking functions, as well as the latest version of the Nanforum Toolkit, a freeware collection of Clipper functions. Please see Appendix C for more information on using the disk.

Introduction to Networks

WHAT IS A NETWORK?

NETWORK HARDWARE

NETWORK SOFTWARE

NETWORKS AND MEMORY

PROGRAMMING ON A NETWORK

Chapter 1

Networks are fast becoming the customary method of operations for personal computers. Many applications that in the past could run only on large-scale mainframe computers have been converted and are now running quite successfully on networked personal computers.

In this chapter, we will introduce basic network concepts and discuss how a personal computer communicates with a network. We will also discuss the hardware and software components of a network, how to manage memory on a network, and some fundamental programming concepts for networks.

WHAT IS A NETWORK?

A network is a group of computers that share resources. The most commonly shared resources are hard-disk drives and printers. In most networks, one computer acts as the *network server*, which means that its hard drive (and all files thereupon) are available to the other computers. These other computers are called *workstations*. In addition, the parallel and serial ports on the server computer are made available to the workstations for printing, which means that all the computers on the network can use the same printer(s).

The workstations can be personal computers, complete with hard drives and printers of their own, or they can be diskless computer terminals that have keyboards and monitors, but no hard-disk storage capabilities.

THE PERSONAL COMPUTER AND DOS

How can a computer designed for a single person share its data? After all, PCs were not designed to be linked together (and some people feel they never should be!). Yet somehow, through a magic combination of hardware and software, they can indeed be linked together to great advantage. In order to understand some of the principles, let's first explore the DOS operating system.

The DOS operating system is a piece of software that coordinates the operations of all the hardware components of your computer system. Users enter commands through the keyboard, and then DOS interprets these commands and issues the appropriate instructions to the hardware. For example, when you enter a simple DOS command to print a file, DOS sends an instruction to the disk to read the file and then sends an instruction to the printer port to print the file. These services are designed into the operating system and made available to PC users.

DOS also makes these services available to application programs through a series of interrupts. An *interrupt* is a piece of code that performs any of the DOS services. These functions have a specific syntax and are available to almost every DOS-compatible compiler. Clipper is a DOS-compatible compiler, and thus can use interrupts to access the DOS services.

In the Summer '87 version, Clipper introduced low-level file functions. While this was a breakthrough in Xbase language, it wasn't exactly a complex piece of coding. DOS provides an internal function (number 61, to be exact) that opens a file and returns a handle. We will not yet go into the details of how to call an interrupt, but the DOS function needs the file name and the access mode. It returns a numeric handle to be used by other DOS functions to work with the file. The Clipper syntax to open a low-level file is

< nHandle> := Fopen(<cFilename>,<nAccess_mode>)

If we could examine the source code for Clipper's FOPEN() function, we would see that the parameters are taken from Clipper and placed into registers. Function 61 (Open File) is then called and voilà ... a file handle is returned. The FOPEN() function also checks whether an error occurred, and if so returns the error value to Clipper.

As with FOPEN(), the other Clipper low-level file functions merely place your Clipper parameters into registers and call the underlying DOS functions. Table 1.1 shows the Clipper low-level file commands and the DOS functions that they call.

Table 1.1: File Functions

Clipper Command	DOS Function
FCLOSE()	62 (hex 3E) Close File Handle
FCREATE()	60 (hex 3C) Create File
FOPEN()	61 (hex 3D) Open File
FREAD()	63 (hex 3F) Read from File or Device
FSEEK()	66 (hex 42) Move File Pointer
FWRITE()	64 (hex 40) Write to File or Device

You may not be familiar with these functions, but you are undoubtedly working with them. For example, whenever you apply the USE command to a .DBF file, Clipper converts that USE command into a call to the DOS Open File function. When you close a database, Clipper converts that command into DOS function 62 (Close File Handle). The DOS functions are probably called numerous times within your Clipper program.

All Clipper's file requests (reading, writing, movement, and so on) are passed to DOS. Fortunately, the designers of DOS built a very flexible system. They made every available DOS service totally replaceable. Each function has a number of parameters and returns a specific value. Programs that use the DOS functions pass the required parameters and expect certain results; they do not know anything about the code that actually gets executed. (This is known as a *black box routine.*) As long as the routine obeys the rules that DOS specifies, it has the flexibility to do anything it needs to, including directing file I/O away from a local disk to a network interface card. It is this flexibility that allows a computer designed for a single person to suddenly become a network workstation.

DOS interrupts In order to get DOS to open a file for you, you need to set up some registers and perform an interrupt. As mentioned, an *interrupt* is a command to the computer to immediately stop what it is doing and to do something else for you. In Clipper terms, the concept is very similar to calling a Clipper function. Listing 1.1 shows a simple Clipper program that calls the ACHOICE() function.

Listing 1.1: Clipper Program That Calls the ACHOICE() Function

```
procedure main
local x := 1
do while ! empty(x)
   x := achoice(5,5,15,25, { "Open customer file", ;
                             "Browse the customers",;
                             "Close the file" } )
   do case
   case x == 1
      if select("customer") == 0
         use customer new
      else
         alert("Customer file already open!")
      endif
   case x == 2
      select customer
      browse(5,5,20,75)         // another Clipper function
   case x == 3
      close databases
   endcase
enddo
return
```

When the code in Listing 1.1 is executed, the computer performs the steps sequentially. When the ACHOICE() function call is reached, the program jumps to the address where the ACHOICE() code is stored, executes the function, and then returns to the next line of code in procedure MAIN().

To open a file, you issue interrupt 33 (21H) and tell the computer to perform function 61 (Open File). Interrupt 33 is the DOS services interrupt. Somewhere in DOS memory is a segment of machine code that tells the computer how to open a file; by requesting the interrupt, we are asking DOS to find that piece of code and execute it. We give DOS the parameters, and it executes the code and returns a value.

In DOS programming, these interrupts do not have names, but rather numbers. How does DOS determine which piece of code to execute? It looks up the number in an *interrupt table*. This is a fixed-size table stored in the first memory locations in the computer's random-access memory (RAM). It is exactly 4,096 bytes long, and consists of memory addresses for each of the interrupts. When an interrupt is requested, the computer determines the interrupt address from this table. It saves the current location and then jumps to the code location pointed to by the interrupt table. Then, it executes the code for that interrupt and returns control to the original location.

DOS flexibility   The designers of DOS decided that, in order to provide maximum flexibility, they would allow a programmer to change the interrupt table. Most of the DOS interrupts, including interrupt 33, can have their table entries changed. By changing an entry in the table, a programmer can cause the computer to execute his or her piece of code instead of executing the normal DOS routine. This means that a program can change the functionality of DOS: As long as the new routine accepts the parameters and returns the proper value, the calling program has no way of knowing whether DOS or some other program performed the requested service.

With this level of control available, a program could easily redirect all DOS file requests (60 through 66, for example) to its own routines. While the standard DOS services translate file requests into the action of accessing the hard disk, a modified set might redirect all file access elsewhere. By changing these DOS addresses, a piece of software can change a single-user computer into a network workstation.

To access a network, a piece of software is run on the computer we wish to use as a workstation. This software changes some of the DOS interrupts to its own routines so that the network can communicate with programs running on the workstation. (We will talk more about this software later in this chapter.)

We have seen how, in theory, a personal computer can act as a network workstation. However, we must keep in mind that every computer we intend to use as a workstation will need some additional hardware and software components in order to access the network. In the next few sections, we will discuss these components in more detail.

NETWORK HARDWARE

Suppose we have installed the network software on the workstation and that it, rather than DOS, is handling our file requests. That's great, but the question is, "What exactly is the network software doing with these requests?" To answer that question, we have to talk about hardware.

Unfortunately for us software people, networks need just as much hardware as they do software, so we need to become familiar with some hardware components. (But the nice thing is that you can now blame the hardware if a problem occurs. After all, hardware people usually blame the software!) Figure 1.1 illustrates the hardware setup needed to access a network through a personal computer.

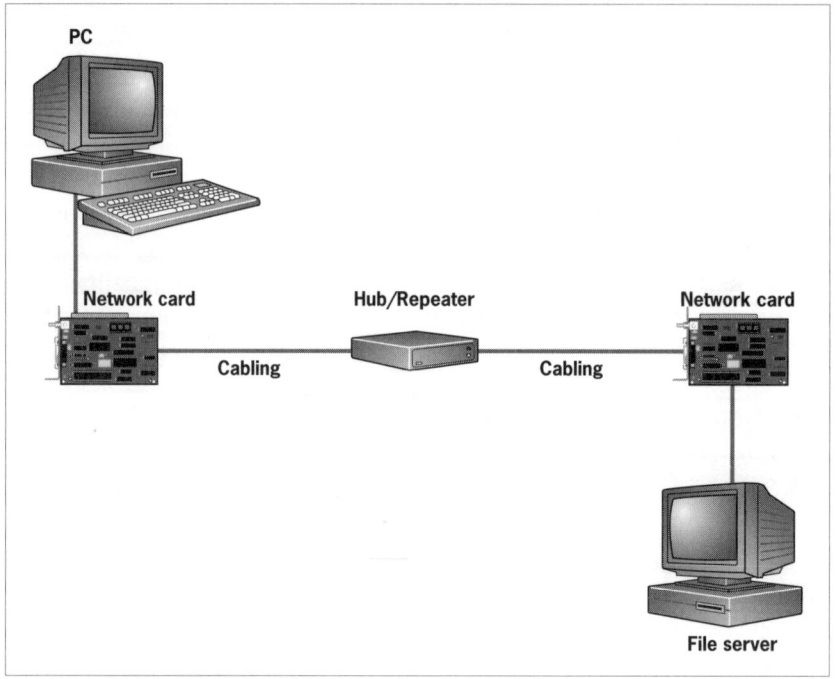

Figure 1.1: Network hardware setup

NETWORK CARDS

If you look in the back of the average PC, you will not find anywhere to hook a cable. You will need a network card, which serves as an interface between the PC and the cable. The network card is an add-in board that occupies one slot in your computer. On the back of the card is an outlet where you connect the cable. This card contains the necessary hardware to translate disk requests from a computer to packets of information sent along the cabling. Usually, each network card will also have a physical address that can be set by switches. This allows the server to uniquely identify each workstation. A network card is also present in the server for the same purpose, converting disk activity into cable traffic.

The network card is also called a network interface card (or NIC). The type of card will vary, depending upon the type of cabling. Every computer in the network will need a network card to access the cabling that connects to the file server.

CABLING

The cable is the thread that connects all the components together. It serves as the conduit for data passed between the workstations and the file server. Many kinds of cabling can be used, depending upon the environment at the network site. When installing a network, be sure that the cable and connectors are good, high-quality components. Cheap connectors or cabling can cause all sorts of problems that will be hard to detect and isolate.

Twisted-pair cable   Twisted-pair cabling is one of the least expensive cabling methods available. It consists of two wires twisted together and wrapped in shielding. Most commercial telephone wiring is of the twisted-pair variety, although twisted-pair cabling for data communications must meet more stringent specifications. Data-grade twisted-pair wiring might also have additional external shielding.

Twisted-pair wiring offers good throughput, but is somewhat susceptible to electromagnetic interference. If the network uses twisted-pair wiring, cables should be no more than 100 yards long, and should be installed to avoid any sources of electronic noise (such as fluorescent lights, elevator motors, and so on).

Coaxial cable   A coaxial cable usually consists of a shielded copper cable surrounded by a plastic casing. A second wire casing is wrapped around the interior plastic casing, and the entire cable is then wrapped in shielding. The cable is terminated at each end by a BNC connector.

This type of cable is most frequently used with ArcNet or EtherNet, and it offers good speed and good data protection. The type of coaxial cable used by ArcNet is called RG-62, and that used by EtherNet is called RG-58.

Fiber optic cable   Fiber optic cables transmit data as a beam of light. While this is a fast transmission method, reliability and distance are the main reasons why fiber optic cabling is used; it is feasible to connect nodes on a network using fiber optic cable over a mile long. Fiber optic cable also does not pick up static or energy from external sources.

In addition to these assets, fiber optic cables are also very secure. It is possible to tap into a coaxial cable and read the data being sent over it, since the cabling radiates electronic signals as it transmits them; in fact, you can even read the signal from outside the cable. A fiber optic cabling system is much more controlled, however, since light does not leak out of the cable, nor can the cable be tapped into without breaking the connection. Hence fiber optic cable is often used in situations where security is extremely important.

Hubs and repeaters   Depending upon the network configuration and the distance between each workstation and the server, a hub or repeater may be necessary. There are two kinds of hubs available: active and passive. An active hub boosts the signal from the cable and passes it along, whereas a passive hub merely passes the signal on. Hubs are used with ArcNet cards and cabling.

A repeater serves the same purpose as an active hub for EtherNet cards and cabling. Both a repeater and a hub have ports to connect to the cables that run into them. These allow a single cable from the server to service multiple workstations.

THE FILE SERVER

The server is the primary computer in your system. It controls the shared resources and handles the data requests. These resources—the server's hard disk and printers—are monitored and made available to other computers by the network. Most servers have large hard disks and lots of RAM. In order to keep performance good, the RAM is used to buffer disk requests.

A server may be *dedicated*, which means that only the network operating system runs on it, or it may be *nondedicated*, which means that the server can function as both a server and a workstation. A nondedicated server has twice the work to do and is usually used only in smaller networks.

> **Note:** When a Clipper application is run on nondedicated server, other functions of the server, particularly printing, may suffer significant performance degradation. This is due to the fact that the server is waiting for idle time in the Clipper program in order to perform its background processes. Since Clipper programs make use of idle time to perform various internal tasks, the server never detects idle time from the Clipper application, and hence, never gives any time to the background programs. In order to allow Clipper programs to run a little less selfishly on a nondedicated server, Clipper includes a replacement terminal library called NOVTERM. While use of this library will slow your application down, it does allow the server to process its background tasks. If you are writing a program to run on a nondedicated server, you should link in the NOVTERM library. To include this library in your application, you must include the GT.OBJ file with your other object files and specify NOVTERM.LIB instead of TERMINAL.LIB when you link. Because performance will degrade, you should only use NOVTERM when absolutely necessary.

As you can see in Figure 1.1, the file server also requires a network adapter card and access to the cabling.

NETWORK SOFTWARE

In addition to the hardware, several software programs must be run to coordinate communications between the workstation and the file server. This section describes these software components.

NETWORK OPERATING SYSTEM

The network operating system is run on the file-server computer. Its primary function is to accept data requests from the workstations and to respond by providing the requested data or results. Most network operating systems can also handle printers and other peripherals, and have extensive built-in security systems.

Although the server runs the network operating system, it is rarely used to its full capacity. When a Clipper program requests data from the network, the network sends *all* the data to the workstation, which then is required to pull out the data it needs. In a client/server relationship, however, the server will become a more intelligent piece of hardware. Instead of just shuffling data around, the server will analyze data requests and send only the appropriate subset of data. If the server selects the needed data, it stands to reason that less data will be sent from the server to the workstation. This greatly improves throughput.

IPX protocol   IPX (or Internet Packet Exchange) is a protocol that transmits data through cables between workstations. The IPX file contains the software to handle the data transmissions. The IPX software implements simple communication capabilities that provide the minimum service for network traffic between the network shell (NETX, discussed below) and the adapter board.

For most applications, IPX is sufficient. However, a superset of commands and functionality called SPX can be added to IPX. Among other things, SPX can confirm that data that was transmitted has been received.

Network shell programs   Most networks have what is known as a *network shell*, which is the program that remaps the DOS file-access routines to its own code. Some network shells also remap DOS printer routines, date and time services, and so on. In this manner, the network can seem transparent to a wide variety of applications running on the workstation.

For example, the network shell for Novell networks is a program called NETX. If we examine the memory map for a workstation with the shell installed, it appears as follows:

MCB	PSP	Files	Bytes	Owner	Hooked Interrupts
09C3	0008	0	7840	Config	
0BAE	0BAF	0	3376	Command	22 23 2E
0C82	0000	0	48	Command	
1091	1096	1	39312	NETX	1B 20 21 24 27 CE CF F0

You can see that the NETX shell program has taken DOS interrupt 21H (33 decimal) and remapped it. This means that all DOS service requests will be passed to the shell for processing. The network shell also takes over the DOS fatal-error and program-termination interrupts. You will also notice that the network shell uses some of DOS's memory, thus making less available for your Clipper application. (In the next section, we will discuss how to maximize the amount of memory available for your Clipper application.)

NETX is the current release of the shell that works with all versions of DOS. There are older versions called NET3, NET4, and NET5, which work with DOS 3.0, 4.0, and 5.0, respectively. There are also versions of the network shell that work in expanded memory. See Appendix C for more information.

Networks and memory

DOS Version 5.0 and other products, such as QRAM, allow the network shell to be loaded into memory above the 640K available to DOS. If your application is tight on memory before going to the network, consider obtaining software to place the shell into high memory. DOS Version 5.0 also allows you to load DOS itself into high memory. These measures will leave more of the base 640K RAM for your Clipper application.

LOADING INTO HIGH MEMORY

The ability to load programs into memory above the 640K limit can mean a dramatic increase in the amount of memory available for your Clipper application. Table 1.2 and Table 1.3 represent two memory maps. The first one has the network software installed in the 640K base memory, and the second uses DOS's LOADHIGH program to place the network software above the 640K limit. You will see that the second option increases memory available to your Clipper program by 55,000 bytes.

Table 1.2: Network Software in Conventional Memory

Name	Size in Decimal
MSDOS	16,544 (16.2K)
COMMAND	3,392 (3.3K)
IPX	16,656 (16.3K)
NETX	43,728 (42.7K)
FREE	64 (0.1K)
FREE	574,976 (561.4K)
Total FREE:	**575,040 (561.5K)**

Largest executable program size:	**574,976 (561.4K)**

Table 1.3: Using DOS 5.0's LOADHIGH Program

Conventional Memory

Name	Size in Decimal
MSDOS	16,544 (16.2K)
HIMEM	1,072 (1.0K)
EMM386	3,232 (3.2K)
COMMAND	3,392 (3.3K)
FREE	64 (0.1K)
FREE	630,768 (616.0K)
Total FREE:	**630,832 (616.1K)**

Upper Memory Blocks

Name	Size in Decimal
SYSTEM	167,472 (163.5K)
IPX	16,656 (16.3K)
NETX	43,728 (42.7K)

Table 1.3: Using DOS 5.0's LOADHIGH Program (Continued)

Upper Memory Blocks

Name	Size in Decimal
FREE	64 (0.1K)
FREE	32,768 (32.0K)
FREE	1,344 (1.3K)
Total FREE:	**34,176 (33.4K)**
Largest executable program size:	630,768 (616.0K)

CONFIG.SYS requirements   To use high memory, you need to load the high-memory device drivers and then specify that DOS should be placed into the high-memory area. Here's the setup you'll need in your CONFIG.SYS file:

```
DEVICE=C:\DOS\HIMEM.SYS
DEVICE=C:\DOS\EMM386.EXE NOEMS
DOS=HIGH,UMB
```

You can obtain more details about CONFIG.SYS in your DOS manual. If Microsoft Windows is installed on the workstation, you might also need to specify different device drivers.

Adding LOADHIGH to AUTOEXEC.BAT   Once the high-memory device drivers are loaded, any network software can be loaded into high memory using DOS's LOADHIGH command. Here is a simple AUTOEXEC.BAT file that loads the network shell and IPX programs into high memory:

```
@ECHO OFF
LOADHIGH C:\NETWORK\IPX
LOADHIGH C:\NETWORK\NETX
```

If you do not want your users to boot directly into the network, you can make a separate batch file to load the network software. Keep in mind that if the software cannot be loaded into high memory, DOS will place the software into conventional memory below the 640K limit.

OTHER MEMORY PROGRAMS

DOS 5.0 is not alone in its ability to move programs into memory above the 640K limit. Two popular programs, QuarterDeck's QEMM and Qualitas's

386Max, also provide memory configuration. If you are in a network environment, it is worthwhile to explore ways to maximize available memory for Clipper, which can use every bit of memory it can find.

LINKING FOR MORE MEMORY

In addition to configuring DOS to maximize available memory, you can also customize your link scripts to minimize the amount of memory that your Clipper application requires. The degree of reduction and the methods to use vary, depending upon the linker. These options are described in this section, although you should refer to your linker's manual for more detail.

Overlays   When a linker combines your object files to create an executable file, it can place each object file in either the root area or an overlay. Object files in the root always remain in memory while the program is running. Object modules in the overlay section are not loaded into memory when you first execute the program—instead, they are loaded from disk as necessary.

When linking, it is important to remember that there are two sources of object files to be placed into the executable file. The first source consists of the actual compiled program files, and the second consists of the library files that the program refers to. Remember that an .LIB file is nothing more than a collection of .OBJ files bundled into a more convenient package.

To reduce the amount of memory your application needs, you should increase the amount of code placed in the overlay area. If your code is entirely Clipper code, the only program in the root should be a one-line program that calls the main application from the overlay area. Listing 1.2 shows an example.

Listing 1.2: Minimize Root Code Example

```
* Program:   STUB.PRG
* Notes..:   This program gets placed into the root area,
*            while the program file containing CustUpdate()
*            should be placed in the overlay area.
**************
procedure main
CustUpdate()
return



* Program:   MAIN.PRG
* Notes..:   This is the main program of the application and
*            is placed into an overlay to minimize the memory
```

Listing 1.2: Minimize Root Code Example (Continued)

```
*           requirements of the application.
**************
function CustUpdate()
//
// Open files, update customers, etc.
//
return NIL
```

Several linkers are available for use with Clipper, and each has its own syntax for moving modules into the overlay area. These linkers require you to create a link script and add commands to move .OBJ files into the overlay area. You will also need to use commands to place modules from your .LIB files into the overlay area. These commands are briefly discussed here, although to fully optimize memory you should also refer to your linker's documentation.

When preparing an overlay strategy, you must determine which code can be overlaid and which code must remain in the root. Third-party libraries available for Clipper fall into three categories: (1) entirely overlayable, (2) entirely nonoverlayable, or (3) partially overlayable. In the third case, the manufacturer will generally provide two libraries required at link time. The smaller one is usually placed into the root and the other library can be placed into the overlay.

If the library consists entirely of Clipper code, you should be able to overlay it. Libraries that consist of C or Assembler modules will have to be reviewed to determine their ability to be overlaid. If the C or assembly library is "well-behaved"—that is, if it uses Clipper's published Extend System interface—it probably can be overlaid. If the library handles interrupts, it must be in the root. Trying to determine the placement of libraries can be a time-consuming practice, but fortunately many third-party vendors will provide instructions for overlaying their libraries.

RTLink   RTLink is the linker that is shipped with Clipper. PocketSoft also publishes a commercial version of RTLink that supports many languages besides Clipper.

To overlay object files created by Clipper, you use the BEGINAREA and ENDAREA commands. These commands form a control structure that marks the beginning and ending of an overlay area. Within the structure, you use the

SECTION FILE command to specify the individual .OBJ files to place in the overlay. Here is an example of a link script:

```
FILE stub
BEGINAREA
    SECTION FILE main
    SECTION FILE reports
    SECTION FILE maint
ENDAREA
```

In addition to the SECTION FILE command, RTLink also has a SECTION MODULE command. This command is used to extract .OBJ files from a specified library and place them into the overlay area. To use this command in RTLink, you must first specify the library name outside of the BEGINAREA/ENDAREA structure and then specify the module names within the structure. Following is an example of a link script that uses both SECTION FILE and SECTION MODULE:

```
FILE stub

LIB reports
BEGINAREA
    # These are compiled Clipper programs
    SECTION FILE main
    SECTION FILE reports
    SECTION FILE maint
    # These are OBJ files found in the REPORTS.LIB
    SECTION MODULE PickPrnt
    SECTION MODULE QueryIt
    SECTION MODULE Display
ENDAREA
```

You can also use RTLink to place modules from the Clipper libraries into the overlay area. For example, if you want to place MEMOEDIT() into an overlay, instead of the root, you could include the commands shown in the following listing to force MEMOEDIT() and family into an overlay:

```
BEGINAREA
    SECTION MODULE memoedit, memoread, memotran
    SECTION MODULE memowrit, memoline
    SECTION MODULE mlpos, mlcount
ENDAREA
```

If you have a library manager, you can use its output to help you determine module names for inclusion in overlays. While it is tempting to overlay all the Clipper libraries, keep in mind that your performance can deteriorate if frequently called code always has to be loaded from the overlay. We suggest that you place into an overlay only modules that will be called infrequently. For example, if your application uses TBrowse extensively and you place the TBrowse modules in the overlay, performance will slow to an excruciating crawl.

Blinker   Blinker is another third-party general-purpose linker that handles many languages. It is published by Assembler Software Manufacturers, Inc., and can be used for either Summer '87 code or Clipper 5.0 code.

The syntax for Blinker is very similar to that for RTLink. To overlay object files created by Clipper, you use the BEGINAREA/ENDAREA pair to mark the beginning and ending of an overlay area. Within the structure, you use the FILE command to specify the individual .OBJ files to place in the overlay. If a library is pure Clipper code, you can also use the ALLOCATE command to place all necessary modules from that library into an overlay. Here is a sample Blinker link script:

```
FILE stub
BEGINAREA
    FILE main
    FILE reports
    FILE maint
    # Three fully overlayable libraries
    ALLOCATE grump
    ALLOCATE clipwks5
    ALLOCATE extend
ENDAREA
```

Like RTLink, Blinker has a MODULE command that allows you to extract .OBJ files from a specified library and place them into the overlay area. To use this command, you need to specify the library name outside of the BEGINAREA/ENDAREA structure and then specify the module names within the structure. Here is an example of a link script that uses ALLOCATE, FILE, and MODULE to reduce memory usage:

```
FILE stub
BEGIN SECTION
    FILE main
    FILE reports
    FILE maint
    # Three fully overlayable libraries
    ALLOCATE grump
    ALLOCATE clipwks5
    ALLOCATE extend
    # Extract OBJ from the reports library
```

```
    MODULE PickPrnt
    MODULE QueryIt
    MODULE Display
END SECTION
LIB reports
```

You can also use Blinker to place modules from the Clipper libraries into the overlay area. For example, if you want to place the various array-handling functions into an overlay (rather than the root, where they would ordinarily reside), you could include the following commands:

```
BEGINAREA
    MODULE acopy, adel, aeval, ains, atail
ENDAREA
```

Keep in mind the aforementioned caveat about performance of overlaid modules.

Blinker also comes with link scripts that you can use to automatically place varying amounts of the Clipper libraries into the overlay areas.

WarpLink   WarpLink is a third-party general-purpose linker that handles many languages, including Clipper. It is published by Hyperkinetix, Inc. and can be used for either Summer '87 code or Clipper 5.0 code.

WarpLink's syntax is very different from either RTLink or Blinker, but is similar to many other linkers. To overlay object files created by Clipper, you need to enclose the overlayable files in parentheses and specify that the overlay manager code is to be included in the root. Here is an example of a WarpLink script:

```
/st:3000/mx/i/xt/r/op:50/ox/clp5 +
stub+(main)+(reports)+(maint)+c5ovlmgr,,
clipper+terminal+dbfntx+(extend)+(grump)+(clipwks5)
```

In this script, MAIN, REPORTS, and MAINT are all Clipper-compiled .OBJ files that are placed into the overlay area. CLIPPER, TERMINAL, and DBFNTX are nonoverlayable Clipper libraries, and EXTEND, GRUMP, and CLIPWKS5 are libraries that can be placed into the overlay area.

You can also use WarpLink to place modules from the Clipper libraries into the overlay area. For example, if you wanted to place all input commands into an overlay (instead of the root), you could include the following commands to force the ACCEPT, READVAR, and GETSYS code into your overlay:

```
(CLIPPER:_accept)+(CLIPPER:_getsys)+;
    (CLIPPER:_readvar)
```

It can be debated that, for many applications, overlaying the GET System (GETSYS) would cause major performance problems. However, imagine a program that collects information only once from the user and then spends the rest of its time processing that information. In this type of application, slower performance during the collection of information is acceptable, since it allows more memory to be used for the program's main process. This shows the tremendous flexibility and consideration required when you are trying to reduce your program's memory requirements by overlaying portions of the Clipper libraries.

Programming on a network

Programming on a network can best be described as the art of designing systems to circumvent Murphy's Laws. One of these laws states that if something can go wrong, it will do so, and at the worst possible moment.

In order to understand the programming considerations for a network environment, we first need to have a brief understanding of what the network operating system is doing for us.

The Efficient Secretary

An analogy I find useful is to think of the network as a massive filing cabinet. In front of this filing cabinet is a single dedicated secretary. His name is Jake; he is 6' 2" and weighs in at 250 pounds, so you are not going to get anything from the files unless he lets you.

In order to access the file cabinet, you have to tell Jake what you want to use and how you want to use it. Unfortunately, Jake's vocabulary is very limited, so you have to tell him exactly what you want in precisely the right terms.

May I have a file, please?   In order to access any information in the filing cabinet, you have to tell Jake the name of the file you want, and whether other people can use it while you are working with it. You do this with the USE command.

```
USE <file_name> EXCLUSIVE (or SHARED)
```

The Clipper USE command instructs Jake to let you work with a file. If you do not want anybody else to use the file, you should request that the file be EXCLUSIVE. If you can let other people work with it also, tell Jake to let the file be SHARED.

Jake determines if he can give you the file by first checking his list to see if anyone else is using it. If nobody else is using the file, it's all yours. Jake writes your name on his pad of paper next to the file. If someone else wants to use the file,

Jake checks his pad of paper. When he discovers your name next to the file, he checks to see if you are using the file exclusively. If not, he then asks the other person if they are willing to share the file or if they need it exclusively. If you are both willing to share, Jake lets the other person have the file. If either of you refuse to share, Jake will not give the second person the file until the first person is finished with it. "First come, first served" is Jake's motto when it comes to files.

Checking for errors with NETERR()   Now that we know how to ask Jake for files, we need to know how to figure out his answer. Unfortunately, since USE is a command rather than a function and commands do not return values, we cannot expect a direct answer. However, we *can* ask the NETERR() function whether an error occurred. If NETERR() says yes, and the previous statement was a USE command, you can be certain that the error occurred because Jake would not let you have the file. The following example shows how the USE command is checked before the operation continues:

```
USE customer EXCLUSIVE    // Jake, may I use the CUSTOMER
                          // file all by myself please?
if .not. neterr()         // Jake said OK!
   // Do something with
   // the file
else                      // Jake said NO!
   // Tell the end-user
   // Jake said NO
endif
```

Each and every time you open a .DBF file in a network environment, you must check the NETERR() function to make sure that you were successful. If you were unsuccessful, you can either wait a few seconds and try again, or do something different that does not need that file.

Let's look at a practical example of opening a file on a network with a ten-second wait period for each file. Listing 1.3 shows a sample method of opening files.

For an actual application, you would probably pass the array to the OPEN_EM() function and continue the program only if all your files were opened successfully. Here is an example:

```
if open_em( flist_ )
   // Main menu
else
   Alert( "Files are unavailable.." )
endif
close databases
```

Listing 1.3: Sample Method of Opening Files

```
#define DATABASE   1
#define INDEX      2
function open_em
//              DBF file      Index file(s)
//              ---------     ---------------
local flist_ :={ {"CUSTOMER", {"CUST1","CUST2"}},;
                 {"VENDOR"  , {"VEND1"}},;
                 {"PARTS"   , {"PART1","PART2"}}  }
local jj
local kk
local lReturn := .T.
local nWait
local nIndexes
local nFiles := len(flist_)
begin sequence
   for jj := 1 to nFiles
      nWait := 10
      use (flist_[jj, DATABASE]) new shared
      if neterr()                        // Didn't open it ok
         do while neterr() .and. nWait > 0  // Let's try a
            inkey(1)                     // few more times
            nWait--                      // before giving up
            use (flist_[jj, DATABASE]) new shared
         enddo
         if neterr()                     // Still couldn't
            lReturn := .F.                // open the file
            break
         endif
      endif
      dbclearindex()
      nIndexes := len(flist_[jj, INDEX])
      for kk := 1 to nIndexes
         dbsetindex( flist_[jj, INDEX, kk] )
      next
   next
recover
   alert("Could not open " + flist_[jj, DATABASE])
end sequence
return lReturn
```

Notice that in OPEN_EM() the indexes are not opened until after we know that we have successfully opened the file. If you use the INDEX option with the USE command, such as

```
use CUSTOMER new shared index cust1, cust2
```

what happens if the USE command fails? We don't know if we'd like the idea of having index files opened without a corresponding database. If you are programming for a network, do yourself a favor and forget about the INDEX keyword on the USE command. You and your computer (and Jake) will be much happier!

In Chapter 3, we will show a function that you can use to handle all file opening operations.

Exclusive vs. shared files   Why would you want to open a file exclusively? Most of the time, you won't want to. After all, nobody else can use the file until you are done. (If you have a sadistic streak, you could code an application to randomly open files exclusively so that the hapless clerk could unknowingly lock out the president of the company.) The main reason to open a file exclusively is if you need to use it with any of the following three Clipper commands: PACK, REINDEX, and ZAP. You should avoid REINDEX like the plague, since it will not correct corrupt index files. PACK and ZAP commands are used very infrequently, so your need for exclusive use of a file should be equally infrequent.

OK, I've got the file open   Once your USE command is successful, you can perform one of two general operations: (1) read information from the database, or (2) write information to it. From Clipper's view of the network, the only time you need to lock the file or a portion of the file is when you need to write to it. Yet there are times when locks are needed even though you are not writing to the file.

Locks? What are locks?   Remember Jake? In addition to opening the files for you, he will also allow you to change the file's contents. However, he will allow only one person to change a file (or a record from the file) at a time. Jake does this by maintaining a lock table. This area of memory in the network operating system lists all sections of the filing cabinet that currently are reserved by some user. Each user may have one of two types of locks active: (1) a file lock, or (2) a record lock. Your program may have (at most) one lock per work area at any given time.

You can mix file locks and record locks in separate work areas. For example, you might have a file lock on the CUSTOMER database at the same time you have a lock on the fifteenth record in the PARTS database.

An entry in the lock table prevents any other users from writing to that file or record. Other users may still read from the file, but cannot update the data in a locked record.

File locks   Locking a file is similar to obtaining exclusive use of a file for a brief period of time. No other users can update any information in the file until you release the lock. A significant difference between a file lock and exclusive use is that other users can continue to read information from a locked file. They cannot change it, however.

Locking an entire file should be done judiciously. If you need to change only a single record, file locking is definite overkill. If you need to change multiple records as part of one process, then Clipper will require a file lock. Here is an example of an unneeded file lock:

```
// File lock here is overkill
select customer
if flock()
   goto 15
   replace customer->name with "Grumpfish"
   unlock
endif
// File lock here is required
select customer
if flock()
   replace all customer->status with "LATE" ;
           for customer->age > 30 .and.      ;
           customer->balance > 0.0
   unlock
endif
```

A file lock should be used only when more than one record will be affected by your operation. Remember that if you lock a file, no one else can update that file until you are done.

The FLOCK() function in Clipper attempts to obtain a file lock for the current work area. It makes one attempt and returns a logical value indicating the success or failure of the attempt.

You can easily expand FLOCK() to wait ten seconds before giving up, by writing a user-defined function that calls it repeatedly. The FILELOCK()

function below accepts a numeric parameter indicating how many seconds to keep attempting to lock the file.

```
function FileLock(nWait)
if nWait == NIL
   nWait := 10
endif
do while .not. flock() .and. nWait > 0   // Let's try a few
   inkey(1)                               // more times before
   nWait--                                // giving up
enddo
return flock()
```

Record locks A record lock allows you to update a single record in the database. It also denies any other user the ability to update that record until you release the lock. As with file locks, another user can read a locked record—he or she simply cannot change it. Any time you need to update only one record, use the record lock to avoid interfering with other users.

The RLOCK() function in Clipper attempts to obtain a record lock for the current work area. It makes one attempt and returns a logical value indicating the success or failure of the attempt.

As with the FLOCK() example shown above, it is simple to write a function that will attempt to lock a record repeatedly. The RECORDLOCK() function below accepts a numeric parameter indicating how many seconds to keep trying to lock the record.

```
function RecordLock(nWait)
if nWait == NIL
   nWait := 10
endif
do while .not. rlock() .and. nWait > 0   // Let's try a few
   inkey(1)                               // more times before
   nWait--                                // giving up
enddo
return rlock()
```

In Chapter 5, we will discuss file and record locks in much greater detail.

NETWORK PROGRAMMING GUIDELINES

Now that we have a basic understanding of networks, there are some guidelines to keep in mind when writing your Clipper applications. These are discussed in this section.

Start networking from the beginning When you are designing and writing a Clipper program, plan for it to run on a network right from the start. Although it might not be specified that the program is to be designed for a network, at some point the program may have to run in a network environment. It is much easier to write all programs for a network than it is to go back and modify your existing code to make it network-ready.

If you run your program on a single-user machine, the network locks will always succeed, since no other process is contending for them. You can always run a network application on a single-user machine; however, you can rarely run a single-user application in a network environment. With networks becoming more and more common in the workplace, you should design all applications with the capability to run well on a network.

Do not make assumptions One of the most frequent problems encountered when programming on a network is that the code assumes all network locking will be successful. For example, the following code, from an actual application, runs and produces no run-time errors:

```
select customer
if rlock()
   replace customer->balance with ;
           customer->balance + nAmount
endif
select trans
if rlock()
   replace trans->amount with nAmount,;
           trans->who with customer->id_code
endif
select TAXES
if rlock()
   replace taxes->amt_due with ;
           taxes->amt_due + (nAmount * .06 )   // sales tax
endif
```

However, precisely because it lacks run-time errors, corrupt-data errors can occur. In this situation, three files are updated each time the code is executed. Almost every time this program is run, the correct results are obtained. However, *almost* is not good enough. The correct results must be obtained *every* time.

Let's take a look at what our databases would contain if the second record lock were not successful: The CUSTOMER database would contain the proper balance and the TAXES database would be up-to-date, but the TRANS database would contain the wrong information. If someone were to call up this customer and view the transactions, they would notice that the total of the transactions did not equal the balance in the customer's account. If the TAXES file were not updated, then the amount of money paid for sales tax would be understated, which would not please the state government.

Listing 1.4 shows a corrected version of the function, which reports to the user that data may have been corrupted. (In Chapter 12, we will discuss transaction processing, which would treat the three file updates as a single unit.)

Listing 1.4: A Better Locking Scheme

```
select customer
if rlock()
   replace customer->balance with ;
           customer->balance + nAmount
   select trans
   if rlock()
      replace trans->amount with nAmount,;
              trans->who with customer->id_code
      select taxes
      if rlock()
         replace taxes->amt_due with ;
                 taxes->amt_due + (nAmount * .06 )   // tax
      else
         Alert("ERROR: Sales tax file is understated..")
      endif
   else
      Alert("ERROR: customer balance is current, but "+;
            " TRANS file and TAXES files are not... ")
   endif
else
   Alert("ERROR: This transaction could not be recorded!!")
endif
```

Although the error messages are sparse and there are no instructions for recovery procedures, at least we have taken the extra step to notify the user that something went wrong with this transaction.

Ask for permission   Another important aspect of the network to keep in mind is that other people are probably using the same files you are. Someone (such as Jake) is in charge of all these files. Among other things, you must ask if it is all right for your application to continue. For example, the following code does not ask for permission before erasing a transaction file:

```
select CUSTOMER
// Some update work
use TRANS new exclusive
//
// Remove prior transactions
//
zap
select CUSTOMER
//
// More code
//
```

For the most part, this code will execute correctly. However, when another user tries to use that transaction file, the file will fail to open. As a result, you will receive a run-time error, which is slightly better than erasing the wrong database file, but is still disconcerting to the user.

Below is the same code, this time including an extra step to ask for permission to open the transaction file. Although users might be a little surprised when they encounter the error message, it is certainly better than possibly zapping the wrong file.

```
select customer
// Some update work
use trans new exclusive
if NetErr()
   Alert("Cannot open the TRANS file..")
   return .F.
else
   //
   // Remove prior transactions
   //
   zap
endif
select CUSTOMER
//
// More code
//
```

Always ask for permission from the network before attempting to do any operation. This is particularly important when you are preparing to perform operations that will affect a large number of records in the file.

Plan for conflicts   While the first three guidelines deal with ensuring that the data is properly updated, they also assume that the user has nothing better to do than wait until the computer is finished with its processing. Your application should assume that every record lock or file lock request *will fail.*

If a file open request fails, what options should the user be presented with? In some cases, the program should simply tell the user it cannot run, because the files are not available. In other cases, the program might switch to another database. For example, consider an application that allows the user to get the name of a person to call for a survey. If all the names are in one file, the only appropriate action is to tell the user that the file is unavailable. However, if the names are spread across ten files, then failure to open one of them should be followed by an attempt to open the next one.

It is vitally important to design your application with the thought that every attempt to open a file will fail and that the program will not be able to obtain any record locks. Does your program handle these conditions gracefully by alerting the user and giving him or her options? Does it merely report the failure and abort the procedure? Or does it ignore the problem and just update what it can? In this book, we will discuss how to design programs that run effectively on a network, not just how to wrap record locks around the appropriate sections of code.

Summary

In this chapter, we introduced some basic network concepts, including how a network communicates with its workstations. We also presented some general guidelines to keep in mind when programming on a network. In subsequent chapters, we will expand upon those guidelines and provide practical working code that you can use to write robust network-ready applications.

How Clipper Operates on a Network

.DBF FILES

CLIPPER .NTX FILES

FOXPRO .IDX AND .CDX FILES

DBASE .NDX AND .MDX FILES

BUFFERS

WHAT HAPPENS WHEN CLIPPER TALKS TO DOS

CLIPPER COMMANDS AND FUNCTIONS FOR ACCESSING FILES

Chapter 2

In this chapter, we will first explore the structures of the data and index files that Clipper uses, and look at how buffers are used by Clipper, DOS, and the network. We will then cover what is happening behind the scenes when a Clipper command or function is used in a network environment.

.DBF FILES

Clipper includes numerous built-in database-management commands and functions, many of which do not require the programmer to have any understanding of the file structure. For example, when you move to a record in a .DBF file, Clipper automatically breaks the record into formatted fields and places those fields in a buffer for your program to use.

Clipper's database management is provided for a file known as the .DBF, or (D)ata (B)ase (F)ile. This file structure was developed by Ashton-Tate in the early 1980s and is still in heavy use today. It is a simple file structure that provides developers with a great deal of flexibility in handling many situations.

The .DBF structure consists of a header section followed by the file's data. The structure of the header is shown in Table 2.1.

Table 2.1: .DBF Header Structure

Byte	Size	Contents
1	1	Signature byte 03 = .DBF file without a memo 131 = .DBF file with a memo 139 = dBASE IV file with a memo 245 = FoxPro .DBF file with a memo
2	1	Year the file was last updated
3	1	Month the file was last updated
4	1	Day the file was last updated
5	4	Number of records in the file
9	2	Location in the file where data section starts
11	2	Size of each record
13	20	Filler, unused space

These first 32 bytes are followed by multiple occurrences of the field information. Each field has 32 bytes with the structure shown below:

Byte	Size	Contents
1	11	Field name, followed by a NULL byte, chr(0)
12	1	Type (C)har, (D)ate, (L)ogical, (N)umeric, (M)emo, (F)loating point—dBASE IV and FoxPro only, (P)icture—FoxPro only
13	4	Field offset in record
17	1	Field size, up to 255 bytes
18	1	Number of decimal places
19	14	Filler, unused space

With this structure, the maximum size of any field is 255 bytes. However, Clipper supports larger character strings by using the decimal size and the field length. Since character strings do not have decimal places, if Clipper sees a value in the decimal field, it multiplies that value by 256 and then adds the field size to the result to determine the actual field length. For example, if the field size were 88 bytes and the decimal places were 2 bytes on a character field, then Clipper would set the actual field size to 600 bytes.

Clipper .NTX files

An index (.NTX) file is a secondary file that allows a logical ordering to be placed on a .DBF that may be in a completely different physical order. The .NTX file consists of a header section, which describes the key field to be used for the ordering, and a data section, which consists of the keys themselves along with the corresponding record numbers. Table 2.2 shows the structure of Clipper's index file.

Table 2.2: .NTX Header Structure

Byte	Size	Contents	
1	2	Signature byte, bit encoded	
		Bits	**Contents**
		7-3	Reserved
		4-1	New lock offset bit
		3-1	Partial index bit
		2-2	Index types
		0-1	Conditional index
3	2	Count of index updates	
5	4	Offset to first index page	
9	4	Offset to list of unused pages	
13	2	Key size +8 bytes for record pointers	
15	2	Key size	
17	2	Decimal places in the key expression	
19	2	Maximum entries per index page	
21	2	Minimum entries per index page	
23	256	Key expression, NULL terminated	
279	1	1 if unique index, 0 otherwise	
280	1	1 if descending index, 0 otherwise	
281	256	Filter expression	
537	11	Order name	

Clipper 5.2 adds additional capabilities to its index file, but still maintains backward compatibility with older Clipper index files. The signature field is now bit encoded to determine which new features are in this index file. If these bits are not set, the index signature byte is the number 6, so older Clipper applications can still use the index. If any of the bits are set, an older Clipper version will report that the index file is corrupt. The new bits are explained in this section.

BIT 4-1: NEW LOCK OFFSET BIT

Clipper does not require that the developer perform index file locks, but rather handles these locks transparently. When Clipper locks the index file, it uses a virtual lock located outside of the physical index file rather than locking the physical file. In earlier versions of Clipper, this lock was stored at an offset one billion bytes past the beginning of the file. Clipper indexes, however, can grow to over one billion bytes, so this offset could actually have ended up being within the file. With Clipper 5.2, the offset has been moved from one billion to hexidecimal FFFFFFFF, which is the largest allowable offset under the DOS operating system. Although this solves the problem, it also means that if a Clipper 5.01 program is using the same index that a Clipper 5.2 program is using, they will be locking at different spots, which can easily cause data corruption and integrity problems.

To get around this problem, a bit has been added to instruct Clipper which offset it should use. Older Clipper index files will have this bit cleared, so the one billion offset will be used. The newer index files will have the bit set, so the FFFFFFFF offset will be used.

When Clipper 5.2 creates index files, it will create the old version to maintain backward compatibility. If you wish to have Clipper create the new indexes, you will need to link the NTXLOCK2.OBJ file into your program. This will instruct Clipper to create the new index format anytime it makes an index file.

BIT 0-1: CONDITIONAL INDEX BIT

Since Clipper indexes now support a FOR clause (so you can restrict the index to only certain records), a bit has been added to designate whether the index is conditional or a full index. If this bit is set to 1, then the index is conditional, otherwise the index is a full index. If a condition is specified, it is stored in the index header.

Keep in mind that if these additional bits are set, they will cause older Clipper programs to assume the index is corrupt. Make sure that all your programs are compiled under Clipper 5.2 with the NTXLOCK2.OBJ installed before you start using Clipper's new index files. If you plan to have both Clipper 5.2 and 5.01 programs running against the same index file, be sure that the NTXLOCK2.OBJ is not linked in so that you can maintain compatibility between the two applications.

The data portion of the index consists of a number of pages, each of which is 1,024 bytes in size. These pages contain the key values and the record numbers that correspond to the keys. When Clipper is moving through a file in indexed order, it locks the current page during the read. This is done to ensure that no other program can change the key before Clipper has gotten the chance to return the proper record number.

Keep in mind that all movement through an indexed file requires that a portion of the index file be locked. If several users are working with that index file, each user will have to wait while the other users lock and unlock the index file. Thus, it is very possible to have file-contention problems even when there is just read-only access to the files.

FoxPro .IDX and .CDX files

Clipper allows you to access FoxPro databases and indexes using the CDXDBF data driver. Although the indexes work similarly to the .NTX files, they are designed differently. They consist of a header section which describes the key field to be used for the ordering, and a data section which consists of the keys themselves along with the corresponding record numbers. Table 2.3 shows the structure of the .IDX file that FoxPro uses.

Table 2.3: .IDX Header Structure

Byte	Size	Contents
1	4	Pointer to first (root) index page
5	4	Point to list of free index pages, -1 if none
9	4	File size
13	2	Length of key expression
15	1	Index options
		1—Unique index
		8—Index with FOR clause
		9—Unique index with a FOR clause

Table 2.3: .IDX Header Structure (Continued)

Byte	Size	Contents
16	1	Reserved for future use
17	220	Key expression
237	220	FOR expression, if Index options are 8 or 9
457	56	Filler, not used

The data portion of the index consists of a number of pages, each of which are 512 bytes in size. These pages contain the key values and the record numbers that correspond to the keys.

FoxPro also has a compact index (.CDX file), in which the keys are stored in compressed fashion. In an index with a large number of similar keys, this can greatly reduce the size of the index. In a network environment, a smaller index size causes less network traffic and can help improve performance.

Table 2.4 shows the structure of the header of the .CDX index file. This header is 1024 bytes in length rather than 512.

Table 2.4: .CDX Header Structure

Byte	Size	Contents
1	4	Pointer to first (root) index page
5	4	Point to list of free index pages, -1 if none
9	4	Reserved for future use
13	2	Length of key expression
15	1	Index options
		1—Unique index
		8—Index with FOR clause
		32—Compact index format
		64—Compound index The numbers may be combined if needed
16	1	Reserved for future use
17	485	Reserved for internal use
503	2	0=Ascending, 1=Descending

Table 2.4: .CDX Header Structure

Byte	Size	Contents
505	2	Reserved for internal use
507	2	Length for FOR expressions
509	2	Reserved for internal use
511	2	Length for key expressions
513	512	Expressions (key and FOR)

The data portion of the index consists of a number of pages, each of which are 512 bytes in size. These pages contain the key values and the record numbers that correspond to the keys. These key values are more complex to express, since they are stored in a compressed manner.

dBASE .NDX AND .MDX FILES

Clipper also allows you to access dBASE IV databases and indexes using the NDXDBF and MDXDBF data drivers. Although the .NDX index file works similarly to the .NTX file, it is designed a bit less efficiently. The .MDX index file, which allows multiple keys in a single file, does not have a counterpart in Clipper indexing schemes.

The .NDX file consists of a header section which describes the key field to be used for the ordering, and a data section which consists of the keys themselves along with the corresponding record numbers. Table 2.5 shows the structure of the .NDX file that dBASE uses.

Table 2.5: .NDX Header Structure

Byte	Size	Contents
1	4	Pointer to first (root) index page
5	4	Number of 512 byte pages in the file
9	4	Filler, not used
13	2	Length of key expression
15	2	Maximum number of keys per index page
17	2	Key type, 1 = numeric, 0 = character

Table 2.5: .NDX Header Structure (Continued)

Byte	Size	Contents
19	4	Size of key records
23	1	Filler
24	1	1 if unique index, 0 if not
25	488	Key expression

The data portion of the index consists of a number of pages, each of which are 512 bytes in size. These pages contain the key values and the record numbers that correspond to the keys.

dBASE IV also has a multiple tag index (.MDX file), in which the multiple keys are stored in a single index file. This index can be used to reduce the number of file handles a program requires and can also ensure that all index files are always updated.

Table 2.6 shows the structure of the header of the .MDX index file. This portion of the header is 48 bytes in length and is followed by individual tag information.

Table 2.6: .MDX Header Structure

Byte	Size	Contents
1	1	Signature byte, (2)
2	3	Last reindex date
5	16	Root name of associated .DBF file
21	2	Block size value
23	2	Block size in bytes
24	1	Production MDX file? 1=Yes
25	1	Filler, not used
26	2	Number of index tags in the file
28	2	Reserved
30	4	Page number of end of file
34	4	Page number of next free block

Table 2.6: .MDX Header Structure (Continued)

Byte	Size	Contents
38	4	Number of pages in next free block
42	3	Date file was created, YMD
45	4	Reserved

The .MDX header structure is followed by tag information for each tag in the file. The tag information has the following structure:

Byte	Size	Contents
1	4	Index page number
5	11	Tag name
16	1	10 if a field tag, 0 otherwise
17	4	Reserved
21	1	Key type (C)har, (D)ate, (N)umeric
22	12	Filler

The tag structure can be repeated up to 47 times, depending upon the number of tags in the index file.

USING INDEX FILES ON A NETWORK

Clipper index files have been known to cause all sorts of problems for applications. Several of the internal errors deal specifically with indexes getting "corrupted." A corrupt index is one that does not agree with the .DBF file it is supposed to represent. While it is possible for index files to become corrupted in a single-user environment, this is much more apt to occur in a network environment.

Most corrupt indexes are the result of programming errors. Programs that run fine when no other process is contending for an index might not run as well when other processes need the index file. The following sections describe some general guidelines to keep in mind when working with indexes on a network.

Do not use keys of varying lengths   The index structure requires that the key size be the same for all records in the index. With Clipper's flexibility in index expressions, it is very easy to create expressions that will result in different sizes. Therefore, it is the programmer's responsibility to make sure that the keys are always the same length.

When Clipper creates an index file, it needs to determine the index key size to store in the header (see Table 2.2). It evaluates your index expression on a blank record to determine the size. If you were to index on the TRIM() of a field, then Clipper would determine the index key size to be zero and create the file accordingly. The moment you tried to insert a record into the index that had a key length greater than zero, you would overwrite pointers and, before long, index corruption messages would begin to appear.

Be very careful if your index expression uses a user-defined function. In one application we managed, the user-defined function was changed in one place, but not in the indexing program. This change caused different index key sizes, so index corruption messages began sprouting up frequently. The solution to the problem of corrupt index files is to recreate them; unfortunately, every time the indexing program was called to recreate them, it changed the key size!

Open all indexes whenever the file is opened   It is a good idea to open all indexes whenever the file is used. Allow Clipper to make the decision as to whether an index should be updated based upon the changes to the database. Clipper will update only index files whose keys are changed by the database operation. If you do not open all index files, you are not giving Clipper the opportunity to decide which index files to update. While it is possible to open only the .NTX files you anticipate that your application will need, it is generally not a good idea.

Do not use REINDEX   At first, the REINDEX command appears to be a godsend. With one quick command, all open indexes (no matter how many) will be instantly recreated. However, the REINDEX command makes the assumption that the header for the index is intact, and therefore simply recreates the data pages. If the index header is corrupted, REINDEX will just produce another corrupt .NTX file rather than fix the problem.

It is better to have an indexing routine that can be called from any location in your program and to always use this routine to recreate all indexes. You should forget that the REINDEX command even exists!

Do not create indexes on shared files   Never, ever create an index file while the file is opened and unlocked. Clipper will oblige such a request, but you risk another program changing key values while you are creating the index.

Note that the INDEX ON command will not only create the desired index file, but will also open it on an exclusive basis. If the file cannot be opened exclusively, the command will fail. By contrast, the SET INDEX TO command causes indexes to be opened in the same mode as that in which the file was opened.

If you need to create an index on a shared file, it is best to attempt to lock the file first and then create the index. Here is an example:

```
use customer shared new      // Open the file
if ! file("cust1.ntx")       // Does index exist
   if Flock()
      index on cust1->id_code to cust1
   else
      Alert("Cannot create index file")
      close databases
      quit
   endif
   use customer shared
endif
set index to cust1
```

In this example, if CUST1.NTX does not exist, the program will attempt to lock the file and create the index. If this is successful, the second USE command closes the CUSTOMER file and reopens it. This way, when the SET INDEX command is done, the CUST1 index will now be opened in SHARED mode.

If you are creating only a temporary index—that is, one that will not be used after the program exits—you can be a little less strict in your locking requirements. However, if your environment can support it, make every effort to index only files that are exclusively used or locked.

Always open index files in the same order   When you open index files, you should always open them in the same order. Since Clipper updates indexes in the order they were opened, it is dangerous to have two programs updating different indexes simultaneously.

For example, here are two programs that normally run simultaneously on the network:

Program One	Program Two
use customer shared new	use customer shared new
set index to rep,repstate	set index to repstate,rep

Let's assume that the two programs are about to update the databases at the same time. Program One updates the REP field and in doing so moves the REP to a different index page. It then proceeds to update the REPSTATE field. Meanwhile, Program Two has updated REPSTATE and as a result has moved the REPSTATE field to a different index page. It goes on to update the REP index. The timing of writes and locks becomes much more critical in this situation than it does in a case where the index files are updated in the same order. With multiple indexes being updated in a scattered function, any timing error can cause the index file to contain the wrong information and become corrupt. To reduce the likelihood of this occurring, it is best to allow Clipper to access the index files in the same order in each program.

Minimize index locking during read operations   Keep in mind that index files are locked during read operations. A program that does an indexed read through a database creates quite a bit of network traffic and file lock activity. If possible, try to minimize the amount of index locking to what is absolutely necessary.

If the database order will not change, you might consider keeping the file in sorted order rather than creating an index. This would allow you to read the database without locking any records or index files. In many cases, databases can be sorted rather than indexed, greatly reducing network traffic and thus improving performance.

If the order is not important, be sure to use the SET ORDER TO 0 command, which will display the information in record number order.

Keep index key expressions simple   While Clipper index expressions can be very complex, even to the point of calling user-defined functions (UDFs), this complexity has a price. First, keep in mind that the index expression's code is executed every time the index is updated. If you have several indexes, each using a UDF as part of the expression, that UDF will be called multiple times. If the UDF is complex, you can greatly slow the index update process.

For example, in one application we developed, a part number had to have leading zeros and other extraneous characters stripped from it. This was a perfect scenario in which to use a UDF. A ten-line program was created to create the key and the UDF() was placed in several index expressions. Whenever a new part was added to the indexed database, the ten-line UDF was called six times for three indexes. The first three times, the indexes were updated with the blank values from the APPEND BLANK command. The second three times, the actual values were written to the record. So two lines of code (an APPEND and a REPLACE operation) caused 60 lines of code to be executed!

If you have complex index keys, consider making a field in the .DBF to hold the key and then index directly on that field. Although this will require additional storage space, it can significantly reduce the time needed for the index operation, as well as the time necessary to update records using the indexes.

IS MY INDEX FILE CORRUPT?

Index corruption is usually not detected until Clipper attempts to process the corrupt key. If it detects something amiss, it stops your program and cries FOUL!! Unfortunately, this detection usually occurs when a person has been using the application for a while and is about to update critical data.

To get around this problem, you could check for index corruption at the beginning of the program, although this would take some time to do. However, Listing 2.1 shows a program that performs a simple check on some aspects of the index. It will not detect every corrupt index condition, but will catch most of them. It is a trade-off between speed and index integrity.

In Chapter 4, we include this index check routine when files are opened.

Listing 2.1: NTXCHK Program

```
*     Program:   NTXCHK.PRG
*     Authors:   Joseph D. Booth and Greg Lief
*     Function:  IndexCorrupt()
*     Purpose:   Spot check an index file's header
*     Syntax:    <logical> := IndexCorrupt( cFile [,cExtension] )
*  Parameter:    cFile       - Name of the index file to check
*                cExtension  - Version of index file this is supposed
*                              to be (NTX,NDX,MDX,IDX, or CDX)
*
*     Notes:     This function makes a guess as to whether or not the
*                file name specified is a valid index file.  Clipper 5.2
*                supports the following index file formats,
*
*                NTX     - Clipper's indexing scheme
*                NDX     - dBASE III+/IV indexes
*                MDX     - dBASE Multiple tag indexes
*                IDX     - FoxPro indexes
*                CDX     - FoxPro compound indexes
*
*
**************************************************************************

#include "FILEIO.CH"
#include "COMMON.CH"

#define   NTX_ENTRY_SIZE    bin2w(substr(cBuf,13,2))
#define   NTX_KEY_SIZE      bin2w(substr(cBuf,15,2))
```

Listing 2.1: NTXCHK Program (Continued)

```
#define    NTX_FILE_OFFSET    bin2l(substr(cBuf, 5,4))
#define    NTX_MAX_ENTRIES    bin2w(substr(cBuf,19,2))

#define    IDX_FILE_SIZE      bin2l(substr(cBuf, 9,4))
#define    IDX_OPTIONS        asc(substr(cBuf,15,1))

#define    NDX_PAGES          bin2l(substr(cBuf, 5,4))
#define    NDX_TYPE           bin2w(substr(cBuf,17,2))
#define    NDX_UNIQUE         asc(substr(cBuf,24,1))

#define    MDX_SIGNATURE      asc(substr(cBuf, 1,1))
#define    MDX_PRODUCTION     asc(substr(cBuf,24,1))
#define    MDX_TAG_COUNT      bin2w(substr(cBuf,26,2))


function IndexCorrupt(cFile,cExt)
LOCAL cBuf   := space(512)       // Read the index header page
LOCAL cVer   := ""               // Version of index file
LOCAL nHandle
LOCAL isBad  := .T.
LOCAL nSize

DEFAULT cExt TO "NTX"

if ! "." $ cFile
   cFile += "."+cExt
endif

nHandle := fopen(cFile, 66)
if nHandle > 0
   fread(nHandle,@cBuf,512)
   nSize := fseek(nHandle,0,FS_END)
   do case
   case cExt == "NTX"
      if NTX_ENTRY_SIZE - 8 == NTX_KEY_SIZE  .and. NTX_KEY_SIZE > 0
         if NTX_FILE_OFFSET % 1024 == 0 // Valid offset?
            isBad := (NTX_ENTRY_SIZE * NTX_MAX_ENTRIES) > 1024
         endif
      endif
   case cExt == "NDX"
      if NDX_PAGES * 512 = nSize
         if NDX_TYPE < 2 .and. NDX_UNIQUE < 2
            isBad := .F.
         endif
```

Listing 2.1: NTXCHK Program (Continued)

```
      endif
   case cExt == "MDX"
      if MDX_SIGNATURE = 2
         if MDX_PRODUCTION <2 .and. MDX_TAG_COUNT <= 47
            isBad := .F.
         endif
      endif
   case cExt == "IDX"
      if IDX_FILE_SIZE = nSize
         isBad := ascan( {1,8,9},IDX_OPTIONS ) == 0
      endif
   case cExt == "CDX"
      if IDX_FILE_SIZE = nSize
         isBad := ascan( {1,8,9,32,33,40,41,64,65,70,96},IDX_OPTIONS ) == 0
      endif
   endcase
   fclose(nHandle)
endif
return isBad
```

INDEX FILE LOCKING

Clipper's indexing scheme is very powerful since it allows any type of expression, including user-defined functions, to be used as an index key. You are not limited to a database field. Unfortunately, this power comes at a slight cost in a network environment: the necessity to lock the index file even for read access. Since another Clipper program could be changing the index file, Clipper attempts to get a stagnant snapshot of the index file before it performs a record movement operation.

When Clipper is reading an index file on a network, it copies information from the header or one of the data pages into a buffer. It also saves the current counter of index file updates. If your program moves to another record, Clipper reads the index file header to see if the index change counter has been updated. The index file is locked during this read. If the change counter has increased, Clipper discards the buffer and rereads the header information. It reads both the header and the data pages until it finds the record, and then unlocks the index file.

The index locking is handled transparently and automatically by Clipper. Prior to Clipper 5.2, applications would continuously try to lock the index file and never give up. Although such persistence has some benefits, it also can cause a workstation to appear hung. If another program dies with an index file locked, every other workstation will appear hung until the failed program is logged out of the network.

Clipper 5.2 now generates a recoverable error if the lock has not been obtained after a certain number of retries. When the default error handler gets control, it merely returns TRUE to retry the operation. If you do not customize the error handler, then the program operates the same as prior releases of Clipper. You can, however, give the user a message indicating that the station is not hung, and allow the user to quit or continue trying. If the user quits, then your recovery strategy should be to recreate the index file as soon as possible.

If you install a custom error handler, the error code is stored in ERROR.CH as EG_LOCK. If this error is encountered, you can return TRUE to keep trying to lock the index, or return FALSE to quit. In either case, your program should either notify a system administrator or log the failure somewhere. If some process is locking the index file and not releasing it, it generally points to another network problem.

The following sample code shows how to install a custom error handler to trap the lock time-out condition.

```
#include "ERROR.CH"
LOCAL bOldError:= ErrorBlock( {|err|LockErr(err,bDefError)})

function LockErr(oError,bOldError)
if oError:genCode == EG_LOCK
   Alert("Index is locked elsewhere, press ENTER to retry")
   return .T.
endif
return eval(bOldError,oErr)   // Original error handler
```

Buffers

A *buffer* is a portion of memory that is used to hold data recently obtained from a disk operation. Since electronic memory (RAM) operates much faster than hard-disk storage, most programs use RAM to speed up overall performance. DOS, Clipper, and NetWare all use buffers for optimal performance.

Clipper Work Areas

For each file you open, Clipper sets aside a buffer in RAM to hold any record retrieved from the .DBF file. The buffer area is also called a work area. In addition to the data, Clipper also keeps various flags stored in this internal table. One such flag is the HOT UPDATE flag, which indicates if the data has been changed. If this flag is set, then Clipper will notify DOS that it has some information to be written to disk.

DOS BUFFERS

DOS also makes use of buffers to improve performance. Each time DOS reads a portion of the disk, it places that disk data into the buffer. If the record size is small, several .DBF records can be placed into the buffer at once, resulting in fewer disk reads to access the data. DOS also keeps track of this data via an internal flag that indicates whether the data needs to be written to the disk. The Clipper COMMIT command (described later in this chapter) checks the Clipper work-area buffers for such HOT UPDATE flags and, if it finds any, issues a request to DOS to write the data to disk.

NETWORK BUFFERS

NetWare also maintains a large buffer for file access to the server's disk. The network operating system keeps track of all data in its memory, regardless of how it got there. For example, if your application requests several records from the server, the network will send them to your workstation and keep them in memory. If another application requests any of those records, NetWare will handle the request by giving the other program records from its memory buffers.

The intermixing of these buffers requires some consideration by Clipper programmers. If you request a record from the network, NetWare will place the record into your DOS buffers and Clipper will place those buffers into its work-area memory. When you make changes to the record, you are actually updating the work-area–memory copies of those records. The changes you make are not visible to other network users until your buffers get sent back to the network disk. For performance reasons, this process is not done after every REPLACE statement, but rather when you unlock the record, move to another record, or commit. It is very important to remember this, because it certainly affects record visibility in other applications.

In addition, if other programs have already read the record, then they too are working with only a copy of the data. In order to see your changes, your program would have to commit them and the other program would have to reread the record. We will discuss this concept more in the Clipper COMMIT and SKIP discussions later in this chapter.

What happens when Clipper talks to DOS

As we mentioned in Chapter 1, many of the Clipper commands are high-level interfaces to the various DOS functions. DOS function 61 is used to open a file, function 62 is used to close a file, DOS function 66 is used to move among records in the file, and so on.

The interaction between Clipper and the network is also handled through a DOS function. Function 92 (5Ch) was added in DOS 3.00 to provide compatibility across a variety of network operating systems. Clipper uses this DOS function to handle its record and file locking. Clipper does not communicate directly with the network operating system, but rather uses the DOS function calls to handle all access to network files. This design decision allows Clipper programs to run on a wide variety of networks. Any network that supports network calls from DOS 3.x and higher (and most of them do) can be used to run your Clipper application.

In this section, we will discuss what happens at the DOS level when certain Clipper commands are executed. By learning what Clipper is asking DOS to do, we can better understand the impact of the commands on the network.

OPENING FILES

When Clipper USEs a .DBF file, it opens the file using DOS function 61 (File Open). This function returns a numeric handle that serves as a pointer to the file. The DOS functions that Clipper calls expect this handle rather than a file name.

The DOS File Open function expects both a file name and an open mode. This mode is numeric and controls how much access is granted to other users to the file. Clipper's FOPEN() function takes the exact same parameters as the DOS function. Table 2.7 lists the available open modes. These modes are covered in more detail in Chapter 4.

Table 2.7: File Open Modes

Numeric Value	Mode
0	Read-only mode
1	Write-only mode
2	Read/write mode
16	Deny read access/write access to others

Table 2.7: File Open Modes (Continued)

Numeric Value	Mode
32	Deny write access to others
48	Deny read access to others
64	Allow read/write access to others

Modes can be combined to create the appropriate open usage. For example, 2+16 (18) would open the file for read/write access and deny other users access to the file. Clipper's USE command provides several parameters that are translated to the appropriate file open modes. These are shown in Table 2.8.

Table 2.8: Clipper USE Parameters

USE Parameter	File Open Modes
Exclusive	18 (2 = Read/Write + 16 = Deny all)
Shared	66 (2 = Read/Write + 64 = Deny none)
ReadOnly	16 if EXCLUSIVE 64 if SHARED

It is important to realize that Clipper does not know if the file it is opening is on a network. Clipper basically hands the file open request to DOS and lets DOS figure out where the file is stored.

LOCKING FILES

DOS function 92 is the lock/unlock file function. It expects the file handle from the open function as the first parameter. The other parameters are the offset into the file, the number of bytes to lock, and a flag meaning either lock (1) or unlock (0) the region. Other applications sharing this file will usually be denied access if they attempt to access the locked portion of the file. Here is the syntax for the function (expressed in Clipper terms rather than DOS's registers):

```
lSuccess := DOSlock( nHandle, ;    // File handle
                     nOffset, ;    // Starting point
                     nLength, ;    // Number of bytes
                     nFlag )       // 0 -Lock, 1 -Unlock
```

Unfortunately, when a portion of a file is locked, all access (both reading and writing) to that portion is denied. Yet it is possible for another Clipper application (as well as other non-Clipper programs) to read a file that is locked by your Clipper application.

Clipper gets around NetWare's read/write lock by adjusting where the lock is requested. Instead of requesting a lock within the range of bytes within the file, Clipper attempts to lock the record by adding one billion to the record number, and locking one byte. Since .DBF files can be only one billion bytes long, no other program will request that byte from the file. Other Clipper applications will check that byte when attempting to lock a record.

Clipper employs a similar scheme to lock a file. It locks the offset at one billion bytes from the beginning of the file. Other Clipper applications will respect this lock when attempting to lock files or records.

Programs not written in Clipper probably use a different locking offset, and hence are not compatible with Clipper locks. For example, you could lock a record in Clipper and lock the same record in FoxPro. Whichever update is written to disk last will overwrite the previous update.

Clipper commands and functions for accessing files

Clipper provides many commands and functions that are used to access files. By reviewing these commands and their effect on a network, we can design a system to keep files and records locked for the shortest possible time. Table 2.9 lists these Clipper commands and functions.

Table 2.9: Clipper Commands and Functions to Access Files

Command or Function	Description
APPEND BLANK	Adds a new record to a shared file
COMMIT	Forces changes to be written to disk
DELETE	Flags a record for deletion
FLOCK()	Attempts to lock all records in a file
NETERR()	Returns the status of network operations
NETNAME()	Returns workstation identification string
RECALL	Recovers a record marked for deletion

Table 2.9: Clipper Commands and Functions to Access Files (Continued)

Command or Function	Description
RLOCK()	Locks one record in the file
SKIP	Moves the record pointer within the file
UNLOCK	Unlocks a previously locked file or record
USE … SHARED	Opens a file that others can also USE

In order to understand these basic commands and functions, their behavior, and their impact on a network, we will cover each one in greater detail. Note that many of the commands listed below have corresponding functions (prefaced by *DB*).

APPEND BLANK / DBAPPEND()

Whenever you want to add a new record to a database, you must first add a blank record and then change the field values as necessary. The APPEND BLANK command adds the blank record and positions the record pointer on that new record.

When the database is opened for shared use, APPEND BLANK will also attempt to lock the new record. From a Clipper point of view, this command results in one locked record. However, from the DOS level at least three locks are needed. If index files are in use, more DOS and network locks will be necessary as well.

If you refer back to Table 2.1, you will notice that part of the header contains a count of records in the file. When an APPEND BLANK command is issued, Clipper needs to add spaces to the end of the file and update the number of records. This results in two network locks. The third lock occurs after the first two are completed, and it locks the record so your program can update the fields.

If any index files are in use when the APPEND BLANK command is given, each of these will be locked and updated. After all, adding a record requires entries in all active indexes.

The APPEND BLANK operation needs a minimum of three locks, as well as another lock for each index that is open in the work area. In addition, the APPEND BLANK command updates each index with blank values. If your index expression is complex or calls a user-defined function, keep in mind that the expression will be executed for each index, even though you are very likely to update the values soon after the append. When you update the blank fields with new values, the index update process will occur all over again.

If your application frequently adds new records to a database file, you might be able to improve performance by reusing records or appending a large number of records at a time. For either of these methods to work, you will need some sort of index to be able to find unused records. The following listing shows the ADDRECORD() function for a file that is indexed on a numeric key. Records with zero in the key field are assumed to be deleted, and therefore are reusable. That is why we first seek a reusable record, and only append if none is found.

```
function AddRecord()
if dbseek(0)              // Look for an empty record
   if Rlock()             // if found, then try to lock it.
      return .t.
   endif                  // If not found or not locked
endif                     // then we should try to add
return AddRec()           // a blank record.
```

COMMIT / DBCOMMIT() / DBCOMMITALL()

The COMMIT command is used to request that the updated information in Clipper's work-area buffers gets written to DOS. The COMMIT command first checks the HOT UPDATE flag in the work area. If it is set, then the information from the work area is transferred to the DOS buffers. The DOS flush function is then called, which will write its buffers to disk unless nothing has changed.

To guarantee a DOS flush, you must use COMMIT or close a database. Though the UNLOCK command does write the information from the work area to the DOS buffers, it does not call the DOS flush.

When DOS detects that a buffer has been changed and writes it to disk, the network might take over if the file is on a network drive. The timing of when the network actually writes the information to disk varies greatly among networks, but the updated information will be made available to the next program requesting that record. Again, as a rule of thumb, you should always use COMMIT after a series of REPLACE statements and prior to the UNLOCK command.

Note that the COMMIT command (and the DBCOMMITALL() function) will force the data in *all* work-area buffers to be flushed. If for performance reasons you want to commit only the data in the current work area, you can use the DBCOMMIT() function rather than the COMMIT command.

DELETE / DBDELETE()

This marks the current record for deletion. Note that this does not physically remove the record from the database. In Clipper, each record in a database has a delete flag associated with it; when you mark a record for deletion, you are simply toggling this flag. The PACK command is what actually removes records that have been flagged for deletion.

If the database is open for shared use, you must lock the current record with RLOCK() prior to marking it for deletion with DELETE. The RLOCK() function will require at least one call to the DOS lock function.

If the scope of the DELETE command is more than just the current record, a file lock will be required, because Clipper work areas are restricted to only one lock per file.

FLOCK()

The FLOCK() function attempts to lock every record in a file. If it succeeds, then no other process can update that file or any individual record in the file. Other users can read the records in the file, but they may not change any of the data.

When FLOCK() is executed, Clipper calls the DOS file lock function with one billion as the offset and the number of records in the file as the length. Therefore, any Clipper process attempting a record lock will fail, since the record lock is one billion + the number of records, which will be marked as locked by the file lock operation.

The FLOCK() function returns a logical true (.T.) if the file was successfully locked, or false (.F.) if the lock failed. FLOCK() is needed if a command is going to update more than one record at a time. For example, the REPLACE command allows you to specify the scope. If the scope is more than merely the current record, then FLOCK() must be called prior to performing the operation.

The FLOCK() function should be used sparingly, since it prevents any other user from updating the file. In many cases, you can avoid the use of FLOCK() by writing loop constructs and locking individual records with RLOCK() within the loop. The following listing shows a REPLACE command to update certain records meeting a condition.

```
select CUSTOMER
if flock()
   replace all CUSTOMER->tax_rate with .07
          for CUSTOMER->state == "NJ"
   unlock
endif
```

If the FLOCK() function returns a true, then all customers in the state of New Jersey will have their tax rates changed. However, let's consider what this function is doing. In essence, the following code is being executed by the single REPLACE ALL command:

```
go top
do while .not. eof()
   if customer->state == "NJ"
      if rlock()
         replace customer->tax_rate with .07
      endif
   endif
   skip 1
enddo
```

While the REPLACE ALL command certainly is easier to code than the seven lines it performs, you can control the network performance much better by not using the ALL option. The benefit of this approach becomes apparent if, for example, another user needs to update a customer from Pennsylvania. If you use the FLOCK() function to lock the entire file, this user cannot update the Pennsylvania customer until the REPLACE ALL command is finished. If the user updating the Pennsylvania customer has the record locked before the FLOCK() function is called, then the FLOCK() function will not be able to update the New Jersey customers. Even though the REPLACE ALL command will never change the Pennsylvania customers, it still locks them for the duration of the replace operation. By using the approach in the previous listing, you lock only the New Jersey records, allowing Pennsylvania records to be updated while the New Jersey tax increase is being applied.

Once again, it is important when designing programs for networks to lock as few records as possible for as short a time as possible. The FLOCK() function frequently locks unneeded records and should thus be used as infrequently as possible.

NETERR()

As mentioned in Chapter 1, the NETERR() function is Clipper's way of communicating the results of network operations to your program. It returns a true (.T.) if the last network command resulted in an error, or a false (.F.) if the command was successful.

The NETERR() function is used to return the results of operations that are done by a command rather than a function call. Since commands do not return a value, we need a foolproof way to determine the command's success or failure.

The APPEND BLANK command and the USE command are two examples in which NETERR() is used. In a network environment, you must check NETERR() after each APPEND BLANK statement to see if the record was successfully appended. In addition, NETERR() must be checked after a USE command is issued to see if the file was successfully opened.

NETNAME()
The NETNAME() function returns a character string that can be up to 15 characters long. This string identifies the name of the workstation. NETNAME() operates only on IBM networks, and returns an empty string on other networks.

If you need to get a workstation name on a Novell network, please refer to Chapter 12, which includes functions to obtain information from the workstation.

RECALL / DBRECALL()
This command toggles the delete flag if the current record was marked for deletion. In Clipper, each record in a database has a delete flag associated with it. When you mark a record for deletion, you are simply toggling this flag. When you recall the record, you are setting the flag back to active record. If the PACK command was used, the deleted record no longer exists and cannot be recalled.

If the database is open for shared use, you must lock the current record with RLOCK() prior to recalling it. The RLOCK() function will require at least one call to the DOS lock function.

If the scope of the RECALL command is more than just the current record, a file lock will be required. As previously mentioned, this is because Clipper work areas are restricted to only one lock per file.

RLOCK()
The RLOCK() function is used when updating a single record. It attempts to lock the current record in the current work area. Commands that require a record lock are REPLACE, DELETE, RECALL, and in-line assignments for assigning values to database fields. The RLOCK() function returns a logical true (.T.) if it successfully locks the record, or a false (.F.) if the lock is unsuccessful. If RLOCK() is successful, the record lock will remain in force until you use UNLOCK, use UNLOCK ALL, close the database, lock another record with RLOCK(), or lock the current file with FLOCK().

The RLOCK() function will call the DOS lock function requesting that one byte be locked at location two billion + the current record number. This will allow other users to still have read-only access to the current database even if you have locked a record. (But your program will be the only one that can change it.)

The RLOCK() function makes only one attempt to lock the record. In some cases, you might want to retry the operation several times before giving up. The REC_LOCK() function discussed in Chapter 3 is Clipper code to retry the RLOCK() for a number of seconds or until the lock is successful.

SKIP / DBSKIP()

The SKIP command (as well as any other record-pointer movement command, such as GO TOP and GO BOTTOM) instructs Clipper to find the next record. If there is no controlling index associated with the work area, finding the next record is easy. However, finding the next record within an index requires more work and at least one lock of the index file.

If your application program is currently positioned on an unlocked record, it is possible that another process has changed the data and the copy of the data with your work area's buffer is no longer current. If you are using a record without a lock, you can use the SKIP command to force the network to reread that record.

If your program has locked the current record and updated key values, when you leave the current record, Clipper will check to see if any keys have been updated. If so, the appropriate index files will be locked and updated. Once the index files are updated, the index file will be locked again so the pointer movement can be safely performed. This is one reason why the corrupt index messages nearly always appear on a SKIP, UNLOCK, or COMMIT statement (rather than the actual REPLACE command). Until you leave the record, commit the changes, or unlock the record, the database and appropriate indexes will not be updated. REPLACE updates only your work area's buffer.

UNLOCK / DBUNLOCK() / DBUNLOCKALL()

The UNLOCK command (or DBUNLOCK() function) removes any locks from the current work area. The UNLOCK command unlocks either the file lock or the record lock, depending upon the last lock function called. UNLOCK applies to the current work area only. UNLOCK ALL (or the DBUNLOCKALL() function) removes all records and file locks from all work areas. The UNLOCK command should be called after the REPLACE operation is performed, so that other users can access the record.

Unlocking does not guarantee that your changes are flushed from the buffer to disk. The work-area buffer is written to DOS, but Clipper does not request that DOS write the data immediately. Instead, Clipper gives the data to DOS and trusts that DOS will write it to disk at the most opportune moment.

USE ... SHARED | EXCLUSIVE / DBUSEAREA()

The USE command opens a .DBF file and assigns it to an available work-area buffer. Since USE is a command rather than a function, you must use NETERR() to check if the open was successful. In Chapter 4, we will provide a much more robust alternative to the USE command.

When a file is opened via USE, you can optionally specify that the file be opened in SHARED mode or EXCLUSIVE mode. In a network environment, SHARED mode will be used most often, since use in EXCLUSIVE will prevent any other program from accessing the file.

The index files are always opened in the same mode that the .DBF is opened in. However, before you open any index files, you should check NETERR() to make sure the file was opened successfully.

The following listing shows the proper technique to use for opening a network file with the USE command:

```
use customer shared new
if ! NetErr()
   set index to cust1, cust2
else
   Alert("Customer file is not available!")
endif
```

The NEW keyword on the USE command tells Clipper to open this file in the next open work area rather than the current work area. You will probably make use of the NEW clause nearly every time that you USE a file.

In Chapter 4, we will provide a function that will not only open files, but also check for any potential problems or corrupt indexes. Since the .DBF files are accessible from many other programs, many unpredictable things can happen to prevent your Clipper program from being able to safely USE the file.

SUMMARY

In this chapter, we covered how Clipper's files are used on a network. We also discussed the Clipper commands that have special network considerations. By understanding the impact of Clipper commands on a network, we can optimize network performance and ensure a smooth-running Clipper operation.

Establishing a Network Library

Enhancing Clipper's LOCKS program

Communicating with NetWare

Chapter 3

In this chapter, we will start to create a library of common functions that can be used in your networking applications. We will begin by enhancing the LOCKS program that comes with Clipper to allow you to easily customize its behavior for the environment your program is running. We will also discuss the services that NetWare provides, as well as explore how DOS interrupts work and how to use them to access NetWare services. Finally, we will create a program to translate information between Clipper and NetWare.

Enhancing Clipper's LOCKS program

The Clipper package includes a sample source-code file entitled LOCKS.PRG. This file contains high-level shell code wrapped around the core network functions. These functions are listed in Table 3.1.

Table 3.1: LOCKS.PRG Functions

Function	Purpose
RECLOCK()	Tries x number of seconds to lock a record
FILLOCK()	Tries x number of seconds to lock the file
ADDREC()	Tries x number of seconds to add a record
NETUSE()	Attempts to open a file on a network

For many applications, the functions in LOCKS.PRG are adequate. But, although these functions provide the basic functionality required to handle file opening and locking, they lack the flexibility to be easily customized for a variety of applications. For example, in some network environments, waiting for ten seconds to lock a record is considered good performance, while in other systems it is totally unacceptable.

Instead of compiling customized versions of LOCKS.PRG for each application, we can write a version that is driven by a configuration file. Our customized version will become the starting point for the network library we will build during the course of this book.

Each network function in the library will be preceded by the letter *N*, followed by an underscore. For example, N_RECLOCK() works the same as the RECLOCK() function in the default LOCKS program. If you wish to maintain the same naming convention as in LOCKS.PRG, you can use the preprocessor directives shown below. These directives translate calls to RECLOCK() to the appropriate N_ functions.

```
#xtranslate RecLock( <n> )   => N_RecLock( <n> )
#xtranslate FilLock( <n> )   => N_FilLock( <n> )
#xtranslate AddRec( <n> )    => N_AddRec( <n> )
```

The code for our modified LOCKS program, called N_LOCKS.PRG, is shown in Listing 3.1.

Listing 3.1: N_LOCKS Program

```
*  Program:  N_LOCKS
*  Author.:  Joseph D. Booth and Greg Lief
*  Purpose:  A more flexible and configurable locking
*            program for use with Clipper.
****************************************

#include "fileio.ch"

#include "common.ch"
* #include "cl501.ch"    \\ If Clipper 5.01

#xtranslate DispMsg( <cText> )  => ;
            setpos(maxrow()-1, 0) ; ;
            dispout(padr(<cText>), maxcol()+1)

#define CRLF   chr(13)+chr(10)

// network configuration file
#define CFGFILE   "network.ini"
```

Listing 3.1: N_LOCKS Program (Continued)

```
// manifest constants delineating structure of file-wide globals_ array
#define N_SHOW_MESSAGE       1
#define N_WAITFOR_RECLOCK    2
#define N_WAITFOR_FILELOCK   3
#define N_WAITFOR_APPEND     4
#define N_WAITFOR_OPEN       5
#define N_ASKFOR_WAIT        6
#define N_FILELOCK_MSG       7
#define N_RECLOCK_MSG        8
#define N_APPEND_MSG         9
#define N_OPEN_MSG          10
#define N_RETRY_MSG         11

#define IDENTIFIER           1
#define VALUE                2

static globals_ := { ;
          { "display wait messages", .F. }, ;
          { "add record wait time" ,  3  }, ;
          { "file lock wait time"  ,  3  }, ;
          { "record lock wait time",  3  }, ;
          { "file open wait time"  ,  5  }, ;
          { "ask user to wait"     , .F. }, ;
          { "file lock message"    , "Trying to lock the file..." }, ;
          { "record lock message"  , "Trying to lock a record..." }, ;
          { "add record message"   , "Trying to add a record..."  }, ;
          { "file open message"    , "Trying to open the file..." }, ;
          { "retry message",         "Continue trying (Y/N)?" } }


*    Function: N_Init()
*    Purpose: Initialize file-wide settings from NETWORK.INI
*       Notes: Recreates NETWORK.INI if it does not exist
***************************
function n_init(cFile)
local x
local y
local nItems := len(globals_)
local cString
local nHandle
default cFile to CFGFILE
// attempt to open configuration file
nHandle := fopen(cFile)
// continue if file opened successfully
```

Listing 3.1: N_LOCKS Program (Continued)

```
if nHandle != -1
   do while gfreadline(@cString, nHandle)
      // loop through the TEXT_ array and compare to this line
      for x := 1 to nItems
         if cString = lower(globals_[x,IDENTIFIER])
            // read in value and convert to correct data type
            y := rtrim(substr(cString, at('=', cString) + 2))
            // convert to correct data type and assign to array
            globals_[x,VALUE] := convert1(y,valtype(globals_[x,VALUE]))
         endif
      next
   enddo
   fclose(nHandle)
else
   // configuration file does not exist, so create it
   if ( nHandle := fcreate(cFile, FC_NORMAL) ) != -1
      fwrite(nHandle, "[network parameters]" + CRLF)
      for x := 1 to nItems
         fwrite(nHandle, padr(globals_[x,IDENTIFIER], 22) + '= ')
         fwrite(nHandle, convert2(globals_[x,VALUE]) + CRLF)
      next
      fwrite(nHandle, chr(26))
      fclose(nHandle)
   endif
endif
return nil
*************************************************************
*
*    Function:  Convert1()
*       Purpose: Convert character to any data type
***************************
static function convert1(data, cType)
local ret_val
do case
   case cType == "L"
      ret_val := data == "YES"
   case cType == "N"
      ret_val := val(data)
   case cType == "D"
      ret_val := ctod(data)
   case cType == "C"
      ret_val := data
endcase
```

Listing 3.1: N_LOCKS Program (Continued)

```
return ret_val
************************************************************


*    Function: Convert2()
*      Purpose: Convert any data type to character
***************************
static function convert2(data)
local cType := valtype(data)
local ret_val
do case
   case cType == "L"
      ret_val := if(data, "YES", "NO")
   case cType == "N"
      ret_val := ltrim(str(data))
   case cType == "D"
      ret_val := dtoc(data)
   case cType == "C"
      ret_val := data
endcase
return ret_val
************************************************************


*    Function: N_Addrec()
*      Purpose: To add a record to a locked file
***************************
function N_Addrec(nWait)
local cSave    := savescreen(maxrow()-1, 0, maxrow(), maxcol())
local keepWait := .T.
local nOrigWait
default nWait to globals_[N_WAITFOR_APPEND, VALUE]

nOrigWait := nWait
append blank                       // Attempt to add the record
if ! neterr()                      // Did we succeed ?
   return (.T.)
endif
do while keepWait
   // Tell user we're waiting
   if globals_[N_SHOW_MESSAGE, VALUE]
      DispMsg(globals_[N_APPEND_MSG, VALUE])
   endif
```

Listing 3.1: N_LOCKS Program (Continued)

```
   nWait := nOrigWait
   do while nWait > 0
      append blank
      if ! neterr()
         if globals_[N_SHOW_MESSAGE, VALUE]
            restscreen(maxrow()-1, 0, maxrow(), maxcol(), cSave)
         endif
         return (.T.)
      endif
      inkey(1)          // Wait 1 second
      nWait--
   enddo
   if globals_[N_ASKFOR_WAIT, VALUE]
      keepWait := yn(globals_[N_RETRY_MSG, VALUE])
   endif
enddo
if globals_[N_SHOW_MESSAGE, VALUE]
   restscreen(maxrow()-1, 0, maxrow(), maxcol(), cSave)
endif
return (.F.)          // Not locked
************************************************************


*   Function: N_Fillock()
*   Purpose: To lock the file in the current work area
***************************
function N_Fillock(nWait)
local cSave    := savescreen(maxrow()-1, 0, maxrow(), maxcol())
local keepWait := .T.
local nOrigWait
default nWait to globals_[N_WAITFOR_FILELOCK, VALUE]
nOrigWait := nWait

if flock()                                    // Did we get the file locked?
   return (.T.)
endif
do while keepWait
   // Tell user we're waiting
   if globals_[N_SHOW_MESSAGE, VALUE]
      DispMsg(globals_[N_FILELOCK_MSG, VALUE])
   endif
   nWait := nOrigWait
   do while nWait > 0
      if flock()
```

Listing 3.1: N_LOCKS Program (Continued)

```
         if globals_[N_SHOW_MESSAGE, VALUE]
            restscreen(maxrow()-1, 0, maxrow(), maxcol(), cSave)
         endif
         return(.T.)
      endif
      inkey(1)           // Wait 1 second
      nWait--
   enddo

   if globals_[N_ASKFOR_WAIT, VALUE]
      keepWait := yn(globals_[N_RETRY_MSG, VALUE])
   endif
enddo
if globals_[N_SHOW_MESSAGE, VALUE]
   restscreen(maxrow()-1, 0, maxrow(), maxcol(), cSave)
endif
return (.F.)          // Not locked
*****************************************************************


*   Function: N_Reclock()
*   Purpose: Attempts to lock a record
***************************
function N_Reclock(nWait)
local cSave     := savescreen(maxrow()-1, 0, maxrow(), maxcol())
local keepWait := .T.
local nOrigWait

default nWait to globals_[N_WAITFOR_RECLOCK, VALUE]
if rlock()                           // Did we succeed ?
   return (.T.)
endif

nOrigWait := nWait

do while keepWait
   // Tell user we're waiting
   if globals_[N_SHOW_MESSAGE, VALUE]
      DispMsg(globals_[N_RECLOCK_MSG, VALUE])
   endif

   nWait := nOrigWait
   while nWait > 0
      if rlock()
```

Listing 3.1: N_LOCKS Program (Continued)

```
         if globals_[N_SHOW_MESSAGE, VALUE]
            restscreen(maxrow()-1, 0, maxrow(), maxcol(), cSave)
         endif
         return(.T.)
      endif
      inkey(1)          // Wait 1 second
      nWait--
   enddo

   if globals_[N_ASKFOR_WAIT, VALUE]
      keepWait := yn(globals_[N_RETRY_MSG, VALUE])
   endif
enddo
if globals_[N_SHOW_MESSAGE, VALUE]
   restscreen(maxrow()-1, 0, maxrow(), maxcol(), cSave)
endif
return (.F.)          // Not locked
**************************************************************


*    Function: YN( <cMsg> )
*    Purpose: Display message, get yes/no response from user
**************************************************************
static function yn(msg)
local cKey := ""
@ maxrow(),0 say padr(msg, maxcol() + 1)
do while ! cKey $ "YN"
   cKey := upper(chr(inkey(5)))
enddo
@ maxrow(),0
return ( cKey == "Y" )
**************************************************************


*    Function: GFReadline(@<cString>, <nHandle>)
*    Purpose: Read one line (to CR/LF) from a text file
*    Excerpted from Grumpfish Library (c) 1989-92 Greg Lief
**************************************************************
function gfreadline(cstring, nhandle)
local ret_val := .t.
local buffer
local ptr
local bytes
local bufsize := 255
```

Listing 3.1: N_LOCKS Program (Continued)

```
local tempstring
cstring := []
buffer := space(bufsize)
do while .t.
   bytes := fread(nhandle, @buffer, bufsize)
   tempstring := left(buffer, bytes)
   if ( ptr := at(CRLF, tempstring) ) > 0
      cstring += substr(tempstring, 1, ptr - 1)
      fseek(nhandle, -(bytes - (ptr + 1)), FS_RELATIVE)
      exit
   else
      cstring += tempstring
      if bytes < bufsize
         ret_val := .f.
         exit
      endif
   endif
enddo
return ret_val
```

CONFIGURATION FILES

If you have Microsoft Windows installed on your computer, you have probably seen files called SYSTEM.INI and WINDOWS.INI. These files contain the parameter settings that tell Windows how to operate. The general format is

```
[Section-name]
keyword = value
```

These ASCII text files can be edited easily with any editor (even good old EDLIN). We will borrow this type of structure to create our own configuration file, which will control our network library. Our configuration file will be called NETWORK.INI.

The first line of data in our configuration file is a section header called [network parameters]. This section contains the default wait times, as well as communication rules for the N_LOCKS.PRG file. Here are the contents of a typical NETWORK.INI file:

```
[network parameters]
display wait messages = YES
add record wait time  = 3
file lock wait time   = 5
record lock wait time = 3
ask user to wait      = YES
```

The N_INIT function at the beginning of Listing 3.1 can allow a configuration file to be used to control lock timings and communication with the user. You can also use the configuration file to alter the text of the wait messages. This would allow your software to be used internationally, with simply a change to the text in the NETWORK.INI file.

Communicating with NetWare

While Clipper provides the basic commands and functions needed to access the network, the network provides a host of other services waiting to be tapped. Later chapters of this book will discuss these services in more detail, but now we will discuss what these services are and, more importantly, how we can access them from within our Clipper program.

Novell Application Program Interface (API)

Novell, Inc., the company that sells NetWare, actively encourages developers to write applications that communicate with the network. To assist the developer, Novell has released a set of APIs that give programmers access to almost all information available with the operating system. In this book, we will use many of the functions available through the API set.

The API set is divided into a number of sections. Here are some of the common API groups:

Accounting services

Apple File Talk services

Bindery services

Communication services

Connection and workstation services

Diagnostic services

Directory services

File services

Messaging services

Printing services

Queue services

Synchronization services

Transaction tracking services

USING THE FT_INT86() FUNCTION TO ACCESS DOS INTERRUPTS

All NetWare APIs are available through the DOS interrupt system. In order to access any of Novell's API functions, we need a function that allows Clipper to directly call a DOS interrupt. Ted Means, an assembly language guru, has contributed such a function—FT_INT86()—to the Nanforum Toolkit, a public-domain collection of functions to enhance Clipper's functionality. The Nanforum Toolkit is included on the disk accompanying this book, and is also available on many BBS systems and on the CompuServe Clipper forum.

The NetWare operating system services are accessed via DOS interrupt 33 (21h). This interrupt is mapped to NetWare when the shell is loaded, and NetWare looks at all calls. If a call is for a network service, NetWare passes control to one of its own routines; otherwise, it passes control to DOS for handling.

DOS interrupts DOS communicates to our programs through its ten CPU registers. Each register contains 16 bits of data. The 16 bits, or two characters, can be used as a whole or as two halves. For example, one register is called AX, and it can be divided into high and low portions called AH and AL, respectively. These registers are used to pass information to DOS and to retrieve information from DOS.

To request a DOS service (execute an interrupt), you would follow these general steps:

1 Load the appropriate registers with the proper values.

2 Execute the desired interrupt.

3 Read the values you need from the registers.

FT_INT86() uses an array in the place of the CPU registers. In order to use FT_INT86(), you must first set up an array containing ten elements. You then initialize the registers by writing to the appropriate array element.

Once we have initialized the array, we then call the FT_INT86() function, passing it the interrupt we wish to execute and the array of registers. If the function returns .T., then the array will be updated to reflect the changed parameters.

As an example, let's use FT_INT86() to determine if a network shell is loaded. Listing 3.2 contains the function N_WHATNET(), which returns the letter *N* if NetWare is loaded and *L* if the LANtastic network is loaded. If neither network is loaded, the function returns an empty string.

Listing 3.2: N_WHATNET() Function

```
*  Program:   N_WhatNet()
*  Authors:   Joseph D. Booth and Greg Lief
*  Purpose:   A function to determine which network, if
*             any, is loaded.
***************************************************************

#define    AX    1
#define    SI    5
#define    DI    6
#define    DS    8
#define    ES    9

function N_WhatNet()
local cReturn := ''
LOCAL nReturn := 0
local aRegs[ 10 ]
//
// First, lets check Novell
//
aRegs[ AX ] := 227 * 256              // Set AH to nService
aRegs[ DS ] := i2bin(1)+chr(70)       // Request packet
aRegs[ SI ] := .T.
aRegs[ ES ] := space(5)               // Send packet
aRegs[ DI ] := .F.

if ft_int86( 33, aRegs )
   nReturn := aRegs[AX] % 256   // Extract low byte
   if nReturn = 0
      cReturn := "N"
   endif
endif
//
//
if empty(cReturn)
   //
   // Now we can check for Lantastic
   //
   aRegs[1] := 47104
   if ft_int86( 47, aRegs )
      if (aRegs[AX] % 256) <> 0   // Extract low byte
         cReturn := "L"
```

Listing 3.2: N_WHATNET() Function (Continued)

```
      endif
   endif
endif
return cReturn
```

NETWARE()—A FUNCTION TO CALL NOVELL'S API

Novell's NetWare API works with packets. A *packet* is a string that contains various information that the function call requires. There are two packets needed: Request and Reply. The two first bytes of either packet are the packet size. The remaining bytes and packet size will vary, depending upon which API we are calling.

Using FT_INT86() to handle the actual DOS call, we can write a general-purpose function to call a NetWare API. Calling an API consists of the following steps:

1 Create a Request packet. This is a Clipper string containing various information needed for the API.

2 Create an empty Reply packet. This packet must be large enough to hold the data returned from the API called.

3 Load the DOS registers, which include the API function to call and the pointers to the Request and Reply packets, with the appropriate function number.

4 Execute the DOS interrupt.

5 Remove the length bytes from the beginning of the Reply packet.

6 Return the success or error code from the DOS call.

Listing 3.3 contains a general-purpose function to execute the NETWARE() API function call.

Listing 3.3: NETWARE() Function

```
*  Program:  NetWare()
*  Authors:  Joseph D. Booth and Greg Lief
*  Purpose:  A shell for calling Netware interrupts
*
***********************************************************
```

Listing 3.3: NETWARE() Function (Continued)

```
#define    NULL_BYTE  chr(0)
#define    AX         1
#define    BX         2
#define    CX         3
#define    DX         4
#define    SI         5
#define    DI         6
#define    BP         7
#define    DS         8
#define    ES         9
#define    FLAGS      10

#define    REG_DS     .T.
#define    REG_ES     .F.
#define    MAX_REGISTERS  10

function Netware( nService, cRequest, cReply )
local aRegs[ MAX_REGISTERS ]
local nReturn := -1
local cSend   := i2bin(len(cRequest)) + cRequest
local cRecv   := i2bin(len(cReply)) + cReply

aRegs[ AX ] := nService * 256   // Set AH to nService
aRegs[ DS ] := cSend             // Request packet
aRegs[ SI ] := .T.
aRegs[ ES ] := cRecv             // Send packet
aRegs[ DI ] := .F.

if ft_int86( 33, aRegs )
   nReturn := aRegs[AX] % 256   // Extract low byte
   if nReturn < 0
      nReturn += 256
   endif
endif

cReply := substr( aRegs[ ES ], 3 )
return nReturn
************************************************************
```

XLATE—A PROGRAM FOR TRANSLATING FUNCTIONS BETWEEN NETWARE AND CLIPPER

In addition to the actual communication with the NetWare function call, we will need some functions to convert the NetWare results into a format that Clipper can use.

When NetWare returns a string value, it is terminated by a null byte. In order for Clipper to work with this string, the null byte and all bytes beyond it must be stripped off. When strings are passed to NetWare, they must be padded to the required length with null bytes.

In addition to strings, there are three kinds of numbers that NetWare works with: bytes, integers, and long integers.

- A *byte* is a number between 0 and 255 and uses one character of storage. The Clipper ASC() and CNR() functions can be used to translate single bytes.

- An *integer* uses two characters of storage and can be signed or unsigned. Signed integers range from -32,767 to 32,768 and unsigned integers from 0 to 65,535. Unlike DOS, NetWare stores the integer from left to right. DOS swaps the bytes so that the left eight bits represent the lower portion of the number and the right eight bits the higher portion. Clipper provides functions to convert a DOS integer into a number, but does not provide functions to convert a NetWare integer into a number. In the XLATE program, we will provide a function to convert integers back and forth.

- A *long integer* uses four characters of storage and can be signed or unsigned. The XLATE program provides methods for translating long integers to and from Clipper numerics.

Listing 3.4 shows the XLATE program, which contains the user-defined functions for converting NetWare data into a format usable by Clipper:

Listing 3.4: XLATE Program

```
*  Program:  XLATE.PRG
*  Authors:  Joseph D. Booth and Greg Lief
*  Purpose:  Translation functions between NetWare and
*            Clipper
************************************************************

#define NULL_BYTE    chr(0)
```

Listing 3.4: XLATE Program (Continued)

```
//  Function:  CleanStr()
//   Purpose:  Removes all characters following the NULL
//             character, including the NULL itself
//
/////////////////////////////
function cleanstr( cString )
local x
return if( (x := at(NULL_BYTE, cString)) == 0, cString, ;
            substr(cString, 1, x-1) )
*************************************************************

//  Function:  Lstring()
//   Purpose:  Pads a string with NULL characters
//
/////////////////////////////////
function Lstring( cString, nSize )
return chr(nSize)+padr(cString, nSize, NULL_BYTE)
*************************************************************

//  Function:  Int2Clip()
//   Purpose:  Converts an integer string to a Clipper
//             numeric value
//
/////////////////////////////
function Int2Clip( cInteger )
local nValue := 0
nValue := 256 * asc(cInteger)+asc(substr(cInteger,2,1))
return nValue


*************************************************************

//  Function:  Clip2Int()
//   Purpose:  Converts a Clipper numeric to an integer
//             string value
//
///////////////////////////////////
function Clip2int( nValue )
return chr( nValue / 256) + chr( nValue % 256 )
*************************************************************

//  Function:  Long2Clip()
//   Purpose:  Converts a long integer string to a
//             Clipper numeric value
//
```

Listing 3.4: XLATE Program (Continued)

```
///////////////////////////////
function Long2Clip( cInteger )
LOCAL nValue := 0
nValue := asc(substr(cInteger,1,1)) * 65536 +;
         asc(substr(cInteger,2,1)) * 4096  +;
         asc(substr(cInteger,3,1)) * 256   +;
         asc(substr(cInteger,4,1))
return nValue
**************************************************************

//   Function:  Clip2Long()
//    Purpose:  Converts a Clipper numeric to an integer
//              string value
//
///////////////////////////////
function Clip2Long( nValue )
 return chr( nValue/65536)  + chr( (nValue%65536)/ 4096) + ;
        chr( nValue/ 256)   + chr( nValue % 256 )
```

Summary

In this chapter, we've expanded the basic functionality of the LOCKS program provided with Clipper. We've also introduced some new functions that allow us to communicate directly with NetWare. These functions will be used quite frequently in subsequent chapters.

Opening Files

OPENING .DBF FILES

OPENING INDEX FILES

OPENEM()—A FILE OPENING PROGRAM

FIXEM()—A FUNCTION TO REPAIR OPEN ERRORS IF POSSIBLE

USING ALTERNATE DEVICE DRIVERS

OPENING OTHER TYPES OF FILES

Chapter 4

Clipper was originally designed to compile the dBASE language into an executable form. Because the dBASE language handles .DBF files and .NDX indexes, Clipper has grown up working with these types of files. Since the inception of dBASE, many other programs have been written to work with .DBF files. Although this proliferation has made the .DBF file format a de facto standard, it can also pose a problem for your Clipper application. While your compiled Clipper code is safe and hidden away inside its .EXE file, the data files your program manipulates might be opened, updated, or even deleted by some other program.

When making a multiuser system, you have to deal with the possibility that anything could happen to your files. In this chapter, we will discuss some of the considerations for opening files and we will design an extremely robust file opener. If your .DBF files can get through these file-opening routines, you can be assured that Clipper will be able to work with the files.

OPENING .DBF FILES

Although Clipper provides a USE command to open a .DBF file, it does very little error checking on that file. In a network environment, many things can occur that would prevent that file from being used. Not all these conditions signal to Clipper that an error has occurred and that the file cannot be used. To ensure safe operation in a network environment, we need to expand what we check before we open the file. These steps are discussed in the following sections.

DOES THE FILE EXIST?

The first consideration is to test that the file exists and is in the appropriate directory. Normally, Clipper assumes that the files are stored in the current directory, but you can override this assumption by using the SET DEFAULT TO command. This command instructs Clipper to look in a different directory for the necessary .DBF and .NTX files. Its syntax is

```
SET DEFAULT TO <cDirectory_name>
```

However, the low-level functions used to open a file do not respect the default directory. You can use the SET() function to determine the default directory, so that the low-level functions can properly open the file. When testing for the presence of a file, it is important that you ensure that Clipper looks in the proper directory.

Fortunately, it is very easy to test for the existence of a file. Clipper provides a function, called FILE(), that returns TRUE if the file exists or FALSE otherwise. Rather than let the application abort with DOS error 2 (file not found), your program should make sure the file exists before trying to open it.

IS THE FILE A DBF?

Unfortunately, you cannot assume that a file is a valid database file just because the extension is .DBF. Clipper's default database driver (DBFNTX) reads standard dBASE III+ files but does not recognize all the other file-format extensions provided by other Xbase-language products. DBFNTX can work with dBASE III files and even some dBASE IV files. However, dBASE IV added a new field type (Floating Number) that DBFNTX does not recognize. As such, DBFNTX cannot work with any dBASE IV file that contains this new field type.

When a USE command is issued, Clipper assumes that the file is a valid .DBF file. If it is not, you usually will not find out until you attempt to update the data in the file. However, by using Clipper's low-level file functions and referring to Table 4.1, you can make sure that the .DBF file you were asked to open appears to be a valid .DBF file.

The low-level file functions allow you to open any file in a raw-data mode. This means that Clipper views the file strictly as a series of characters or bytes. When using the low-level functions, it is up to your program to interpret the data read from the file. Clipper also provides an error system for trapping errors that can occur when working with the low-level file functions.

In Listing 4.1, shown in a moment, we will use the low-level file routines to ensure that a file ending with ".DBF" is indeed an Xbase file that Clipper can use.

DOES THE FILE NEED A MEMO FILE AS WELL?

If the .DBF file contains a memo field, then there must be a file with the same root name and a .DBT extension in the directory. For a FoxPro memo file, the extension is .FPT. We need to validate that this memo file exists. The memo file does not have any signature byte, but the first 4 bytes represent a count of the number of 512-byte blocks in the memo. This number, multiplied by 512, should equal the file size, except that the last block is not padded out to 512 bytes. This means the file size can be anywhere from 1 to 511 bytes different from 512 times the count in the header. Although this method is not as reliable as reading the signature byte in a .DBF file, it makes for a pretty good guess as to whether the file is a .DBT file.

If a memo field is present in the .DBF file, but the memo file does not exist, it is possible to create an empty memo file to allow Clipper to work with the .DBF. If you do not have a memo file when one is expected, Clipper will not complain until you attempt to update the data.

Listing 4.1 contains a function called VALIDDBF(), which can be used to validate that the file name exists and appears to be a valid .DBF file. It also checks for a valid memo file, if one should exist. VALIDDBF() returns a zero value if no problems are detected, or a numeric error code if a problem occurred. These error return codes are shown in Table 4.1.

Table 4.1: Error Return Codes for VALIDDBF() Function

Code	Meaning
−1	.DBF/.NTX appears corrupt
−2	.DBF's required memo file is missing
−3	File is set to read-only
−4	Memo file appears corrupt
2	File does not exist
3	Path does not exist
4	Too many files are open
5	Access denied
6	Invalid handle
8	Not enough memory
32	Sharing violation

The positive numbers correspond with DOS errors that can occur when using low-level files. The negative numbers represent error codes unique to the VALIDDBF() function. For the most part, the DOS errors are nonrecoverable, although the FIXEM() function discussed later in this chapter will provide code to recover from DOS error 2 (file not found).

Listing 4.1 contains the source code for the VALIDDBF() function call. Note that our version of NET_USE(), shown later in this chapter, will use this function.

Listing 4.1: VALIDDBF() Function

```
*    Function:  ValidDbf()
*    Authors:   Joseph D. Booth and Greg Lief
*    Purpose:   To check that the file specified is a valid DBASE file.
*
*
*
*************************
#define    VALID_SIGNATURE_BYTES    { 3,131,139,245 }
#define    DBT_FILE_NEEDED_BYTES    { 131,139,245   }
#define    MEMO_FILE_EXTENSIONS     { "DBT","FPT","DBT" }


#include "SET.CH"
#include "FILEIO.CH"

function ValidDbf(cFile)

local cDir      :=  set(_SET_DEFAULT)
local nHandle   :=  fopen(cDir+cFile+".DBF",66)
local cBuf      :=  space(12)
local nSign     :=  0
local nReturn   :=  0
local nBlocks   :=  0
local nSize     :=  0
local nRecs     :=  0
local nRecSize:=    0
local nOffset   :=  0
local x

if nHandle <> -1
   //
   // Read the signature byte to make sure this
```

Listing 4.1: VALIDDBF() Function (Continued)

```
// is a .DBF file
//
///////////////////////////
fread(nHandle,@cBuf,12)
nSize    := fseek(nHandle,0,FS_END)
fclose(nHandle)
nSign := asc(cBuf)
if ascan( VALID_SIGNATURE_BYTES,nSign ) > 0
   nRecs    := bin2l(substr(cBuf, 5,4))
   nRecSize := bin2w(substr(cBuf,11,2))
   nOffset  := bin2w(substr(cBuf, 9,2))
   if nRecs > 0
      nReturn  := if(abs( (nRecs*nRecSize)+nOffset-nSize ) < 3,0,-1)
   else
      nReturn  := if(nOffset <= nSize+1,0,-1)
   endif
else
   nReturn := -1
endif

if nReturn == 0

   if (x := ascan(DBT_FILE_NEEDED_BYTES,nSign)) > 0
      //
      nReturn := -4
      //
      nHandle := fopen(cdir+cFile+"."+MEMO_FILE_EXTENSIONS[x],64)
      if nHandle <> -1
         if MEMO_FILE_EXTENSIONS[x] == "DBT"
            cBuf    := space(4)
            fread(nHandle,@cBuf,4)
            nSize   := fseek(nHandle,0,FS_END)
            nBlocks := bin2l( cBuf ) * 512
            if nSize <= nBlocks .and. nSize > (nBlocks-512)
               nReturn := 0
            endif
            fclose(nHandle)
         else
            nReturn := 0
         endif
      elseif ferror() == 2
```

Listing 4.1: VALIDDBF() Function (Continued)

```
            nReturn := -2
         endif
         //
      endif
   endif
else
   //
   // If -1 is returned from the FOPEN call, then a DOS
   // error occurred which caused the function to fail.
   //
   if Ferror() == 5
      nReturn := -3
   else
      nReturn := Ferror()
   endif
endif
return nReturn
```

FILE ATTRIBUTES

Another problem that you might encounter when trying to open a .DBF is finding that the file is flagged as read-only. Clipper 5.*x* allows you to open a read-only file only if you specify READ-ONLY on the USE command.

DOS has a useful set of functions that allow you to manipulate file attributes. Each DOS file has a byte in its directory entry that determines the file attributes. These attributes are listed in Table 4.2.

Table 4.2: DOS File Attributes

Letter	Meaning
N	Normal file, can be read or written to
R	Read-only file
H	Hidden, does not appear in DIR listings
S	System file, relic from CP/M days
V	Volume label
D	Directory name, not file name
A	File has been archived

DOS function 33 (21H) has a subfunction 4300H, which returns the attribute byte. We can access this function by using the FT_INT86() function described in Chapter 3. Listing 4.2 shows the function GETFATTR(), which returns a character string containing the file's attributes. Its syntax is

`<cAttributes> := GetFattr( cFilename )`

GETFATTR() will return a string of attributes for the specified file. The string will contain an uppercase letter from Table 4.2 if the appropriate attribute is set. If not, the letter will not be included in the string. If an *R* is present in the returned string, then the file is set to read-only and the .DBF cannot be opened for update purposes. Note that *N* will never be returned, since a normal file lacks any attributes.

Listing 4.2: GETFATTR() Function

```
*  Function:  GetFattr()
*  Authors:   Joseph D. Booth and Greg Lief
*  Purpose:   To get the file attributes for the
*             specified file name.
*  Syntax:    <string>  := GetFAttr( cFile )
*
*******************************************

#define CX                 3
#define DX                 4
#define DS                 8
#define FLAGS             10

function getfattr(cName)
*
* 4300h - Get file attributes
*
LOCAL aRegs := { 17152, 0, 0, 0, 0, 0, 0, 0, 0, 0 }
LOCAL cAttr :=""
aRegs[ DS ] := cName  // File name
aRegs[ DX ] := .T.    // Tell interrupt we are using a string
Ft_int86(33,aRegs)              // Execute interrupt
if aRegs[FLAGS] % 2 == 0        // Check carry flag
   cAttr += if( isbiton(aRegs[CX],5), "A", "" )
   cAttr += if( isbiton(aRegs[CX],4), "D", "" )
   cAttr += if( isbiton(aRegs[CX],3), "V", "" )
```

Listing 4.2: GETFATTR() Function (Continued)

```
   cAttr += if( isbiton(aRegs[CX],2), "S", "" )
   cAttr += if( isbiton(aRegs[CX],1), "H", "" )
   cAttr += if( isbiton(aRegs[CX],0), "R", "" )
endif
return cAttr
*******************************************************
/*
* Thanks....: Ted Means
* Source....: Nanforum Toolkit
*/

STATIC function isbiton( nWord, nBit )
  nWord := int(nWord * (2 ^ (15 - nBit)))
  nWord := int(nWord % 65536)
  nWord := int(nWord / 32768)

return (nWord == 1)
```

SHARED VS. EXCLUSIVE MODE

Once we have established that the file appears to be a valid and usable .DBF file, we need to check whether the opening mode is SHARED or EXCLUSIVE. Fortunately, the USE command, in conjunction with NETERR(), can provide that information and open the file.

Listing 4.3 shows a new version of Clipper's NET_USE() function. This function expects the first three parameters to be the same as those in Clipper's version. Table 4.3 lists these standard parameters.

Table 4.3: NET_USE() Standard Parameters

Parameter	Meaning
cFile	Name of the .DBF (without an extension) to open.
lExclus	TRUE to open the file in EXCLUSIVE mode or FALSE to open the file in SHARED mode. The default is SHARED mode.
nWait	Number of seconds to wait before giving up the attempt to open the file.

Listing 4.3: Modified NET_USE Function

```
*  Program:  N_OPEN()
*   Author:  Joseph D. Booth and Greg Lief
*  Purpose:  A more robust file opening routine for
*            network programming for use with Clipper.
*
*************************************************************
#include "fileio.ch"

#xtranslate DispMsg( <cText> )  => ;
            setpos(maxrow()-1, 0) ; ;
            dispout(padr(<cText>), maxcol()+1)

#include "CL501.CH"              // Clipper 5.01
* #include "COMMON.CH"            // Clipper 5.2

#define DEFAULT_DRIVER          "DBFNTX"

#define N_SHOW_MESSAGE          1
#define N_ASKFOR_WAIT           2
#define N_WAITFOR_OPEN          3
#define N_RETRY_MSG             4
#define N_OPEN_MSG              5

#define IDENTIFIER              1
#define VALUE                   2

static globals_ := { ;
           { "display wait messages", .F. }, ;
           { "ask user to wait"     , .F. }, ;
           { "file open wait time"  ,  5  }, ;
           { "retry message",         "Continue trying (Y/N)?" } ,;
           { "open file message",     "Trying to open the file..." } }


function Net_Use( cFile,lExclusive,nWait,cAlias,;
                  lNewArea,lReadOnly,cDriver )

local nOldWait := 0
local lReturn  := .F.
```

Listing 4.3: Modified NET_USE Function (Continued)

```
local keepWait := .T.
local cSave    := savescreen(maxrow()-1, 0, maxrow(), maxcol())
local x

if cFile <> NIL
   DEFAULT  lExclusive  TO  .F.
   DEFAULT  nWait       TO  globals_[N_WAITFOR_OPEN,VALUE]
   DEFAULT  cAlias      TO  cFile
   DEFAULT  lReadOnly   TO  .F.
   DEFAULT  lNewArea    TO  .T.
   DEFAULT  cDriver     TO  DEFAULT_DRIVER

   nOldWait   := nWait

   x := ValidDbf( cFile )
   if x = 0 .or. x = -3

      if "R" $ GetfAttr( cFile+".DBF" ) .and. !lReadonly
         return .F.
      endif

      if ascan( RddList(),cDriver ) = 0
         return .F.
      endif

      dbUseArea( lNewArea,cDriver,cFile,cAlias,;
                 !lExclusive,lReadonly )
      if !NetErr()
         return .T.
      endif

      do while keepWait
        // Tell user we're waiting
        if globals_[N_SHOW_MESSAGE, VALUE]
           DispMsg(globals_[N_OPEN_MSG, VALUE])
        endif
        do while nWait > 0
           dbUseArea( lNewArea,cDriver,cFile,cAlias,;
```

Listing 4.3: Modified NET_USE Function (Continued)

```
                    !lExclusive,lReadonly )
         if ! neterr()
            if globals_[N_SHOW_MESSAGE, VALUE]
               restscreen(maxrow()-1, 0, maxrow(), maxcol(), cSave)
            endif
            return (.T.)
         endif
         inkey(1)           // Wait 1 second
         nWait--
      enddo
      if globals_[N_ASKFOR_WAIT, VALUE]
         keepWait := yn(globals_[N_RETRY_MSG, VALUE])
         nWait    := nOldWait
      endif
    enddo
  endif
endif
return lReturn
*************************************************************************




*    Function: YN( <cMsg> )
*       Purpose: Display message, get yes/no response from user
***************************************************************
static function yn(msg)
local cKey
@ maxrow(),0 say padr(msg, maxcol() + 1)
do while ! cKey $ "YN"
   cKey := upper(chr(inkey(5)))
enddo
@ maxrow(),0
return ( cKey == "Y" )
*************************************************************************
```

Table 4.4 lists the additional parameters in our version of NET_USE(). These optional parameters are not present in the version of NET_USE() that comes with Clipper.

Table 4.4: Additional NET_USE() Parameters

Parameter	Meaning
cAlias	Optional work-area alias to use. Defaults to the name of the file.
lNewArea	TRUE to open the file in the next available work area or FALSE to open it in the current work area. Note that if the file is open in the current work area, it will close any file currently open in the work area. The default is TRUE to use a new work area.
lReadOnly	Should the file be open for read-only access only. The default is FALSE, which indicates to open the file for update purposes.
cDriver	Database driver to use to open file.

This version of NET_USE() internally calls the VALIDDBF() function and the GETFATTR() function to make sure that the file you wish to open is valid and flagged properly. You can use this version as a direct replacement for NET_USE() in your applications if you want to reduce the likelihood of .DBF problems. Although this code is self-contained, a version of NET_USE() that is controlled by the NETWORK.INI we discussed in Chapter 3 can be made by copying the NET_USE() and VALIDDBF() functions into the N_LOCKS.PRG from Chapter 3. Note that this code also contains a function called DBFFAIL_CODE(), which will return a numeric value from Table 4.1 if the NET_USE() function fails.

OPENING INDEX FILES

As mentioned in Chapter 2, an index file is a subsidiary file that imposes a logical order on the corresponding data file. It can be used to provide very rapid access to any record and to order the records by something other than record number. If you need an index file to display or look up data, you must specify the index name(s) after the file is opened. This is done using the SET INDEX TO command or the DBSETINDEX() function. Unfortunately, neither method provides any feedback as to the success or failure of the index opening operation.

When Clipper opens index files, it performs very little error checking on the index file. If one of the files is locked by another program, Clipper will not open the index file, but will not report that the index file was not opened. As mentioned in Chapter 2, this situation can lead very quickly to index corruption.

In addition, if the index file does not appear to be a proper index file, Clipper will not detect the problem until you attempt to update the .DBF file and the index file. Listing 4.4 contains a function to make sure that the index exists and appears valid. If the index file does not exist and you have specified a key expression, the function will re-create the index file.

CREATING INDEX FILES ON A NETWORK

When index files are opened on a network, they are opened in the same file-sharing mode as the corresponding .DBF. If you open a file for shared access, the index file is opened for shared access as well. When index files are opened in SHARED mode, bytes 3–2 in the header are incremented each time a program updates the index file. This serves as a semaphore to tell other programs to re-read the disk file instead of using the buffer for determining the next record.

Clipper allows you to create an index file on a .DBF opened in SHARED mode, but the index file will be created for exclusive use. If you are creating a temporary index file for only the current program, then the EXCLUSIVE mode is appropriate. However, if the index file needs to be accessed and updated by other network programs, you need to first create the index and close the databases. You can then reopen the file in SHARED mode and the index will be available for shared use, as well. Here is an example of indexing and reopening a file:

```
if net_use("CUSTOMER",.F.,5)     // Open in SHARED mode
   if !file("CUST1"+INDEXEXT())
      index on upper(id_code) to CUST1
      use
      Net_Use("CUSTOMER",.F.,5)
   endif
   set index to CUST1
endif
```

Although this shows a missing index file being created, it does not have any provision for communicating to other programs that it is creating the index. In Chapter 8, when we discuss semaphores, we will provide an example that allows the indexing program to notify other programs to wait until it is finished before opening the file.

IS IT AN INDEX FILE?

Listing 4.4 contains a function called VALIDNTX(), which can be used to validate that the file name exists, that it appears to be a proper index file, and that the index key is what the program is expecting. VALIDNTX() will return a value of zero if the index appears proper, or one of the error codes listed in Table 4.1 otherwise. This allows you to detect any problems before attempting to update the data files.

VALIDNTX() also has a third parameter that indicates whether the function should re-create a missing index. The default is TRUE, which will allow the function to create the index file if it is missing. The program will create the index on the file in the current work area and then close it. Normally, you would follow your index check functions with the SET INDEX TO command.

Listing 4.4: VALIDNTX() Function

```
*     Program:  VALIDNTX.PRG
*     Authors:  Joseph D. Booth and Greg Lief
*     Purpose:  Spot check an index file's header
*      Syntax:  <numeric>  := VALIDNTX( cFile,cExpr,lCreate )
*****************************************************
//
//                         EXT   Key   Size
//
STATIC    aOffset :=    { {".IDX",  17,   13},.;
                          {".NDX",  25,   13},.;
                          {".NTX",  23,   15},.;
                          {".CDX",513,   13} }


function ValidNTX(cFile,cExpr,lCreate)
LOCAL nReturn     := 0
LOCAL cFullName   := cFile +OrgBagExt()
LOCAL x
LOCAL nHandle
LOCAL nSize
LOCAL cFileExpr
LOCAL buf
LOCAL cExt := OrgBagExt()

lcreate := if(lCreate==NIL,.F.,lCreate)

if !file( cFullname )
   if lCreate
      dbclearind()
      index on &cExpr. to (cFIle)
      dbclearind()
```

Listing 4.4: VALIDNTX() Function (Continued)

```
         nreturn := 0
      else
         nReturn := -2
      endif
   elseif "R" $ GetFattr( cFullname )
      nReturn := -3
   else
      if !IndexCorrupt( cFile,OrgBagExt() )
         //
         nHandle := fopen( cFullname,64 )
         if nHandle = -1
            nReturn := Ferror()
         else
            x := ascan( aOffSet, { |zz| zz[1]=upper(cExt) } )
            if x > 0
               buf := space(1024)
               fread(nHandle,@buf,1024)
               fclose(nHandle)
               nSize    := bin2w(substr(buf,aOffset[x,3],2))
               cFileExpr := upper(cleanstr(substr(buf,aOffset[x,2],nSize)))
               if cFileExpr = cExpr
                  nReturn := 0
               else
                  nReturn := -1
                  if lCreate
                     dbclearind()
                     index on &cExpr. to (cFIle)
                     dbclearind()
                     nreturn := 0
                  endif
               endif
            else
               nReturn := -1
            endif
         endif
      endif

      //
   else
```

Listing 4.4: VALIDNTX() Function (Continued)

```
      nReturn := -1
   endif
endif
return nReturn
```

While Listing 4.4 validates that the file exists and checks for the correct header and key expression, this does not solve all the potential index problems we discussed in Chapter 2. In the next section, we will use the two validation functions we have discussed so far to create a robust file opening program.

OPENEM()—A FILE OPENING PROGRAM

In Chapter 2, we discussed many of the considerations to keep in mind to reduce the likelihood of corrupt indexes. As mentioned, two important aspects of index integrity include opening all indexes at all times, and always opening indexes in the same order. Products such as Novell's Btrieve include the index in the data file, so opening one guarantees that the other will be opened. With Clipper, much more flexibility is provided for opening indexes.

Since Clipper does not know which indexes belong to which files, we need to tell it the relations between .DBF files and indexes when we open the files. We can do this by creating a STATIC array that contains the file names, index names, and index expressions. The array is multidimensional, with the following structure:

Element	Description
1	File name
2,1	Index file name
2,2	Index file expression

For example, assume that the customer and vendor files in an application both contain two indexes, one on ID_CODE and the other on the SOUNDEX() of the name. The following STATIC array could be used to represent these files:

```
STATIC file_list  := ;
    { {"CUSTOMER",{"CUST1","id_code"},;
                  {"CUST2","soundex(custName)"} },;
      {"VENDOR"  ,{"VEND1","id_code"},;
                  {"VEND2","soundex(vendName)"} } }
```

The OPENEM() function uses this array to handle the opening of all files. It scans the array to see if the file name you passed is in the array. If it is found, the function uses the STATIC array to determine the necessary file and index information. For actual application use, you should replace the contents of the array with your application's files and indexes.

OPENEM() is called with two parameters. The first parameter is either a character string or an array of character strings indicating the file or files to be opened. The second is the mode, which can be *S* for SHARED or *E* for EXCLUSIVE. The return value will be a logical value indicating whether all the files were opened. In addition, an error array is maintained by the function. This contains the name of the file that failed, as well as a numeric status code indicating why the failure occurred. In the case of the index file, it also contains the index expression. Refer back to Table 4.1 to see the numeric codes. (They are the same as those for the VALIDDBF function.) The negative numbers indicate that the file could be opened but that something is wrong with it. These conditions frequently can be corrected within the code. The positive numbers represent error values returned by DOS when attempting to open the files. DOS error 2 can be corrected by re-creating the file (if appropriate), but most of the other errors are beyond the ability of Clipper to fix without intervention.

If you called the OPEN_ERR() function, this array will be returned. If you choose, you can explain to the end user why the file failed to open, or you can have your application attempt to fix the problem. Alternatively, you can log the errors to an error file for review.

The OPENEM() function is usually called via the following preprocessor directives:

```
#xtranslate Shared( <xFiles> ) => OpenEm(<xFiles>,"S" )
#xtranslate NonShared( <xFiles> ) => OpenEm(<xFiles>,"E" )
```

The following code fragment shows a sample application module that uses the SHARED() or NONSHARED() functions to open files:

```
if Shared( {"CUSTOMER","INVOICE","ITEMS" } )
   //
   // Now all files and indexes are open and
   // ready for use
   //else
     Alert( "Files are unavailable...." )
endif
```

This code allows you to check that all files are available before the user can start to update files. Although the user might see an unfamiliar error message, it is preferable to some databases being updated or, even worse, the corrupt index syndrome.

Listing 4.5 contains the complete source code for the OPENEM() program. Note that it calls the NET_USE() and VALIDNTX() functions discussed earlier in this chapter.

Listing 4.5: OPENEM() Function

```
*  Function:  OpenEm()
*  Authors:   Joseph D. Booth and Greg Lief
*  Purpose:   A robust file opening program
*             for network applications
*    Syntax:  <logical>  := OpenEm( {cFile(s)} )
*
* The file_list array will vary for each application
*
************************************************************

#define    CAN_CREATE    .T.

STATIC afile_list  := ;
    { {"CUSTOMER",{"CUST1","id_code"},;
                  {"CUST2","soundex(custName)"} },;
      {"VENDOR"  ,{"VEND1","id_code"},;
                  {"VEND2","soundex(vendName)"} } }

STATIC aErrors := {}

function OpenEm( aFiles,cMode )
local nOpened      := 0
local x            := 0
local ntx_problem := .F.
local nMax, y, z, cNtx, cExpr, nn

//
// Clear out the error array
//
aErrors := {}

if valtype( aFiles ) == "C"
   aFiles := { aFiles }
endif
```

Listing 4.5: OPENEM() Function (Continued)

```
nMax := len(afiles)
for x :=1 to nMax
   //
   // Was file opened ok?   //
   if Net_use( aFiles[x],cMode=="E" )
      y := ascan( aFileList,{|z|z[1]==aFiles[x] })
      if y > 0
         //
         // Check out the index files
         set index to
         for z := 1 to len(aFileList[y]) - 1
            cNtx  := aFileList[y,z+1,1]
            cExpr := aFileList[y,z+1,2]
            if (nn := validNtx(cNtx,;
                      cExpr,CAN_CREATE) ) == 0
               dbsetindex( cNtx )
            else
               ntx_problems := .T.
               Aadd(aErrors, { cNtx+".NTX",nn,cExpr})
            endif
         next
         if ntx_problems
            set index to
            use
         else
            nOpened++
         endif
         //
      else
         nOpened++
      endif
   else
      Aadd(aErrors,{aFiles[x]+".DBF", DBFFail_Code(),""})
   endif

next
return nMax == nOpened
```

Listing 4.5: OPENEM() Function (Continued)

```
*     Function: Open_err()
*       Purpose: returns array of file open error codes
***************************************************************
function Open_err()
return aErrors
```

FIXEM()—A FUNCTION TO REPAIR OPEN ERRORS IF POSSIBLE

If OPENEM() returns FALSE, you can attempt to fix the errors by using the FIXEM() function in this section. You call FIXEM() and pass it the array of errors returned from OPEN_ERR(). If all errors can be fixed, FIXEM() will fix the files and return TRUE. You might want to modify the FIXEM() code to log any errors it fixes, since these types of errors generally indicate an environment where some other application is using the .DBF files that your Clipper program is working with.

FIXEM() requires some setup on your part if you'd like the program to be able to create missing .DBF files. This would allow your program to be self-installing; the first time installed, the files would be created automatically by FIXEM().

The function MKFILE() would be customized for your application. It expects as a parameter the name of the file it is to create, and returns TRUE if the file was created or FALSE otherwise. By embedding the structure in the code, you can be sure that the file structure always agrees with the .EXE file that installed it. You could even write a program to compare the file structure with the array definition, if it is absolutely critical that the file structure be the same. For example, if you expect a certain field to be at a certain position during FIELDGET() and FIELDPUT() function calls, and then somebody adds a field in dBASE, you could experience TYPE MISMATCH errors or data integrity problems that would be difficult to catch.

Listing 4.6 contains the FIXEM() function's code.

Listing 4.6: FIXEM() Function

```
*   Function:  FixEm()
*    Authors:  Joseph D. Booth and Greg Lief
*    Purpose:  A program to fix problems detected
*              while open network files
*     Syntax:  <logical>  := FixEm( {aErrors} )
```

Listing 4.6: FIXEM() Function (Continued)

```
*
**********************************************************

#define   FIX_READONLY      .T.
#define   FIX_MISSING_DBT   .T.
#define   FIX_CORRUPT_DBT   .T.
#define   FIX_CORRUPT_DBF   .T.


function FixEm(aErrors)
LOCAL nFixed := 0
LOCAL nSize  := len(aErrors)
LOCAL x
LOCAL cFile
LOCAL nMode
LOCAL cExpr
LOCAL cAttr
LOCAL nHandle

for x:= 1 to nSize
   cFile := aErrors[x,1]
   nMode := aErrors[x,2]
   cExpr := aErrors[x,3]
   do case
   //
   // Corrupt DBF, save the old data and
   // create a new DBF file.  This is a way
   // to fix the problem, but would not recover
   // the data.
   //
   case nMode == -1 .and. FIX_CORRUPT_DBF
      rename (cFile+".DBF") to (cFile+".OLD")
      if mkfile(cFile)
         nFixed++
      endif
   //
   // Missing DBT, we can just create an empty
   // one, however the memo data will be lost
   //
   case nMode == -2 .and. FIX_MISSING_DBT
      nHandle := Fcreate(cFile)
      if nHandle <> -1
         Fwrite(nHandle,l2bin(1)+space(508))
```

Listing 4.6: FIXEM() Function (Continued)

```
            fclose(nHandle)
            nFixed++
        endif
    //
    // Here is an easy one, just change the
    // attribute to READ-WRITE instead of READONLY
    //
    case nMode == -3 .and. FIX_READONLY
        cAttr := GetFAttr(cFile)
        cAttr := strtran(cAttr,"R","")
        SetFAttr(cFile,cAttr)
        nFixed++
    //
    // Corrupt DBT, we can save the old .DBT and
    // just create an empty one, however the memo
    // data will still need to be recovered
    //
    case nMode == -4 .and. FIX_CORRUPT_DBT
        rename (cFile+".DBT") to (cFile+".OLT")
        nHandle := Fcreate(cFile)
        if nHandle <> -1
            Fwrite(nHandle,l2bin(1)+space(508))
fclose(nHandle)
            nFixed++
        endif
    //
    // If the file does not exist, we can call the
    // MKFILE() function to create a new DBF
    //
    case nMode ==  2
        if mkfile(cFile)
            nFixed++
        endif
    endcase
next
return nFixed == nSize


***************************************************************
* Function:   setfattr()
* Purpose:    Set a file's attributes
* Syntax:     setfattr()
* Parameters: cFile
*             cAttr
```

Listing 4.6: FIXEM() Function (Continued)

```
* Returns:     lChanged - were attributes modified?
********************
function setfattr(cName,cAttr)
* 4301h - Get file attributes

#define    CX      3
#define    DX      4
#define    DS      8
#define    FLAGS   10

LOCAL aRegs := { 17153, 0, 0, 0, 0, ;
                     0, 0, 0, 0, 0 }  // Save registers
LOCAL nAttr := 0
nAttr += if("R" $ cAttr, 1, 0)
nAttr += if("H" $ cAttr, 2, 0)
nAttr += if("S" $ cAttr, 4, 0)
nAttr += if("A" $ cAttr,32, 0)
aRegs[ CX ] := nAttr            // Place attributes in a register
aRegs[ DS ] := cName            // Directory name
aRegs[ DX ] := .T.              // Tell interrupt we are using a string
Ft_int86(33,aRegs)              // Execute interrupt
return aRegs[FLAGS] % 2 == 0    // Check carry flag


**************************************************************
function MkFile(cName)
LOCAL lReturn := .F.
//
// The code within the DO CASE structure would be the
// appropriate file structures for your application.
//
do case
case cName == "CUSTOMER"
   DbCreate("CUSTOMER", { {"ID_CODE","C",8,0},;
                          {"CUST_NAME","C",20,0},;
                          {"STREET"   ,"C",30,0},;
                          {"CITY"     ,"C",15,0},;
                          {"STATE"    ,"C", 2,0},;
                          {"COUNTRY"  ,"C",15,0},;
                          {"PHONE"    ,"C",22,0},;
                          {"BALANCE"  ,"N",11,2} })

case cName == "VENDOR"
```

Listing 4.6: FIXEM() Function (Continued)

```
    DbCreate("VENDOR"   , { {"ID_CODE","C",8,0},;
                            {"VEND_NAME","C",20,0},;
                            {"STREET"   ,"C",30,0},;
                            {"CITY"     ,"C",15,0},;
                            {"STATE"    ,"C", 2,0},;
                            {"PHONE"    ,"C",22,0},;
                            {"BALANCE"  ,"N",11,2} })
endcase
return lReturn
```

Both OPENEM() and FIXEM() rely on data stored in STATIC arrays that are unique to your application. It is possible to integrate these functions to work from a .DBF or some other data dictionary if you desire, although such a project is left to your application.

Keep in mind that the FIXEM() program corrects the problems only temporarily, to allow your users to continue working with the program. Many of the problems that FIXEM() corrects will still require intervention to recover any data that was lost (and probably not backed up!).

Here is an example of application code that relies on the OPENEM() and FIXEM() functions to handle all file-opening logic:

```
procedure main
LOCAL aErrors := {}
LOCAL ok      := .T.
do while ok
   if Shared( {"CUSTOMER","INVOICE","ITEMS" } )
      exit
   endif
   Alert("Not all files were opened!  Press any key...")
   aErrors := Open_Err()
   ok      := FixEm(aErrors)
   if ok
      Alert("Problems have been corrected...")
      exit
   endif
enddo
if ok
   //
   // Now all files and indexes are open and
   // ready for use
   //
```

```
else
    Alert( "Files are unavailable...." )
endif
```

Using alternate device drivers

Clipper is not limited to working with .DBF files and .NTX indexes. If dBASE compatibility is required, you can use the DBFNDX driver available from Computer Associates to create and use dBASE .NDX files instead of Clipper's .NTX files. (Note, however, that dBASE .NDX files were not designed for a network environment and Clipper's .NTX file would be a better option.) The DBFSIX driver is a replaceable device driver written by a third-party company, Successware, to offer access to FoxPro's indexing options. The FoxPro indexing scheme provides a plethora of features that the current release of Clipper does not offer. The DBFSIX driver offers the programmer complete access to this indexing scheme. It will also allow your Clipper application to run simultaneously with the indexes being updated by someone else's FoxPro program.

To use either library, you need to specify an alternate driver by using the VIA option on the USE command. Its syntax is

```
USE (cFile)  VIA  "DBFSIX"    // Use DBFSIX FoxPro driver
```

You can also use the DBSETDRIVER() function to set the default driver to something other than DBFNTX, which is the normal Clipper data driver. This command will ensure that all subsequent file opens are handled by the alternate driver.

Opening other types of files

In addition to .DBF files and .NTX indexes, Clipper can open other types of files and allow low-level access to the files. Using Clipper, you can open a text file, a spreadsheet, or even an executable file. The FOPEN() function is used to open any file for low-level access. However, the documentation for Clipper does not cover the modes necessary to use the function in anything other than exclusive file use.

FOPEN() allows you to open an existing file in any of the three modes shown in Table 4.5. These modes determine the allowed actions on the file, but do not address the shared use of the file.

Table 4.5: FOPEN() Modes

Mode	FILEIO.CH	Open Mode
0	FO_READ	Open for reading (default)
1	FO_WRITE	Open for writing
2	FO_READWRITE	Open for reading or writing

The sharing parameter consists of a number that is added to the file-open mode to determine how other programs are allowed to use this file. The sharing parameters are shown in Table 4.6. The listing below contains additional #define statements that can be added to FILEIO.CH if you need to open low-level files in a network environment. You should add the contents of this listing to your FILEIO.CH header file:

```
#define  FO_DENY_ALL      16
#define  FO_DENY_WRITE    32
#define  FO_DENY_READ     48
#define  FO_DENY_NONE     64
```

Table 4.6: File Access Parameters

Value	FILEIO.CH	Open Mode
16	FO_DENY_ALL	Deny read/write access to others
32	FO_DENY_WRITE	Deny write access to others
48	FO_DENY_READ	Deny read access to others
64	FO_DENY_NONE	Allow others read/write access

For example, if you need to open a text file for read-only access (to get network parameters, for example), you could use the FOPEN() function with parameter 64, which opens the file for reading and allows others full access to the file.

Although Clipper allows you to open other files in SHARED mode, there are no direct provisions in Clipper for locking any portion of the file. In Chapter 5, we do provide a function that will allow you to lock a portion of a low-level file, similar to the way in which Clipper allows you to lock individual records.

Summary

In this chapter, we described some of the problems that can occur when opening files. We also wrote a general purpose function that can be used to open all your .DBF files and indexes. By routing all file openings through this routine, you know that all indexes will be opened and updated in the proper order. In Chapter 5, we will touch upon index locking and show potential problems that can easily be avoided by careful file-opening routines.

File and Record Locking

Levels of locking

Clipper's locking mechanism

Designing a locking strategy

Locking problems

Chapter 5

Whenever two applications have the potential to access the same information, chaos can quickly result. You may recall the anecdote about how the first two cars in the world managed somehow to bump into each other; even if a file is used by only two people, it is likely that, at some point, they too will bump into each other. While the car problem can be addressed by traffic lights and signals, the file problem requires more sophisticated methods of communication. When two applications share the same data, the network ensures that the applications communicate with each other about their file needs. One of the most common ways this can be done is through a method known as locking.

A lock is a signal that indicates that a program needs access to a file or a portion of a file. The network operating system usually keeps track of locks and informs other processes about them. Unfortunately, when one program has exclusive access to some section of the file, the network denies all other programs access to that section; therefore, a network application should be designed to minimize the amount of time that any process needs exclusive use of a file or any portion of it. However, this has to be balanced with the need for data integrity. Clipper's locking mechanism gives you the control necessary to perform this balancing act.

In this chapter, we will discuss how to optimize your application's performance and still maintain complete data integrity.

LEVELS OF LOCKING

There are several different levels at which locking can occur. Each level offers the ability to update some portion of the file and allows a varying degree of access to other processes. The appropriate locking level depends upon the application and the command being performed at the time.

EXCLUSIVE USE

EXCLUSIVE is the default mode of locking in Clipper. If you open a file for exclusive use, you are asking the operating system to deny other programs any access to this file until you are done.

While this seems a greedy approach, there are times when it is the most appropriate method. For example, consider a spreadsheet program. When you use a file, the file is loaded into RAM. When you are finished updating the spreadsheet, the contents of the spreadsheet in RAM are written out to the disk file. If another user could access the file while your application had the spreadsheet in RAM, that user's changes would be lost when you finished and wrote your file back to disk. Word processing programs operate in a similar fashion, loading the document into RAM and not allowing other applications access to the disk file.

The biggest advantage to this type of locking is simplicity. A program designed for a single user could run on a network, since the operating system handles the file access and does not inform the program whether the files are on a local drive or on a network driver. The obvious disadvantage of using files exclusively is that only one user can work with the files at a time. For most network applications, this locking level is a bit restrictive.

Clipper has a few commands that can radically change a file's contents and, because of this, require that your application have exclusive use of the file. These commands are listed in Table 5.1.

Table 5.1: Commands Requiring Exclusive Use

Command	Purpose
PACK	Removes all records flagged for deletion
REINDEX	Re-creates all indexes in this work area
ZAP	Removes all records from the database

The PACK command is usually done off line when no one else is on the system. The REINDEX command should be avoided, since it re-creates only the data keys, and not the header portion of the index. Because the REINDEX command will not repair a corrupted index header, most Clipper programmers use the INDEX ON command rather than REINDEX to re-create index files. The ZAP command removes every record from a file. Although certainly not the kind of operation you'd see on a main menu, it can be very useful if you create temporary file structures in your application. These temporary files would be local to your application, however, so exclusive use of them should not present a problem.

Clipper provides two methods you can use to specify the file-opening mode. The first, the SET EXCLUSIVE command, is a global toggle. Its syntax is

```
SET EXCLUSIVE on|off  <logical>
```

If you specify ON or a logical TRUE, then all subsequent file open commands will be in EXCLUSIVE mode. Specifying OFF or FALSE will cause all subsequent open commands to be attempted in SHARED mode.

The problem with the SET EXCLUSIVE command is that it has a global impact. If your program relies only upon the value of SET EXCLUSIVE when opening files, and some other portion of the program changes the setting, you might find that your program is suddenly opening files in EXCLUSIVE mode and preventing other programs from using the files.

The preferred way to specify the file-opening mode is to use the EXCLUSIVE or SHARED keyword on the USE command. By specifying explicitly the mode on each USE command (or by using the file-opening routines discussed in Chapter 3), you can ensure that another portion of the program does not change how your files are opened.

FILE LOCKING

The file lock is the next level of locking. It allows other processes to read from the file, but does not allow any update to the file. While this approach is less restrictive than exclusive use, it still allows only one user full access to the file.

You use a file lock if the application is going to update more than one record (since Clipper does not support more than one lock per work area). Clipper will also require a file lock if you use a command that can change multiple records. For example, a REPLACE command with a scope condition of ALL (or anything other than just the current record) will require that the file be locked.

Table 5.2 lists the commands that require a file lock. In some cases, these commands can be written in a looping construct with single-record replaces.

Although it requires more code to build the loop, it reduces the likelihood of conflicts with other applications that need to update records in the file.

Table 5.2: Commands Requiring a File Lock

DELETE <scope> when scope is more than one record

RECALL <scope> when scope is more than one record

REPLACE <scope> when scope is more than one record

SORT

UPDATE ON

If a file is opened in EXCLUSIVE mode, it is not necessary to obtain a file lock, since exclusive use denies *any* access to the file. The commands that need a file lock require only that no other program write to the file while the command is executing. A file opened in EXCLUSIVE mode provides that, as well as read protection.

Other commands for which you might want to consider obtaining a file lock are discussed in the following list:

- The APPEND FROM command adds records from another database into the current work area. Although Clipper does not require that the current file be locked (it will automatically handle the necessary locking contention while adding the records), by performing the lock, you can keep the appended records together in the file. If the file were not locked, it would be possible for another program to add a record to the group you were appending. If your application went on to perform some calculations on the newly appended records, you would have no way of distinguishing between records from the new file and records that might have been added by another program.

- The AVERAGE command is used to determine a numeric mean of the specified fields in a database file. Although the command will run without the file being locked, there is no guarantee of the accuracy of the data, since other records could have been added or changed since the AVERAGE command was started.

- The COUNT command returns a count of the records in a database that meet a certain condition. The command does not require that the database be locked, although the same caveat about the accuracy of results applies as for the AVERAGE command. If the file is locked during the COUNT command, then the number returned is accurate, at least for that moment.

- The INDEX ON command can create an index on a file that is opened in SHARED mode, but the file should be locked for the duration of this command. Clipper does not require the lock, but a lock will ensure that records are not added or updated during the operation.
- The SUM command returns the total of the values from specified numeric fields of those database records that meet a certain condition. The command does not require that the database be locked, although the same caveat about the accuracy of results applies as with previous commands. If the file is locked during the SUM command, then the total returned is accurate, at least for that moment.
- The TOTAL command creates a new database from the totals of the specified fields from the current work area. The work area does not have to be locked to perform the command, but a lock will ensure that the data in the TOTAL database is accurate and up-to-date.

THE FLOCK() FUNCTION

You lock a file by using the FLOCK() function. Its syntax is

```
<logical>  := Flock()
```

If the file is successfully locked, then a TRUE value will be returned and the operation can proceed. If FALSE is returned, then the file cannot be locked. The file lock might fail if another program has a record or file lock in place.

RECORD LOCKING

The third level of locking is that of a record lock. This approach is much less restrictive than either of the file-locking approaches discussed previously.

When a network file is opened in SHARED mode, the network operating system maintains a table of the file locations that are locked. Write requests are granted or denied based on this table; if the requested location is found in the table, the request is denied.

A record lock is a request to the network to lock a portion of the file for use by this application. If the requested portion of the file is available, the lock succeeds and the network updates the table to reflect that your program is using this location. If the portion of the file is being used by someone else, then the network operating system returns FALSE and does not lock the portion of the file.

The RLOCK() function   When Clipper requests a record lock, it first converts the record number to a file offset and size. It then sends this information to the network and returns TRUE if the network grants the lock or FALSE if the network denies it.

The RLOCK() function makes a single request to the network to attempt to lock a single record in the file. The syntax for RLOCK() is

```
<logical> := Rlock()
```

If the lock is granted, TRUE is returned and the record can be updated. If the network does not grant the lock request, FALSE is returned and your application needs to take the appropriate action to resolve the failed lock.

SEMAPHORE LOCKING

A semaphore lock is the least restrictive form of locking: The only processes controlled by it are programs that agree upon the semaphore. In Chapter 8, we will provide functions to access NetWare's semaphore services.

Generally, the semaphore is a string of characters and a numeric value. Each process that relies upon the semaphore opens the semaphore and passes it an initial value. If the semaphore does not exist, it is created and assigned the value; otherwise, the existing numeric value is incremented.

Once created, the semaphore can be queried to determine if other processes are currently using the semaphore. These queries can be designed to wait until the semaphore reaches a particular value.

Although NetWare provides semaphore services, you can reproduce semaphores by using a Clipper .DBF file. The file would consist of two fields: the name and the value. Listing 5.1 shows a program to create and query semaphores.

Listing 5.1: Semaphore Functions

```
*  Program:   SEM.PRG
*  Authors:   Joseph D. Booth and Greg Lief
*
*******************************
#define   SEMAPHORE_DBF      "Semafore"

function OpenSemaph(cName,nValue)
LOCAL nReturn := -99
if !empty(cName)
   use (SEMAPHORE_DBF) new shared alias SEMAFORE
   locate all for cName == SEMAFORE->name
   if eof()
```

Listing 5.1: Semaphore Functions (Continued)

```
      if AddRec()
         replace SEMAFORE->name  with cName,;
                 SEMAFORE->value with nValue
      else
         use
         return -99
      endif
   else
      if RecLock()
         nReturn := SEMAFORE->value++
         replace SEMAFORE->value with nReturn
         unlock
      endif
   endif
   use
endif
return nReturn

function QuerySemaPh(cName)
LOCAL nReturn := -99
if !empty(cName)
   use (SEMAPHORE_DBF) new shared alias SEMAFORE
   locate all for cName == SEMAFORE->name
   if found()
      nReturn := SEMAFORE->value
   endif
   use
endif
return nReturn

function CloseSemaPh(cName)
LOCAL nReturn := -99
if !empty(cName)
   use (SEMAPHORE_DBF) new shared alias SEMAFORE
   locate all for cName == SEMAFORE->name
   if found()
      if RecLock()
         replace SEMAFORE->value with 0
         unlock
      endif
```

Listing 5.1: Semaphore Functions (Continued)

```
    endif
    use
endif
return nReturn
```

Using semaphores instead of Clipper's normal locking protocols can be useful in some applications. For example, since Clipper does not allow multiple records in a work area, you could create a semaphore to handle them. Once you had obtained the necessary semaphore locks, you could then lock the file and update the appropriate records.

Semaphore locking is discussed in much greater detail in Chapter 8.

CLIPPER'S LOCKING MECHANISM

The locking mechanisms of the network deny read access to a locked portion of a file, but Clipper allows programs to read data even when it is locked by another application. To resolve this difference, Clipper locks records by calculating an offset of one billion bytes plus the record number, and then requesting that the network lock this offset for one byte.

Although use of this offset allows programs to read data on which Clipper has a record lock, it also poses compatibility problems when Clipper is used with dBASE or FoxPro, since these programs use different offsets. You must be careful when programming for an environment in which Clipper is not the sole program accessing files. It is very possible that another program could be allowed to change the data in a file locked by Clipper. If you are programming in such an environment, you should plan to check the data before writing it back to the file, since you cannot depend solely upon Clipper's locking.

DOS AND LOCKING

Clipper's networking commands work across a wide variety of networks and work transparently when on a single-user machine. This flexibility is inherent in DOS, and the Clipper developers wisely chose to take advantage of it.

DOS versions 3.1 and above added a new function call to the list of interrupts: Number 92, the Lock/Unlock file function, either denies or allows access to a specified region of the file. Clipper calls this function whenever it locks or unlocks a file. This is why Clipper's networking commands work only on DOS versions above 3.0.

The function takes four parameters: the file handle, the offset, the length, and a 0 to lock the file or a 1 to unlock the file. If the operation is successful, then TRUE is returned; if an error occurs, then FALSE is returned.

.DBF LOCKING

In order to update the fields within a file, Clipper requires a record lock in the .DBF file. Any operation that can change the record buffer's contents must be surrounded by a lock request if the file is open in SHARED mode.

Although Clipper requires the lock to update the buffer, it does not write the data to the disk at the time of the REPLACE command. Using the COMMIT command or moving to another record will write the buffer's contents to the disk.

INDEX FILE LOCKING

When Clipper writes the data to disk, it needs to lock the index file before it writes the keys into the file. Keep in mind that the index files are not updated during the REPLACE statement, but rather during a flush action, which can be either a COMMIT statement or some record pointer movement.

Clipper's index locking uses a semaphore system to communicate index status between programs. The header record of an index file contains a counter that is updated every time the file is changed. When Clipper needs to write to an index file, it locks the header of the file and performs the update. It then increments the counter, rewrites the header, and unlocks the file.

When a Clipper program is reading through a database in indexed order, it needs to lock the index file before each record movement (such as SKIP or GO TOP). The program reads an index page into memory. When the movement is requested, Clipper locks the header and reads the counter. If the counter has changed since the buffer's contents were read, then the program will discard the buffer and reread the index file. This lock is attempted infinitely, so if another process locks the index file, the movement operation will wait until the lock is released.

Since Clipper must lock the index file for each record movement, you should consider turning the index off if you need to read all the records or if the data is sorted already. For example, if a report needs to summarize the contents of a database, use the SET ORDER TO 0 command before you run the report. This will not only improve performance, but also reduce contention of the index file by other programs.

DESIGNING A LOCKING STRATEGY

Now that we have covered the basic locking concepts, we need to discuss how you decide when to lock and which level of locking to use. When devising a locking strategy, you should plan to use record locking as much as possible. This allows most of the file to be used freely by other applications.

TWO LOCKING CONSIDERATIONS

Whatever level of locking your application uses, there are two issues that you must keep in mind: persistency, and techniques for resolving failed locks.

Locking persistency   If either a record lock or a file lock fails on the first attempt, you need to decide whether you should try again and, if so, how often. There are two extremes: You could try just once and give up, or you could wrap the lock request in a do-while loop and try an infinite number of times. For most applications, however, you will probably want to try an approach somewhere in between.

In Chapter 3, we provided a version of RECLOCK() that would try to lock a record for a specified time or until the user pressed the Escape key. This function, and the function of the same name in LOCKS.PRG, both provide useful alternatives to the one-attempt and infinite-retry methods.

Resolving failed locks   If a lock fails, you need to make a decision as to how to handle the failure. In some cases, the most appropriate action might be to try a different record. For example, if an application randomly selects a record for the user to update, then selecting a different record might be the proper reaction to a failed lock. In other cases, a failed lock is a critical error and should be treated as such. Each lock in your program should be reviewed to determine the proper action in the event of a failure.

A general strategy would be to communicate the failure to the user and present a list of options. The options might consist of the following:

RETRY	Try the lock again after a period of time.	
ABORT	Cancel the updates, warning the user that the updates might be lost.	
SELECT	Select a different record to update.	

The RETRY option makes no attempt to determine why the lock failed, but merely makes another attempt to lock the record. The failure of a lock indicates the possibility that the record you are attempting to update has been changed since you last read the data.

ABORT will cancel the current action and return to a prior screen. This option is often the most appropriate selection.

SELECT will move on to a different record for a new set of edits. This is often the proper action when the program has multiple users updating a list of potential records.

TEMPORARY FILES AND MULTIPLE-RECORD UPDATES

The first step in determining the lock levels is to look at all files with which the program needs to work. If any file is local to the application, such as a temporary work file, it should be opened in EXCLUSIVE mode. Other applications then would not be allowed to open that file, which is exactly the result you want for a localized file.

When creating temporary files, you should come up with a scheme that creates unique names for each workstation's file. Listing 5.2 shows a function that will return a unique file name.

Listing 5.2: UNIQUE File Name Program

```
*   Program:   UNIQUE.PRG
*   Authors:   Joseph D. Booth and Greg Lief
*
************************************************

function N_Unique
LOCAL cName := "TEMP"
LOCAL nCtr  := 1

do while file( cName+alltrim(str(nCtr))+".DBF" )
   nCtr++
enddo
return cName+alltrim(str(nCtr))+".DBF"
```

Once you've isolated the temporary files, you should look for files that will have multiple records updated at one time. The files in these processes are candidates for file locking. Although Clipper does not allow you to lock multiple records in a single work area, you can lock the entire file and update several records.

Locking a file that is visible to other programs will restrict those programs from using the file; it should be kept to a minimum and used only if absolutely necessary.

SINGLE-RECORD UPDATES

Once you've completed processing the exclusive files and the functions that need file locks, you need to design the record-locking strategies. Timing is the most important consideration in record-lock design.

Many programmers, when writing a networked application, do the bare minimum required for the application to run on a network. If you place an RLOCK() function around every REPLACE statement, your program will run and allow shared access to the data. However, RLOCK() is a form of communication that returns a value indicating success or failure. If the lock is successful, then the program can update the data. If the lock fails, it may be because some other program has updated this data already; this means that your updates are no longer current and might not be accurate.

There are two strategies you can use for your record-locking needs. One is to attempt the lock first and, if successful, then allow edits to be made. This approach is preferable for most applications, but could potentially keep a record locked for a long time. The second approach is to read the data, allow the user to update it, and then lock the record before writing the changes back. While this approach minimizes the amount of the time the record is locked, it also increases the opportunity for another user to change the record after it is read and before the data update is requested.

Lock-Read-Edit-Write-Unlock   This approach is the safest method to use when allowing multiple programs to update a file. A lock should be a signal to other applications that this record is currently being updated and hence is off-limits to other programs. If you consider the lock a method of communication between programs rather than a requirement for database update, then this approach is the only one you should use.

With this approach, you should first locate the record and attempt to lock it. If the lock succeeds, then keep the record locked and allow the user to edit it. After the user finishes updating the record, replace the edits to the buffer and unlock the record. You should also consider issuing a COMMIT command to write the buffer's contents to the network's cache or the hard disk.

Here is an example of this approach to editing:

```
use CUSTOMER index CUSTNAME
seek cId
if found()
   if Rlock()
      //
      // Edit this customer
      //
      replace commands
      unlock
   else
      Alert("Someone else is updating this customer")
   endif
else
   Alert("Customer not found..." )
endif
```

You can use this code example as a template for database edit functions in which you view the lock as a message between two programs. Later in this chapter, we will address the problem that can occur if the user does not update the record fairly quickly.

Read–Edit–Lock–Write–Unlock   This approach keeps the record locked for the shortest possible time and is the minimum lock duration required. It is also the more dangerous of the two locking methods, because it is possible for another user to read the record and update it before the current user saves any changes.

Here is an example of this approach to record locking:

```
use CUSTOMER index CUSTNAME
seek cId
if found()
   //
   // Edit this customer
   //
   if Rlock()
      replace commands
      unlock
   else
      Alert("Someone else is updating this customer")
   endif
else
   Alert("Customer not found..." )
endif
```

Notice that the only difference between the two methods is the placement of the RLOCK() function call.

LOCKING PROBLEMS

There are some special considerations that need to be discussed when dealing with record and file locks. Some of these are limitations of Clipper and some are general problems with locking strategies.

LOCKING MULTIPLE RECORDS

Clipper 5.2 allows you to lock more than one record in a work area. Previous versions of Clipper restricted the work area to only one lock at a time. The DBRLOCK() function, which is new to Clipper 5.2, allows you to lock multiple records. Its syntax is

```
<logical>  := DBRLOCK( record_number )
```

If the record number is succesfully locked, then TRUE will be returned. If the record cannot be locked, FALSE will be returned.

With the DBRLOCK() function, you can easily build looping constructs to lock multiple records. Listing 5.3 shows a couple of examples.

Listing 5.3: MULTLOCK Program

```
*  Program: MULTLOCK
*  Authors: Joseph D. Booth and Greg Lief
*  Purpose: Examples of locking multiple records
*
*********************************
function LockRange( nLow, nHigh )
LOCAL jj
for jj := nLow to nHigh
   if ! dbrlock( jj )
      dbrunlock()        // Failed - unlock everything
      return {} endif
next
return dbRlockList()

function LockArray( aRecords )
LOCAL jj
for jj := 1 to len(aRecords)
    if ! dbrlock( aRecords[jj] )
```

Listing 5.3: MULTLOCK Program (Continued)

```
    dbrunlock()         // Failed - unlock everything
    return {} endif
next
return dbRlockList()
```

The functions return an array. If any locks failed, then all locks are released using the DBRUNLOCK() function. An empty array is returned in this case. If all locks are granted, then the function uses the DBRLOCKLIST() function, which returns an array of locked record numbers.

The enhanced locking capability is just one feature of Clipper 5.2 that addresses some of the problems encountered in earlier versions of Clipper.

LOCKING TEXT AND MEMORY FILES

Although Clipper provides record and file locking for .DBF and .NTX files, it provides no support for locking other types of files. Fortunately, since a lock is a signal between two programs, if both programs agree to the same lock, we can use the Novell API's semaphores discussed in Chapter 8 or the semaphore function from Listing 5.1.

To implement such a signal system, each program could specify the name of the file to be locked as a semaphore value. It would query the system to determine if the file could be locked. If the semaphore indicated that nobody else was using the file, the file could be used or updated. When the program finished the update, it would release the semaphore lock, making the file available to another user.

LUNCH-TIME LOCKING

A common problem with multiuser programs is the "lunch-time lock." This calamity can occur when you choose the "lock before editing" method outlined earlier in this chapter. In this scenario, the user is free to lock a record, commence data entry, and then walk away from the computer for lunch or other extended break. Meanwhile, all other users of the program are unable to access the record that has so carelessly been left locked.

The solution lies in writing some simple code to use the reader instance variable provided with Clipper's GET objects. We also need to make some very minor (but far-reaching) modifications to the GETREADER() function, which processes GETs.

The Get:reader instance variable The get:reader instance variable (added with release 5.01 of Clipper) allows individual GETs to have specialized read behaviors without requiring you to modify the standard READMODAL() function (contained in GETSYS.PRG). This maintains compatibility for GETs that are to be handled in the customary fashion, as well as eliminating potential conflicts between different extensions to the GET/READ System.

If get:reader contains a code block, the GET System will evaluate that block in order to read the GET. In this case, the currently active GET object is passed as a parameter to your code block. The block will in turn call your alternate GETREADER() function, passing along the GET object as a parameter. If get:reader does not contain a code block, READMODAL() uses the default GETREADER() function contained in the GETSYS.PRG file.

The following line of code demonstrates the structure for a typical get:reader code block. This particular example will pass the currently active GET object to the TIMEREADER() function, discussed in a moment.

```
@ 1,1 get x
atail(getlist):reader := { | g | TimeReader(g) }
```

In case you haven't seen the ATAIL() function before, it too was added with release 5.01. ATAIL() refers to the last element in an array. Because this GET was just added to the Getlist array, ATAIL() will be pointing to the new GET. This allows your code to be completely generic, because it will not matter how many GETs are in the Getlist array.

The GETREADER() function The GETREADER() function implements the standard read behavior for GETs. It performs the following fundamental actions:

1 Evaluates the WHEN clause (if one exists)

2 If the WHEN is satisfied, activates the GET for editing

3 Accepts keystrokes from the user and processes them accordingly

4 When the user exits the GET, evaluates the VALID clause (if one exists)

5 Once the VALID clause is satisfied or when the user escapes from the read, deactivates the GET

The crucial part of this logic is item 3. The stock GETREADER() uses the INKEY(0) statement to receive a keypress from the user. As you already know, this causes the program to halt dead in its tracks until a keypress is received, regardless of how long the wait might be. Therefore, we can simply rewrite that part of the code to allow for a time-out period.

Instead of INKEY(0), we should use the following loop:

```
do while ( nkey := inkey() ) == 0
enddo
```

This accomplishes the same thing as INKEY(0) with one important difference: It is completely open-ended, because it continuously checks the incoming keypress buffer. We can then expand upon this by adding another clause to break out of the loop if a keypress is not detected within a certain period of time, as demonstrated here:

```
nstart := seconds()
ntimeout := 600
do while ( nkey := inkey() ) == 0 .and. ;
        seconds() - nstart < ntimeout
enddo
if nkey != 0                    // a keypress was received
   getapplykey(oGet, nkey)
else
   // perform timeout action
endif
```

We can further expand this to permit ourselves the flexibility of specifying a variety of time-out actions. The following example tests for a code block named EXIT_EVENT and evaluates it if specified. Otherwise, an Escape key is stuffed into the keyboard buffer, which will force an exit from the read.

```
if nkey != 0                    // a keypress was received
   getapplykey(oGet, nkey)
elseif exit_event != NIL        // timeout action was specified
   eval(exit_event)
else
   keyboard chr(K_ESC)
endif
```

The GFTIMEOUT() function   The next hurdle is to specify to our alternate GETREADER() the values to be used for the time-out period and exit event. Although it might be possible to tweak the get:reader instance variable to pass those two items as additional parameters, it would be an exercise in convolution. The get:reader instance variable is, obviously enough, tied to each GET, whereas a time-out period should be tied to the READ command.

Therefore, we will add a small function, GFTIMEOUT(), to the bottom of the same .PRG file that contains our alternate GETREADER() function.

GFTIMEOUT() will maintain a two-element static array. The first element of this array will contain the number of seconds to wait for a keypress, and the second element will contain an optional code block specifying the exit event in case of time-out. The function is configured like the Clipper SET() function, in that you can retrieve and/or assign the values of these two items. We will assign the values at the instant that the READ command is issued, and retrieve them from within our GETREADER() function.

Please note that GFTIMEOUT() can reset the static array, should you not pass it any parameters. This enables you to use different waiting periods and/or exit events for different areas of your program.

```
function gftimeout(nitem, val)
static settings_ := { 60000, }
local ret_val
if nitem == NIL      // reset array
   settings_ := { 60000, }
else
   ret_val := settings_[nitem]
   if val != NIL
      settings_[nitem] := val
   endif
endif
return ret_val
```

Preprocessor directive The final step is to provide a preprocessor directive that will properly assign these values. This READ directive is based on the stock version provided with Clipper, but adds the necessary calls to our GFTIMEOUT() function. (This is contained in the TIMEREAD.CH header file on the source-code disk accompanying this book.)

```
#define    R_SECONDS     1
#define    R_EXITEVENT   2

#xcommand  READ TIMEOUT <seconds>                            ;
           [EXITEVENT <exitevent>]                       =>  ;
           gftimeout(R_SECONDS, <seconds> )                  ;
           [ ; gftimeout(R_EXITEVENT, <{exitevent}>) ]       ;
           ; ReadModal( getlist )                            ;
           ; getlist := {}                                   ;
           ; gftimeout()
```

First, the GFTIMEOUT() function is called to set the number of seconds to wait. Next, if you specify the optional EXITEVENT, GFTIMEOUT() is called again to set that as well. The READMODAL() function is then called to start the ball rolling. After you exit from the READ, GFTIMEOUT() is called once more to clear out the two values.

This construction is designed for flexibility—you can switch back and forth between this READ TIMEOUT directive and the stock READ command at will. However, if you anticipate that all your reads will be timed, then you could (and should) enhance performance by simply calling GFTIMEOUT() directly in your code and using the stock READ command, as shown in the following code fragment:

```
// at the top of your program
gftimeout(R_SECONDS, 60)      // time out after
                              // one minute of inactivity
gftimeout(R_EXITEVENT, { || cleanup() })
```

Listing 5.4 contains the complete source code for our alternate GETREADER(), called TIMEREADER(), along with the GFTIMEOUT() function. This is contained in TIMEREAD.PRG on the source-code disk accompanying this book.

Listing 5.4: Alternate GETREADER() Function

```
/*
   Function: TimeReader()
   Purpose:  Alternate to GetReader() to allow timed READs
   Author:   Greg Lief
   Copyright (c) 1992 Greg Lief
   Dialect: Clipper 5.01
*/

#include "getexit.ch"

#define    R_SECONDS     1
#define    R_EXITEVENT   2

function TimeReader( get )
local nStart, nTimeout, exit_event, nKey
// read the GET if the WHEN condition is satisfied
if ( GetPreValidate(get) )
   // activate the GET for reading
   get:SetFocus()
   do while ( get:exitState == GE_NOEXIT )
      // check for initial typeout (no editable positions)
      if ( get:typeOut )
         get:exitState := GE_ENTER
      endif
      // apply keystrokes until exit
```

Listing 5.4: Alternate GETREADER() Function (Continued)

```
      do while ( get:exitState == GE_NOEXIT )
         nStart := seconds()
         nTimeout := gfTimeOut(R_SECONDS)
         exit_event := gfTimeOut(R_EXITEVENT)
         do while ( nKey := inkey() ) == 0 .and. ;
            seconds() - nStart < nTimeout
         enddo
         if nKey != 0                    // a keypress was received
            getapplykey(get, nKey)
         elseif exit_event != NIL        // timeout action was specified
            eval(exit_event)
         else
            keyboard chr(K_ESC)
         endif
      enddo
      // disallow exit if the VALID condition is not satisfied
      if ( !GetPostValidate(get) )
         get:exitState := GE_NOEXIT
      endif
   enddo
   //de-activate the GET
   get:KillFocus()
endif
return nil

//----- end function TimeReader()

/*
   Function: GFTimeOut()
   Purpose:  Assign/retrieve timeout period and exit event
   Author:   Greg Lief
   Copyright (c) 1992 Greg Lief
   Dialect: Clipper 5.01
*/
function gftimeout(nItem, val)
static settings_ := { 60000, }
local ret_val
if nItem == NIL     // reset array
   settings_ := { 60000, }
else
   ret_val := settings_[nItem]
```

Listing 5.4: Alternate GETREADER() Function (Continued)

```
      if val != NIL
         settings_[nItem] := val
      endif
   endif
endif
return ret_val
```

Putting it all together   The following sample code demonstrates the use of the items outlined in the previous sections to implement timed reads. Note the use of the AEVAL() function to change all the GET's reader instance variables in one fell swoop.

```
#include "inkey.ch"
#include "timeread.ch"

function test
local a := { 1, 2, 3, 4, 5 }
local getlist := {}
scroll()
@ 1,1 get a[1]
@ 2,1 get a[2]
@ 3,1 get a[3]
@ 4,1 get a[4]
@ 5,1 get a[5]
aeval(getlist, { | g | g:reader := { | g | timereader(g) } } )
read timeout 50 exitevent shutdown()
return nil

static function shutdown
close data
scroll()
? "program terminated due to inactivity"
keyboard chr(K_ESC)
return nil
```

Summary

In this chapter, we covered the concepts of locking files or portions of files to allow shared use of files. We also discussed the various levels of locking and how to devise a locking strategy for your programs.

Next, we discussed the two methods for updating records and described some problems with these methods. Finally, we offered solutions for some of the common locking problems that can occur on a network.

Browsing Network Data

TBROWSE—A QUICK REVIEW

TBROWSE() EXAMPLE 1—AN ACCOUNTING APPLICATION

TBROWSE() EXAMPLE 2—MONITORING A TELEPHONE PROCESS

Chapter 6

Applications often need to display data on the screen for the user to review. In a network environment, however, it is possible for other programs to change this data even as it is being displayed. If the data is changed, your applications should change the display so that the screen shows the latest data. Fortunately, with Clipper's new TBROWSE construct, building this capability into your programs is not only possible, but very easy to do.

This chapter offers a quick review of the basics of TBROWSE and a more detailed discussion of TBROWSE and networks. It also provides several examples to show how TBROWSE can be made network aware. We hope that these examples will stimulate your imagination with regard to the many ways that networks and TBROWSE() can work beautifully together.

TBROWSE—A QUICK REVIEW

Clipper provides us with the TBROWSE object class, which is perfect for browsing databases and arrays. TBROWSE includes an exported method named REFRESHALL() that allows us to force the entire screen to be redisplayed. This provides an exceptionally high degree of control, which is particularly important on networks.

It is beyond the scope of this discussion to provide an exhaustive description of how to program TBROWSE configurations. (For further TBROWSE illumination, we highly recommend *Clipper 5.0 Insights: Object Classes,* published by

Grumpfish, Inc., 1992.) Nonetheless, we will dissect the rudiments of the TBROWSE configuration, which consists of the following seven basic steps:

1. First, we create a TBROWSE object with the TBROWSEDB() function. At this point, the TBROWSE object is nothing but an empty shell. The syntax for this function call is

   ```
   TBROWSEDB(<top>, <left>, <bottom>, <right>)
   ```

   The four parameters are all numerics corresponding to the screen coordinates to be used for the browse. Note that there is another function, TBROWSENEW(), which can also be used to create TBROWSE objects.

2. Next, we fill the TBROWSE object with columns so that it can actually be useful. For each field in the database, we create a TBCOLUMN object with TBCOLUMNNEW(). The syntax for the TBCOLUMNNEW() function is

   ```
   TBCOLUMNNEW(<heading>, <block>)
   ```

   where <heading> is a character string to be used as the heading for the column. If you do not want to use a heading for a column, skip the first parameter entirely. If you want to set up a generic database browser and wish to use the field names as column headings, the Clipper 5.0 FIELD() function is your best bet for this parameter.

   The <block> parameter is a code block that, when evaluated, determines the contents of this column. For a generic database browser, the FIELD-BLOCK() function is ideal for creating a retrieval/assignment code block for each field in the database.

3. Next, each column must be added to the TBROWSE object with the TBROWSE:ADDCOLUMN() exported method.

4. The data in the TBROWSE object is displayed by calling the TBROWSE STABILIZE() exported method repeatedly in a do-while loop. Although its name is hardly intuitive, this is nonetheless the primary mechanism for displaying the data in the TBROWSE window.

   Whenever you create a TBROWSE object, each row in the data window has a corresponding logical flag that tracks whether the data for that row has been properly displayed. At the time of creation, all these flags will be set to FALSE (.F.) because none of the data has yet been displayed.

   The STABILIZE() method redisplays one row of data and sets the flag for that row to TRUE (.T.), indicating that it was properly displayed. It returns the logical value TRUE (.T.) if all the data in the TBROWSE window has been properly displayed, or FALSE (.F.) if it has not. For this reason, it is necessary to call the STABILIZE() method until it returns TRUE. If you called it only once, you would end up with only one row of data on the screen.

5 After displaying the data with the stabilization loop, we wait for a keypress, generally with the INKEY(0) statement.

6 The keypress is acted upon, usually by testing it against a conditional logic structure and executing a TBROWSE movement method (UP(), DOWN(), LEFT(), RIGHT(), and so on).

7 Items 4 through 6 are repeated until an arbitrary exit condition is fulfilled (for example, the user presses the Escape key).

Item 5 is the most crucial for the purposes of this discussion. We generally wait for a keypress with the INKEY(0) statement. As already mentioned in Chapter 5, this statement causes the program to stop and wait indefinitely for a keypress. When we looked at timed reads in Chapter 5, we saw how to derive greater control by using a do-while loop to continuously poll the incoming keypress buffer. We can use similar logic to force the screen to refresh automatically after a specified period of inactivity.

THE TBROWSE:REFRESHALL() EXPORTED METHOD

TBROWSE:REFRESHALL() marks all data rows as invalid, which will force the entire screen to be redrawn when you come back to the stabilization loop. This is necessary when the data in the TBROWSE object is being changed. The most common example of this would be add/edit routines. Adding a record would require the REFRESHALL() method because there is no way to tell where the new record might appear, especially if you have one or more active index files. Editing one record might require only a REFRESHCURRENT() method, because only the current row would be affected (unless you happened to edit a key field in the controlling index).

The example in Listing 6.1 demonstrates this logic. When the user sits at the screen without typing anything, the screen will be refreshed automatically every ten seconds. You might instead wish to use semaphores to refresh the screen only when the database is edited on another workstation.

Listing 6.1: TBROWSE Example

```
#include "box.ch"
#include "inkey.ch"
#include "setcurs.ch"

// the following manifest constant
// sets # of seconds for auto-refresh
#define REFRESH_TIME  10

function refresh(dbf_file, ntx_file)
local x
local b := TBrowseDB(1, 1, maxrow()-1, maxcol()-1)
local c
local nKey
local nseconds
set scoreboard off
setcursor(SC_NONE)
if dbf_file != NIL
   use (dbf_file) shared
   if ntx_file != NIL
      dbsetindex(ntx_file)
   endif
   scroll()
   for x := 1 to fcount()
      c := TBColumnNew(field(x), fieldblock(field(x)))
      b:AddColumn( c )
   next
   @ b:nTop - 1, b:nLeft - 1, ;
     b:nBottom + 1, b:nRight + 1 box B_SINGLE + ' '
   do while nKey != K_ESC
      dispbegin()
      do while ( nKey := inkey() ) == 0 .and. ! b:stabilize()
      enddo
      dispend()
      if nKey == 0
         // use another loop so we can refresh
         // while waiting for keypress
         do while ( nKey := inkey() ) == 0
            if seconds() - nseconds > REFRESH_TIME
               nseconds := seconds()
               b:refreshAll()
               dispbegin()
               do while ! b:stabilize()
               enddo
               dispend()
            endif
```

Listing 6.1: TBROWSE Example (Continued)

```
         enddo
      endif
      do case
         case nKey == K_UP
            b:up()
         case nKey == K_DOWN
            b:down()
         case nKey == K_LEFT
            b:left()
         case nKey == K_RIGHT
            b:right()
         case nKey == K_PGUP
            b:pageUp()
         case nKey == K_PGDN
            b:pageDown()
         case nKey == K_CTRL_PGUP
            b:goTop()
         case nKey == K_CTRL_PGDN
            b:goBottom()
         case ( nKey == K_ENTER .or. (nKey > 32 .and. nKey <= 255) ) ;
                  .and. b:stable
            // stuff any alphanumeric keys back
            // into the keyboard buffer
            if nkey != K_ENTER
               keyboard chr(nkey)
            endif
            if editcell(b)
               if b:getColumn(b:colPos):heading $ upper(indexkey(0))
                  b:refreshAll()
               else
                  b:refreshCurrent()
               endif
            endif
      endcase
   enddo
endif
dbclosearea()
return nil



/*
   Function:   EditCell()
   Parameter:  Browse object in question
   Returns:    True (.T.) if edit was consumated,
               False (.F.) otherwise
```

Listing 6.1: TBROWSE Example (Continued)

```
   Note:      Operates on copy rather than
              directly on database field
*/
static function editcell(b)
local lReadexit := readexit(.t.)    // allow up/down arrows to exit READ local c
:= b:getColumn(b:colPos)
local oldvalue := eval(c:block)     // save old contents for comparison
local nKey
local v := oldvalue                 // variable to be edited
local oldcursor := setcursor()
local oldscore  := set(_SET_SCOREBOARD, .f.)   // ugh...
local ret_val   := .f.

//----- remap insert key to toggle shape of cursor
local oldinsert := setkey( K_INS, {|| setcursor( ;
    if(readinsert(! readInsert()), SC_NORMAL, SC_SPECIAL1))} )
//----- set initial cursor size based on current mode
setcursor( if(readInsert(), SC_SPECIAL1, SC_NORMAL) )
readmodal( { getnew(Row(), Col(), { | _1 | if(pcount() == 0, v, v := _1) }, ;
c:heading, '@K', b:colorSpec) } )
setcursor(oldcursor)
if v != oldvalue                    // i.e., variable was changed
   if rlock()                       // make sure record is locked
      eval(c:block, v)              // this changes the field
      dbunlock()
      ret_val := .t.
   endif
endif

//----- if user exited with an up or down arrow, pass it through
nKey := lastkey()
if nKey == K_UP .or. nKey == K_DOWN
   keyboard chr(nKey)
endif

readexit(lReadexit)                 // restore prior readexit() setting
set(_SET_SCOREBOARD, oldscore)      // does anybody really use this?
setkey(K_INS, oldinsert)
return ret_val

//----- end static function EditCell()
```

TBROWSE AND NETWORKS

Perhaps the most important TBROWSE object method for networks is the REFRESHALL() method. The REFRESHALL() method causes TBROWSE() to mark all rows in the browse as invalid. This action in turn causes each row to redisplay the next time the screen is redrawn. The data is read from the network, reflecting any changes made since the last refreshing of the screen.

In the remainder of this chapter, we will provide a couple of examples that illustrate how TBROWSE can work in a network environment. These examples also show some of the flexibility that the TBROWSE object class offers us.

TBROWSE() EXAMPLE 1—AN ACCOUNTING APPLICATION

You have been called in to write an accounting application for a midsize firm. The program is going to be used to allow for better collection efforts in cases where the client's balance is past due.

Traci, who works for the company's controller, is in charge of calling clients whose balances are past due. The controller wants you to design a screen that will show a list of clients with past-due balances. This list should be sorted first by balance due, and then by date. Traci should be able to scroll through the list, select a customer, and make the necessary phone calls to expedite payment.

The information is stored in a file called CLIENTS, which has the indexes

```
upper(CLIENT_ID)
str(BALANCE,8,2)+dtos(DUE_DATE)
```

and has the structure shown below:

Field Name	Type	Size
CLIENT_ID	Char	8.0
CUSTNAME	Char	30.0
ADDRESS	Char	40.0
CITY	Char	15.0
STATE	Char	2.0
ZIP	Char	10.0
PHONE	Char	14.0
FAX_NO	Char	14.0

Field Name	Type	Size
CONTACT	Char	25.0
LAST_CALL	Date	8.0
BALANCE	Numeric	8.2
DUE_DATE	Date	8.0
LAST_PAID	Date	8.0
NOTES	Memo	10.0

When Traci selects a customer from the list, a window with the customer's phone number, contact information, notes, and the rest should be displayed. When Traci makes the phone call, the date is recorded to the customer file for display purposes. This allows Traci to keep track of whom she has called and who still needs to be called. She should then be able to update the notes to record the result of the phone call.

After some preliminary discussion, you come up with the screen layout shown in Figure 6.1.

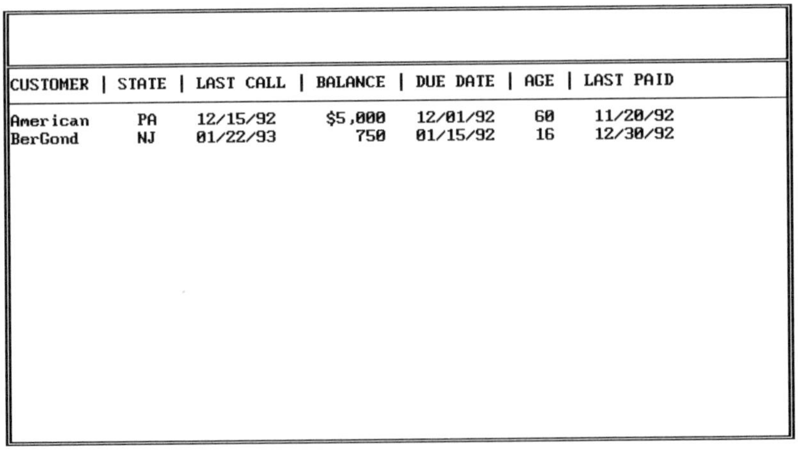

```
|CUSTOMER  | STATE | LAST CALL | BALANCE | DUE DATE | AGE | LAST PAID|
|American    PA      12/15/92    $5,000    12/01/92   60    11/20/92 |
|BerGond     NJ      01/22/93       750    01/15/92   16    12/30/92 |
```

Figure 6.1: Customer Past Due calling screen

The Clipper code shown in Listing 6.2 opens the CLIENTS file and creates a simple TBROWSE() loop to display the screen.

Listing 6.2: Basic PASTDUE Program

```
* Program...: PASTDUE.PRG
* Author....: Joseph D. Booth and Greg Lief
* Function..: PastDue()
* Purpose...: To display the clients with past-due
*             account balances and update notes
**************************************************

#include "box.ch"
#include "inkey.ch"
#include "setcurs.ch"

function pastdue()
local x
local b := TBrowseDB(1, 1, maxrow()-1, maxcol()-1)
local c
local nKey
local nseconds
set scoreboard off
setcursor(SC_NONE)
use CLIENTS shared
set index to CLIENTS,PAST_DUE
set order to 2
c := TBColumnNew(, { || ShowPastDue() } )
b:AddColumn( c )
@ b:nTop - 1, b:nLeft - 1, ;
  b:nBottom + 1, b:nRight + 1 box B_SINGLE + ' '
do while nKey != K_ESC
   dispbegin()
   do while ( nKey := inkey() ) == 0 .and. ! b:stabilize()
   enddo
   dispend()
   do case
   case nKey == K_UP
      b:up()
   case nKey == K_DOWN
      b:down()
   case nKey == K_LEFT
      b:left()
   case nKey == K_RIGHT
      b:right()
   case nKey == K_PGUP
      b:pageUp()
   case nKey == K_PGDN
      b:pageDown()
```

Listing 6.2: Basic PASTDUE Program (Continued)

```
   case nKey == K_CTRL_PGUP
      b:goTop()
   case nKey == K_CTRL_PGDN
      b:goBottom()
   case nKey == K_ENTER .or. nKey == 32
      select CLIENTS
      if Rec_Lock()
         PhoneCall()
      endif
   endcase
enddo
dbclosearea()
return nil


*
* function:  ShowPastDue()
*
*********************************

static function ShowPastDue
field client_id,state,last_call,balance
field due_date,last_paid
local nAge := date() - due_date
return client_id+" "+state+"   "+dtoc(last_call)+;
       str(balance,9,2)+" "+dtoc(due_date)+" "+;
       str(nAge,3)+"  "+dtoc(last_paid)


*
* function:  Phonecall()
*
*********************************
static function Phonecall
//
// Code to update customer's notes with details
// of this phone call.
//
local cSave  := savescreen(6,10,20,70)
local cNotes := CLIENTS->notes
if empty(cNotes)
   cNotes := dtoc(date())+space(500)
endif

dispbox(6,10,20,70,2)
@ 7,11 clear to 19,69
```

Listing 6.2: Basic PASTDUE Program (Continued)

```
@  7,11 say "CLIENT..: "+CLIENTS->custname
@  8,11 say "CONTACT.: "+CLIENTS->contact
@  9,11 say "PHONE #.: "+CLIENTS->phone
@ 10,11 say "BALANCE.: "+str(CLIENTS->balance,9,2)
@ 11,11 say "NOTES...: "
cNotes := memoedit(cNotes,12,11,19,69,.T.)
if lastkey() <> K_ESC
   replace CLIENTS->notes     with cNotes,;
           CLIENTS->last_call date()
endif
restscreen(6,10,20,70,cSave)
return NIL
```

MAKING THE APPLICATION NETWORK AWARE

To add some real-life complexity to the design of our application, let's say that Don in the accounting department is in charge of recording checks when they come in. As soon as the mail arrives, he posts the checks to the CLIENTS accounts. As part of that posting program, the computer updates the last paid date and recomputes the balance due.

With this knowledge in hand, we realize that the PASTDUE browsing program needs to be aware of the updates performed when checks are posted. This is going to require two sets of changes to our browsing program.

Updating the display screen   The first change is to the display screen. It is possible for the customer record to be displayed in the PASTDUE browser and for checks to be posted simultaneously. This means that, periodically, the browse loop must reread the data from the network and refresh the screen display. The code fragment shown below would be inserted before checking the keystrokes, to ensure that the screen is updated after a certain number of seconds have passed. You would also need to define the manifest constant REFRESH_TIME in the beginning of the .PRG file.

```
if nKey == 0
   // use another loop so we can
   // refresh while waiting for keypress
   do while ( nKey := inkey() ) == 0
      if seconds() - nseconds > REFRESH_TIME
         nseconds := seconds()
         b:REFRESHALL()
         dispbegin()
         do while ! b:stabilize()
```

```
        enddo
        dispend()
     endif
  enddo
endif
```

Checking that the client can be called The second change involves checking that the record of the client about to be called is not being worked on elsewhere when Traci presses the Enter key to select that client. This can be accomplished by attempting an RLOCK() on the record. The RLOCK() will make only one attempt; if it is successful, then Traci can call the client and the lock will be kept for the duration of the phone call. The following code illustrates how this check can be done.

```
select CLIENTS
if Rlock()
   //
   PhoneCall()
   //
else
   Alert( "This customer is being updated..." )
endif
```

ALL TOGETHER NOW

Listing 6.3 contains the final code that implements our application's primary screen. It communicates with the network on a timed basis and checks to make sure that the requested client record is available before allowing the phone call to be made.

Listing 6.3: Accounting TBROWSE() Example

```
* Program...: PASTDUE.PRG
* Author....: Joseph D. Booth and Greg Lief
* Function..: PastDue()
* Purpose...: To display the clients with past-due
*             account balances and update notes
****************************************************

#include "box.ch"
#include "inkey.ch"
#include "setcurs.ch"

#define REFRESH_TIME   10
```

Listing 6.3: Accounting TBROWSE() Example (Continued)

```
function pastdue()
local x
local b := TBrowseDB(1, 1, maxrow()-1, maxcol()-1)
local c
local nKey
local nseconds
set scoreboard off
setcursor(SC_NONE)
use CLIENTS shared
set index to CLIENTS,PAST_DUE
set order to 2
c := TBColumnNew(, { || ShowPastDue() } )
b:AddColumn( c )
@ b:nTop - 1, b:nLeft - 1, ;
  b:nBottom + 1, b:nRight + 1 box B_SINGLE + ' '
do while nKey != K_ESC
   dispbegin()
   do while ( nKey := inkey() ) == 0 .and. ! b:stabilize()
   enddo
   dispend()
   if nKey == 0
      // use another loop so we can refresh
      // while waiting for keypress
      do while ( nKey := inkey() ) == 0
         if seconds() - nseconds > REFRESH_TIME
            nseconds := seconds()
            b:refreshAll()
            dispbegin()
            do while ! b:stabilize()
            enddo
            dispend()
         endif
      enddo
   endif
   do case
   case nKey == K_UP
      b:up()
   case nKey == K_DOWN
      b:down()
   case nKey == K_LEFT
      b:left()
   case nKey == K_RIGHT
      b:right()
   case nKey == K_PGUP
```

Listing 6.3: Accounting TBROWSE() Example (Continued)

```
         b:pageUp()
   case nKey == K_PGDN
         b:pageDown()
   case nKey == K_CTRL_PGUP
         b:goTop()
   case nKey == K_CTRL_PGDN
         b:goBottom()
   case nKey == K_ENTER .or. nKey == 32
         select CLIENTS
         if Rlock()
            PhoneCall()
            commit
            unlock
         else
            Alert( "This customer is being updated..." )
         endif
   endcase
enddo
dbclosearea()
return nil


static function ShowPastDue
field client_id,state,last_call,balance
field due_date,last_paid
local nAge := date() - due_date
return client_id+" "+state+"    "+dtoc(last_call)+;
       str(balance,9,2)+" "+dtoc(due_date)+" "+;
       str(nAge,3)+"   "+dtoc(last_paid)


static function Phonecall(b)
//
//  Code to update customer's notes with details
//  of this phone call.
//
local cSave  := savescreen(6,10,20,70)
local cNotes := CLIENTS->notes
if empty(cNotes)
   cNotes := dtoc(date())+space(500)
endif

dispbox(6,10,20,70,2)
@ 7,11 clear to 19,69
@ 7,11 say "CLIENT..: "+CLIENTS->custname
@ 8,11 say "CONTACT.: "+CLIENTS->contact
```

Listing 6.3: Accounting TBROWSE() Example (Continued)

```
@  9,11 say "PHONE #.: "+CLIENTS->phone
@ 10,11 say "BALANCE.: "+str(CLIENTS->balance,9,2)
@ 11,11 say "NOTES...: "
cNotes := memoedit(cNotes,12,11,19,69,.T.)
if lastkey() <> K_ESC
   replace CLIENTS->notes     with cNotes,;
           CLIENTS->last_call with date()
endif
restscreen(6,10,20,70,cSave)
return NIL
```

It is easy to imagine possible enhancements to this program. For example, a record could assume a different color if the bill were extremely late. Another color might indicate that the record was currently being updated, presumably because Don received a check.

TBROWSE() is a powerful tool that provides enough control to properly handle a network environment. This sample program shows some of the TBROWSE() construct's ability to work hand-in-hand with other Clipper programs.

TBROWSE() EXAMPLE 2—MONITORING A TELEPHONE PROCESS

TBROWSE is not limited to displaying data from the file. You can also use a TBROWSE loop to monitor the status of .DBF files being updated by another application.

In this example, assume that a Clipper program is used to call people for donations. A file lists the callers as they log on to the system and keeps track of various stages of the phone call.

The first step is to select a person to call, and the second step is to dial the number. Once the call has been answered, the caller determines whether the person is not available and must be called back, or if contact has been made and the person can be requested to make the donation. For each person being called, there is a suggested donation amount. We would like this information displayed on the screen if the caller makes actual voice contact with the person.

We need to design the screen shown in Figure 6.2. This screen shows a horizontal bar chart indicating the status of the various callers.

```
┌─────────────────────────────────────────────────────────────────┐
│                                                                 │
├─────────────────────────────────────────────────────────────────┤
│CALLER NAME    |   SELECT  |  DIALING  |  CONTACT  |  REQUEST  |  AMOUNT │
│Sandy Booth    ▓▓▓▓▓▓▓▓▓▓▓▓                                       │
│Greg Lief                  ▓▓▓▓▓▓▓▓▓▓▓▓▓▓▓▓▓▓▓▓                  │
│                                                                 │
│                                                                 │
│                                                                 │
│                                                                 │
│                                                                 │
│                                                                 │
│                                                                 │
└─────────────────────────────────────────────────────────────────┘
```

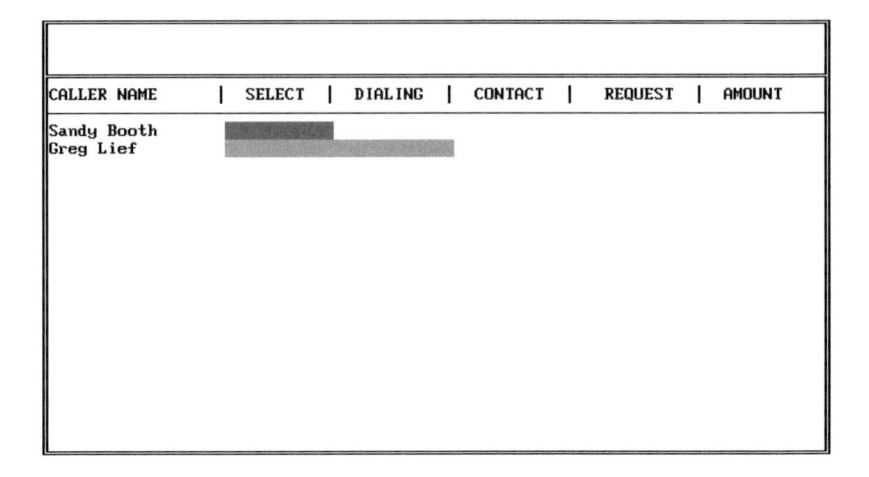

Figure 6.2: Caller Status screen

By looking at the screen, we can tell at a glance what each of the callers is doing and how the phone calls are going in general.

The code example in Listing 6.4 can be used to monitor a telephone process such as the one we've described. It assumes that the people making the phone calls are in a file called CALLERS. Each stage of the program updates a STATUS field with one of the following numbers:

1. Selecting a person to call
2. Dialing the phone
3. Trying to contact the person
4. Requesting the donation

Keep in mind that each time the program updates the STATUS field, it must issue a COMMIT statement to make those changes visible to the monitoring program. Also, once a person reaches the request stage, the CALLERS file is updated with the requested donation amount.

Listing 6.4 shows the monitor program that can be run from another workstation while the main program is being used. Usually, this program would be run by the manager so she or he could see how each person is doing.

Writing a monitor program allows you to quickly check on the status of any running program. You could enhance the monitor program to interactively communicate with the person making the call, offering suggestions.

Listing 6.4: A TBROWSE Example for Monitoring Calls

```
* Program...: MON_CALL.PRG
* Author....: Joseph D. Booth and Greg Lief
* Function..: Mon_Call()
* Purpose...: To display the callers currently on
*             telephone requesting donations
***************************************************
#include "INKEY.CH"

function Mon_Call()

STATIC nWait :=5

LOCAL cSave     := savescreen(1,0,maxrow()-1,maxcol())
LOCAL oldcolor := setcolor()
LOCAL iBrow,key,cSave2,moveit := .T.

if Shared( "CALLERS" ) == 0
   //
   // Display framed headings
   //
   select CALLERS
   set filter to INTVRS->active
   go top
   if !empty( lastrec() )        // If not interviewers, add one
      DispBegin()
      DispBox(2,0,23,78,2)
      @ 3,1 say " Caller Name    Select     Dialing "+;
              "Contact    Request    Amount    "
      @ 4,1 say replicate("-",77)

      dispend()
      ibrow := TbrowseDB(5,1,maxrow()-1,maxcol()-1)
      ibrow:addColumn(TBcolumnNew(,{ || ShowMon()}))
      //
      while .T.
         Footing( "Display updates every "+;
           if(nWait=1,"second.   + to increase.",;
           alltrim(str(nWait))+" seconds.   +/- to change." ))
         ibrow:Refreshall()
         ibrow:gotop()
         dispbegin()
         while .not. ibrow:stabilize()
         enddo
         dispend()
```

Listing 6.4: A TBROWSE Example for Monitoring Calls (Continued)

```
            key     := inkey(nWait)
            do case
            case chr(key)$"+"
               nWait++
            case chr(key)$"-" .and. nWait > 1
               nWait --
            case key == K_ESC   .or. key == K_F10
               exit
            case key == K_UP
               ibrow:up()
            case key == K_DOWN
               ibrow:down()
            case key == K_HOME
               ibrow:gotop()
               ibrow:RefreshAll()
            case key == K_END
               ibrow:gobottom()
               ibrow:Refreshall()
            case key == K_PGUP
               ibrow:pageUp()
            case key == K_PGDN
               ibrow:pageDown()
            endcase
         enddo
      else
         Alert("There are no callers in the file")
      endif
   else
      Alert("Files are not available...")
   endif
   restscreen(1,0,maxrow()-1,maxcol(),cSave)
   setcolor( oldcolor )
   close databases
   return .T.
   *************************

   //   Function:   ShowMon()
   //    Purpose:   To display a single line for each caller
   //     Syntax:   ShowInt()
   // Parameters:   <NONE>
   //    Returns:   <character>
   //      Notes:   Usually this function is called
   //               from within a TBROWSE object
   //
```

Listing 6.4: A TBROWSE Example for Monitoring Calls (Continued)

```
//////////////////////
function ShowMon
FIELD name,status,req_amt
return padr(substr(name,1,12)+" "+;
            replicate("2",status*9)+;
            if(status=4,str(req_amt,9,2),""),maxcol()-1)
**************************************************************************
```

Summary

TBROWSE() is a powerful extension to Clipper, exceeding by far the BROWSE command of other Xbase dialects. The degree of control offered, as well as the flexible file- and record-handling constructs, allow us to create network-aware applications very easily.

This chapter should whet your appetite for opportunities to use TBROWSE() effectively on a network. Keep in mind two rules: First, your program should automatically refresh its screen periodically, not just in response to your actions at the keyboard; and second, if another program is editing the record, you should use the failed RLOCK() to signal that the data has been changed and will need to be refreshed before it can be updated.

Using Configuration Files

WHAT ARE CONFIGURATION FILES?

WORKING WITH PASSIVE CONFIGURATION FILES

WORKING WITH ACTIVE CONFIGURATION FILES

Chapter 7

Once an application starts running, it may use information from a variety of sources. Some of this information, such as the results of calculation, is generated internally by the program. Other information is extracted from database files for the program to use. Still other information, such as the date and time, is obtained from the operating system itself.

While it is common for most of the data the program uses to come from outside sources, we should also consider using an outside data source to control the application's behavior. For a simple example, imagine an order-entry system that checks the credit limit against a maximum amount stored in a database. By updating the database, you can control how large or small an order the application will accept.

In this chapter, we will discuss the use of a database file to contain the global parameters and settings that the program uses to operate. By using an active database as the configuration file, we can easily control many aspects of the program's performance.

What are configuration files?

A *configuration file* is simply a file that contains global information that your program uses to operate. If you produce an application for more than one client, you probably have configuration information—such as the company name and address—already stored in a .DBF or .MEM file.

The configuration file can be active or passive. The NETWORK.INI file discussed in Chapter 3 is an example of a passive file. When the program starts running, it transfers the information from that file into the program's memory and uses those values for the duration of the program. An active file is checked before any major process, to see if another user has updated the information since the program began.

WHY USE A CONFIGURATION FILE?

By using a configuration file, you can change the way a program operates without having to rewrite and recompile the code. This can be a real time-saver in applications where the rules frequently change.

Configuration files are helpful in situations where there are multiple users, each of whom may have his or her own set of preferences as to screen color, confirm key, and so on. Instead of writing a complete file for each user, different versions of the information that needs to change from user to user can be kept in a configuration file.

You can also use a configuration file to accommodate other variables. You could, for example, store a country code in the configuration file. If the software were being used in the United States, then the ZIP code format would be *99999–9999*. In Canada, the format would be *A9A 9A9*. Your code might look like the following:

```
#define COUNTRY_CODE    aConfig[1]

LOCAL aConfig := LoadPassive()

@ 10,20 get cCity
    @ 10,38 get cState  picture "!!"
if COUNTRY_CODE == "USA"
    @ 10,41 get cZip    picture "99999-9999"
else
    @ 10,41 get cZip    picture "A9A 9A9"
endif
```

Although extra code is required to handle the various options, this approach allows for more flexibility in your software.

ACTIVE VERSUS PASSIVE CONFIGURATION FILES

A configuration file can be either active or passive, depending upon the application. A passive file is read in when the program begins and the data from it is saved in the program's memory. Once read in, the values do not change until the user exits the program. The example in the previous section shows a passive configuration file.

Passive configuration files usually contain all global settings and parameters that apply to the current user. Since they are read only once, when the application is loaded, the user must exit the application and enter it again in order for any changes to be made.

A program that handles passive configuration files must perform two major functions. First, it must transfer the information from the file into some variables or an array. Second, it must give your program access to all the configuration variables.

An active configuration file does not transfer its contents into memory, but rather is queried for parameters each time your program needs a value. Although performance is a bit slower using this approach, it allows the system to respond immediately to parameter changes. In a network environment, such a configuration file can be used for real-time control purposes. Your entire program can be controlled by another user who updates the configuration file. An application using an active configuration file is shown later in the chapter.

You should review your global parameters and classify each as active or passive. Passive parameters are stored in the program's memory and are static throughout the program. Since they are in memory, access to them is very quick and you do not need to worry about another user locking the file. Active parameters require a disk read, and so this method performs slightly slower than the passive method.

WORKING WITH PASSIVE CONFIGURATION FILES

Clipper's scoping capabilities provide a solid mechanism for implementing passive files. We can place all the parameters in a STATIC array in a single .PRG file. This way, you do not have to worry about another function changing the values.

Listing 7.1 contains two functions that can be used to implement passive configuration. The first function, READCONFIG(), reads the configuration file and fills the static array with the file's contents. The second function, called WHAT_IS(), returns the value for a specified parameter. Normally, your calls to WHAT_IS() will be handled by the preprocessor to improve code readability. Listing 7.2 shows a sample program that uses the functions from the PASSIVE.PRG program.

Listing 7.1: PASSIVE.PRG

```
*  Program:  PASSIVE
*  Author.:  Joseph D. Booth and Greg Lief
*  Purpose:  A generic program for creating passive
*            configuration files for use with Clipper.
****************************************

#include "fileio.ch"

#include "COMMON.CH"              // Clipper 5.2
* #include "cl501.ch"             // Clipper 5.01

#define CFGFILE           "user.ini"
#define IDENTIFIER        1
#define VALUE             2
#define CRLF         chr(13)+chr(10)

STATIC globals_ := { ;
          { "Regular color"     , "W/B"     },;
          { "Header line color" , "GR+/GR"  },;
          { "Footer line color" , "N/BG"    },;
          { "Bold color"        , "W+/B"    },;
          { "Highlight color"   , "GR+/B"   },;
          { "Fill character"    , "▇"       },;
          { "Box style"         , "┌─┤┘═╡"},;
          { "Data path"         , "F:\MAIL\"} }


*   Function: ReadConfig()
*     Purpose: Initializes file-wide settings
*       Notes: Recreates FILE if it does not exist
***************************
function ReadConfig(cFile)
local x
local y
local z
local nItems := len(globals_)
local cString
local nHandle
default cFile to CFGFILE
// attempt to open configuration file
nHandle := fopen(cFile)
// continue if file opened successfully
if nHandle != -1
   do while gfreadline(@cString, nHandle)
```

Listing 7.1: PASSIVE.PRG (Continued)

```
      // loop through the TEXT_ array and compare to this line
      cString := lower(cString)
      for x := 1 to nItems
         if cString = lower(globals_[x,IDENTIFIER])
            // read in value and convert to correct data type
            y := rtrim(substr(cString, at('=', cString) + 2))
            // convert to correct data type and assign to array
            globals_[x,VALUE] := convert1(y, valtype(globals_[x,VALUE]))
         endif
      next
   enddo
   fclose(nHandle)
else
   // configuration file does not exist, so create it
   WriteConfig(cFile)
endif
return nil
************************************************************

*    Function: WriteConfig()
*    Purpose: Writes configuration information to a disk
****************************
function WriteConfig(cFile)
LOCAL nHandle,x
LOCAL nItems := len(globals_)
if ( nHandle := fcreate(cFile, FC_NORMAL) ) != -1
   fwrite(nHandle, "[global parameters]" + CRLF)
   for x := 1 to nItems
      fwrite(nHandle, padr(globals_[x,IDENTIFIER], 22) + '= ')
      fwrite(nHandle, convert2(globals_[x,VALUE]) + CRLF)
   next
   fwrite(nHandle, chr(26))
   fclose(nHandle)
endif
return NIL



*    Function: What_Is()
*    Purpose: Returns the select parameters value
****************************
function What_Is( xWhich )
LOCAL cReturn := NIL
LOCAL x
if valtype( xWhich ) = "N"
```

Listing 7.1: PASSIVE.PRG (Continued)

```
   if xWhich > 0 .and. xWhich <= len( globals_ )
      cReturn := globals_[xWhich,VALUE]
   endif
else
   x := ascan( globals_,;
      { |zz| upper(zz[IDENTIFIER])==upper(xWhich) } )
   if x > 0
      cReturn := globals_[x,VALUE]
   endif
endif
return cReturn
**************************************


*    Function:   Convert1()
*       Purpose: Convert character to any data type
***************************
static function convert1(data, cType)
local ret_val
do case
   case cType == "L"
      ret_val := data == "YES"
   case cType == "N"
      ret_val := val(data)
   case cType == "D"
      ret_val := ctod(data)
   case cType == "C"
      ret_val := data
endcase
return ret_val
***********************************************************


*    Function:   Convert2()
*       Purpose: Convert any data type to character
***************************
static function convert2(data)
local cType := valtype(data)
local ret_val
do case
   case cType == "L"
      ret_val := if(data, "YES", "NO")
   case cType == "N"
      ret_val := ltrim(str(data))
   case cType == "D"
```

Listing 7.1: PASSIVE.PRG (Continued)

```
      ret_val := dtoc(data)
   case cType == "C"
      ret_val := data
endcase
return ret_val
**********************************************************
*    Function: GFReadline(@<cString>, <nHandle>)
*    Purpose:  Read one line (to CR/LF) from a text file
*    Excerpted from Grumpfish Library (c) 1989-92 Greg Lief
**********************************************************
static function gfreadline(cstring, nhandle)
local ret_val := .t.
local buffer
local ptr
local bytes
local bufsize := 255
local tempstring
cstring := []
buffer := space(bufsize)
do while .t.
   bytes := fread(nhandle, @buffer, bufsize)
   tempstring := left(buffer, bytes)
   if ( ptr := at(CRLF, tempstring) ) > 0
      cstring += substr(tempstring, 1, ptr - 1)
      fseek(nhandle, -(bytes - (ptr + 1)), FS_RELATIVE)
      exit
   else
      cstring += tempstring
      if bytes < bufsize
         ret_val := .f.
         exit
      endif
   endif
enddo
return ret_val
```

Listing 7.2: Example Using PASSIVE.PRG

```
#define  SYS_COLOR     What_Is( 1 )
#define  SYS_HEADER    What_is( 2 )
#define  SYS_FOOTER    What_Is( 3 )
#define  SYS_BOLD      What_Is( 4 )
#define  SYS_FILLCHAR  What_Is( 5 )
```

Listing 7.2: Example Using PASSIVE.PRG (Continued)

```
#define  SYS_BOXSTYLE  What_Is( 6 )


procedure main
LOCAL nChoice :=1

ReadConfig( "USER.INI" )
set scoreboard off
DispBox( 0,0,maxrow(),maxcol(),;
        replicate(SYS_FILLCHAR,9),SYS_COLOR )
@ 00,00 say padr("APPLICATION NAME",72) color SYS_HEADER
@ 00,72 say dtoc( date() ) color SYS_HEADER

@ maxrow(),00 say padr("Press <F10> when done",80) ;
      color SYS_FOOTER

do while !empty(nChoice)
   DispBox(4,30,10,50,SYS_BOXSTYLE,SYS_BOLD)
   setcolor( SYS_COLOR )
   @ 5,31 prompt "Update customers    "
   @ 6,31 prompt "Record invoices     "
   @ 7,31 prompt "Enter cash receipts"
   @ 8,31 prompt "Post to ledger      "
   @ 9,31 prompt "Display reports     "
   menu to nChoice
   do case
   case nChoice == 1
      // Call update customers
   case nChoice == 2
      // Record invoice program
   case nChoice == 3
      // Enter cash receipts
   case nChoice == 4
      // Post transaction to ledger
   case nChoice == 5
      // Display reports
   endcase
enddo
```

Working with active configuration files

Clipper provides network access to .DBF files more or less painlessly, so a .DBF file can be used to hold active system settings. This system file could be designed to have one record and a number of fields representing the various parameters you wish your application to respond to. If you want to have different configurations for each user, then the file might have multiple records; each user would locate his or her record as he or she logged on to your program.

Regardless of the number of records in the system file, it would be opened in SHARED mode at the beginning of your program. It would remain open and unlocked until your program completed.

The system file can be modified from another workstation while your application is running, so it is important that the most up-to-date information is read from the system file. In order to ensure that current information is being used, we have to understand what happens when Clipper reads a record.

Reading the System File

When Clipper opens a file and reads a record into memory, it transfers the contents of that file from the disk into an internal buffer. If you ask for the contents of a field, Clipper looks in the buffer to determine the field value. If someone else has changed the system file from another workstation, Clipper will not immediately update the contents of the buffer. It is therefore your program's responsibility to check the file for changes before acting upon the settings in the file. Fortunately, this is very easy to do.

The SKIP command instructs Clipper to move to another record <n> places away from the current record. Once Clipper moves to a new record location, it reads the disk and updates its internal buffer. By using SKIP 0, you can instruct Clipper to read from the disk. It does this because Clipper performs the command and reads the buffer, even if the <n> value after the SKIP command does not change the current record location. This allows you to easily make sure that the data in Clipper's internal buffer is up-to-date with the disk file.

The program that updates the system file must also force its data to be visible; it does this by using the COMMIT command. As soon as the changes are made to the file, an UNLOCK command and a COMMIT should be executed. In this way, the changes immediately become visible to other network users. (The COMMIT command is discussed in more detail in Chapter 2.)

Example Using the System File

As an example, let's look at an appointment calendar. In this code, the system file controls the last date for which an appointment can be scheduled and whether weekend appointments are allowed. Listing 7.3 shows a calendar function that allows the user to select a date from the screen by moving the cursor. Once a date has been selected, a time is entered and confirmed.

The function returns three parameters in an array: the date of the appointment; the time of the appointment; and a description of this appointment, entered by the user in a memo field. If the user presses the Escape key without setting an appointment, then an empty array is returned.

The system file that controls this appointment calendar contains the fields shown in Table 7.1. It probably would contain several other fields as well, but these are the fields of interest to the appointment program. Listing 7.3 contains the code for the appointment function.

Table 7.1: System File Structure

Field Name	Type	Size	Contents
LastDate	Date	8	Last date appointment can be set
GoodDays	Char	7	String of Y or N indicating if day is allowed to have appointments set for it
Start1	Number	4	Starting appointment time for Sunday
Start2	Number	4	Starting appointment time for Monday
Start3	Number	4	Starting appointment time for Tuesday
Start4	Number	4	Starting appointment time for Wednesday
Start5	Number	4	Starting appointment time for Thursday
Start6	Number	4	Starting appointment time for Friday
Start7	Number	4	Starting appointment time for Saturday
End1	Number	4	Ending appointment time for Sunday
End2	Number	4	Ending appointment time for Monday
End3	Number	4	Ending appointment time for Tuesday
End4	Number	4	Ending appointment time for Wednesday
End5	Number	4	Ending appointment time for Thursday
End6	Number	4	Ending appointment time for Friday
End7	Number	4	Ending appointment time for Saturday

Listing 7.3: SETAPPT() Function

```
*    Function:  SETAPPT
*    Authors:   Joseph D. Booth and Greg Lief
*    Purpose:   Allows an appointment date and time to be set
*    Syntax:    <aApptInfo> = SetAppt()
*    Returns:   Three element array containing the
*               appointment date in element one and
*               the appointment time in element two.
*               The third element is the notes about
*               the appointment.  If the user pressed the
*               escape key then an empty array will be returned.
*********************************

#include "inkey.ch"

function SetAppt()
local getlist    := {}
local tdate      := date()                    // Current date
local ttime      := substr(time(), 1, 5)      //     and time
local cNotes     := space(200)
local cSaveScr
local oldcolor
local oldscore   := set(_SET_SCOREBOARD, .f.)
local oldcursor  := setcursor(0)
local x
local ok         := .T.
local dFirst     := date()
local arr_       := {}
local oldf10
use system
if tdate > system->lastdate
   Alert("No appointments can be set past " + ;
         dtoc(system->lastdate) )
   return {}
endif

oldcolor := if( iscolor(), ;
                setcolor("N/G,N/W,,,N/G"),;
                setcolor("W/N,N/W,,,W/N") )

cSaveScr := savescreen(3, 1, 12, 56)
```

Listing 7.3: SETAPPT() Function (Continued)

```
dispbegin()
@ 03, 01 say "┌─────────────────────────┬─────────────────────────────┐"
@ 04, 01 say "║   Su Mo Tu We Th Fr Sa  | Date:                       ║"
@ 05, 01 say "║                         | Time:                       ║"
@ 06, 01 say "║                         ├─────────────────────────────╢"
@ 07, 01 say "║                         | Note:                       ║"
@ 08, 01 say "║                         |                             ║"
@ 09, 01 say "║                         |                             ║"
@ 10, 01 say "║                         |                             ║"
@ 11, 01 say "║                         |                             ║"
@ 12, 01 say "└─────────────────────────┴─────────────────────────────┘"
dispend()

do while ok
   if tdate <> system->lastdate
      x     := 32
      tDate := dFirst := ChkGoodDay( date() + 1, "F" )
      cal_head(dFirst, system->lastdate)
      do while x <> K_ENTER .and. x <> K_ESC
         x := inkey(50)

         // move record pointer in system file to force
         // Clipper to re-read contents from disk
         system->( dbskip(0) )

         do case

         case x == K_ESC
            ok := .F.

         case chr(x) $ "Dd"
            tDate := dFirst
            cal_head(tdate, system->lastdate)

         case chr(x) $ "Tt"          // Jump to (T)omorrow
            if Date() + 1 <= system->lastdate
               tDate := ChkGoodDay( dFirst + 1, "F" )
            else
               tDate := system->lastdate
            endif
            cal_head(tdate, system->lastdate)

         case x == K_UP              // Previous week
            tDate -= 7
            if tDate <= dFirst
```

Listing 7.3: SETAPPT() Function (Continued)

```
               tDate := dFirst
            endif
            cal_head(tdate, system->lastdate)

         case x == K_DOWN        // Next week
            if tDate + 7 <= system->lastdate
               tDate += 7
            else
               tDate := system->lastdate
            endif
            cal_head(tdate, system->lastdate)

         case x == K_LEFT        // Back one day
            tDate := ChkGoodDay(tdate - 1, "B" )
            if tDate <= dFirst
               tDate := dFirst
            endif
            cal_head(tdate, system->lastdate)

         case x == K_RIGHT       // Forward one day
            if tDate + 1 <= system->lastdate
               tDate := ChkGoodDay(tdate + 1, "F" )
            else
               tDate := system->lastdate
            endif
            cal_head(tdate, system->lastdate)
         endcase
      enddo
   else
      cal_head(tdate, system->lastdate)
   endif
   if ok
      @ 04,35 say dtoc(tDate) + "  " + padr(cDow(tDate), 10)
      @ 05,35 get tTime picture "99:99" valid ChkGoodTime(tdate, ttime)
      setcursor(1)
      read
      if lastkey() == K_ESC
         ok := .F.
      else
         // remap F10 to allow exit from the memo
         oldf10 := setkey(K_F10, { || __keyboard( chr(K_CTRL_W) ) } )
         cNotes := memoedit(cNotes, 8, 29, 10, 54)
         setkey(K_F10, oldf10)
         setcursor(0)
         @ 11,32 say "Is this okay? (y/n)"
```

Listing 7.3: SETAPPT() Function (Continued)

```
          x := 1
          do while ( ! chr(x) $ "YyNn" .and. x <> K_ESC )
             x := inkey(500)
          enddo
          scroll(11, 32, 11, 50, 0)
          if chr(x) $ "Yy"
             asize(arr_, 3)
             arr_[1] := tDate
             arr_[2] := tTime
             arr_[3] := cNotes
             ok := .f.
          else
             scroll(4, 35, 5, 54, 0)
          endif
       endif
    else
       exit
    endif
 enddo
 restscreen(3, 1, 12, 56, cSaveScr)
 setcolor(oldcolor)
 set(_SET_SCOREBOARD, oldscore)
 return arr_
 *******************************************************
 static function ChkGoodDay( dDate, cDir )
 local nX    := if(cDir = "F", 1, -1)
 local nDay  := dow(dDate)
 //
 // Check the current day to see if it is an allowed day.
 // If not, move the appropriate direction.
 //
 do while substr(system->GoodDays, nDay, 1) == "N"
    dDate += nX
    nDay := dow(dDate)
 enddo
 return dDate
 *******************************************************
 static function ChkGoodTime(dDate, cTime)
 local nStart    := system->( fieldpos("START1") ) - 1
 local nEnd      := system->( fieldpos("END1")   ) - 1
 local nDay      := dow(dDate)
 local nCurrent  := val(substr(cTime, 1, 2)) * 100 + ;
                    val(substr(cTime, 4, 2))
 local x
 local ret_val   := .t.
```

Listing 7.3: SETAPPT() Function (Continued)

```
// force re-read from disk
system->( dbskip(0) )

x := system->( fieldget(nStart + nDay) )
if nCurrent < x
   alert("Earliest time allowed for this day is " + ;
         substr(ltrim(str(x)), 1, 2) + ':' + ;
         substr(ltrim(str(x)), 3, 2))
   ret_val := .f.
else
   x := system->( fieldget(nEnd + nDay) )
   if nCurrent > x
      alert("Latest time allowed for this day is " + ;
            substr(ltrim(str(x)), 1, 2) + ':' + ;
            substr(ltrim(str(x)), 3, 2))
      ret_val := .f.
   endif
endif
return ret_val
*********************************************************
static function cal_head( dToday, lastdate )
local nStart
local jj, nEnd, nToday, nFrow, nFcol, endmonth
local mm := month(dToday)
local yy := year(dToday)
// save current date format and set to American to
// accommodate the date-twiddling below
local cDateformat := set(_SET_DATEFORMAT, "mm/dd/yy")
@ 04, 04 say padr(cMonth(dToday) + ", " + str(yy, 4), 20)
nStart := dow( ctod( str(mm, 2) + "/01/" + str(yy, 4) ))
mm++
if mm > 12
   mm := 1
endif
EndMonth := ctod(str(mm,2) + "/01/" + str(yy,4)) - 1
if lastdate < EndMonth
   nEnd := day(lastdate)
else
   nEnd := day(EndMonth)
endif
dispbegin()
scroll(06, 03, 11, 24, 0)
nFcol  := nStart * 3 + 1
nFrow  := 6
nToday := day(dToday)
```

Listing 7.3: SETAPPT() Function (Continued)

```
for jj := 1 to nEnd
   if nFcol - 1 > 21
      nFrow++
      @ nFrow, 4 say space(21)
      nFcol := 4
   endif
   if jj == nToday
      @ nFrow, nFcol say str(jj, 2) color "B+/W"
   else
      @ nFrow, nFcol say str(jj, 2)
   endif
   nFcol += 3
next
dispend()
// reset prior date format
set(_SET_DATEFORMAT, cDateformat)
return nil
***************************************************
```

If you review the code from Listing 7.3, you will see three areas where the system parameter file is controlling the program's behavior. The first, towards the beginning of the code, checks the last date for which an appointment can be set. If you were to change the LASTDATE field in the system file, the calendar would reflect the new last appointment date.

The second use of the system file is found in the function CHKGOOD-DAY(). If the day of the week is set to <n> in the system file, then the function prevents the cursor from moving to that day (by adjusting the date to the closest "good day"). If the flag for that day is set to TRUE, the code accepts the day for the appointment.

The third use is in the time-setting routine, which is validated through the CHKGOODTIME() function. This function makes sure that the selected appointment time is within the normal range of appointment hours for the selected day.

Controlling the appointment process Listing 7.4 contains a function called APPT_CFG() that is used to configure the appointment program's parameters. The user can toggle any day on or off; for days that are toggled on, the user can also specify a starting and ending appointment time.

Listing 7.4: APPT_CFG() Function

```
*      Function:  CfgAppt
*      Authors:   Joseph D. Booth and Greg Lief
*      Purpose:   Update system appoint fields
*       Syntax:   <logical> := Appt_Cfg()
*      Returns:   TRUE if fields were updated, FALSE
*                 if an error occurs
*
*********************************

#include "INKEY.CH"

#define  START          1
#define  ENDING          2


function Appt_Cfg
LOCAL getlist    := {}
LOCAL lReturn    := .F.
LOCAL aGoodDays := array(7)
LOCAL aGoodTime := array(7,2)
LOCAL cSaveScr  := ""
LOCAL x
LOCAL cTmp

use SYSTEM shared new
if ! NetErr()
   //
   //
   for x:=1 to 7
      aGoodDays[x]          := substr(SYSTEM->GoodDays,x,1)=="Y"
      aGoodTime[x,START]    := fieldget( fieldpos("START"+str(x,1)) )
      aGoodTime[x,ENDING]   := fieldget( fieldpos("END"+str(x,1)) )
   next

   cSaveScr := savescreen(3,1,12,31)
```

Listing 7.4: APPT_CFG() Function (Continued)

```
@ 03,01 say "┌─────────────────────────────┐"
@ 04,01 say "│ DAY      │ OK  START   END │"
@ 05,01 say "│ Sunday   │                 │"
@ 06,01 say "│ Monday   │                 │"
@ 07,01 say "│ Tuesday  │                 │"
@ 08,01 say "│ Wednesday│                 │"
@ 09,01 say "│ Thursday │                 │"
@ 10,01 say "│ Friday   │                 │"
@ 11,01 say "│ Saturday │                 │"
@ 12,01 say "└─────────────────────────────┘"

for x:=1 to 7
   @ x+4,15 get aGoodDays[x] picture "Y"
   @ x+4,19 get aGoodTime[x,START] picture "9999" ;
            when aGoodDays[ row()-4 ]
   @ x+4,25 get aGoodTime[x,ENDING] picture "9999" ;
            when aGoodDays[ row()-4 ]
next
read
if lastkey() <> K_ESC
   cTmp := ""
   for x:=1 to 7
      cTmp += if(aGoodDays[x],"Y","N")
      if !aGoodDays[x]
         aGoodTime[x,START]  := 0
         aGoodTime[x,ENDING] := 0
      endif
   next
   if Rlock()
      replace SYSTEM->GoodDays with cTmp
      for x:=1 to 7
         fieldput( fieldpos("START"+str(x,1)), aGoodTime[x,START] )
         fieldput( fieldpos("END"+str(x,1)), aGoodTime[x,ENDING] )
      next
      unlock
      commit
      lReturn := .T.
   endif
endif
select SYSTEM
```

Listing 7.4: APPT_CFG() Function (Continued)

```
   use
   restscreen(3,1,12,31,cSaveScr)
endif
return lReturn
```

Summary

In this chapter, we discussed active and passive configuration files and the differences between them. We wrote a function to handle passive configuration files and covered the network considerations for active configuration files. We also provided a couple of examples to illustrate how the entire application can be controlled by use of configuration files.

Semaphores

WHY USE SEMAPHORES?

CREATING SEMAPHORES IN CLIPPER

ACCESSING NETWARE'S SEMAPHORE SERVICES

TWO SEMAPHORE EXAMPLES

Chapter 8

The word *semaphore* comes from two Greek words: *sēma*, which means a sign, and *pherein*, which means to bear. In computer parlance, a semaphore is a sign between two processes that can be used to indicate how those processes should operate. As an example, a traffic light is a sign between two cars. By interpreting the light's color, each car knows whether to go or to stop (assuming both cars agree on the meaning of the colors).

A network semaphore is a label or string of characters that can be used to communicate information. In addition to the label, a semaphore also has a value. It is entirely up to the application to determine how and when to use the semaphore and its value. In network programming, semaphores are used to control access to network resources, such as files, printers, and more.

WHY USE SEMAPHORES?

Semaphores can be used to bridge the gap between Clipper's file- and record-locking ability and full control over network resources. As long as all programs agree on the use of the semaphore, it can be a very powerful tool for the network programmer. For example, you could use a semaphore to control access to a CD-ROM device, so that only one person at a time could extract data from it. The following pseudocode illustrates the concept of semaphore-controlled access:

```
if CD_ROM_SEMAPHORE > 0
   //
   // Tell user that the CD-ROM device is busy
   //
else
   //
   // Set the semaphores value to one and
   // then load the CD-ROM software
   //
endif
```

This example shows one attempt to access the CD_ROM device; it could easily be wrapped in a loop to allow the user to retry the device later. You could also build a similar system to redirect output to the least busy network printer or to handle locking of text files.

The primary rule to remember when using semaphores is consistency. They work only with programs that agree to play by their rules. You could hardly expect a FoxPro application to respect semaphores designed for printer access. If, however, you could determine which semaphores FoxPro used, you could modify your Clipper program to respect them.

CREATING SEMAPHORES IN CLIPPER

In this chapter, we will explore how you can use .DBF files to create a simple semaphore system. We will also discuss how to access NetWare's semaphore services from within our Clipper application.

CREATING A SEMAPHORE .DBF FILE

You can create a semaphore file in Clipper that can be used on any network, regardless of whether that network provides semaphore services. You do this by creating a master .DBF file that contains three fields:

- The semaphore label, which identifies the particular semaphore
- The current counter, which represents the current number of processes that have accessed the semaphore
- The maximum value, which represents the total number of processes allowed to access the semaphore simultaneously

The structure of the file SEMAPHOR is shown below:

Field Name	Type	Size
S_LABEL	Char	55
S_CURRENT	Number	4
S_MAX	Number	4

Each time you wished to create a semaphore, you would look up its label in the SEMAPHOR.DBF file. If the label were found, then the contents of S_CURRENT would be returned. If the label were not found, then it would be added to the table and its value would be set to zero. The S_MAX field is set to the value you specify; this number indicates how many people can access the semaphore. Listing 8.1 shows a function to use a semaphore.

Listing 8.1: USESEMA( ) Function

```
*    Function:  UseSema()
*    Authors:   Joseph D. Booth and Greg Lief
*    Purpose:   To allow semaphore communication by using
*               a DBF file.
*******************************
#define  DEFAULT_MAXIMUM     3

function UseSema( cLabel,nMax )
local oldarea := select()      // Save current area
local is_ok   := .F.
if nMax == NIL
   nMax := DEFAULT_MAXIMUM
endif

if select("SEMAPHOR") = 0       // If not yet opened
   use SEMAPHOR shared new      // then open the file
   if file("SEMAPHOR.NTX")      // and see if an index
      set index to SEMAPHOR     // exists
   endif
endif
select SEMAPHOR
if indexord() == 0
   locate all for upper(SEMAPHOR->s_label) = upper(cLabel)
else
   seek upper(cLabel)
endif
if found()
   if N_Reclock()
```

Listing 8.1: USESEMA( ) Function (Continued)

```
      is_ok := SEMAPHOR->s_current < SEMAPHOR->s_max
      if is_ok
         replace SEMAPHOR->s_current with ;
                 SEMAPHOR->s_current +1
      endif
      unlock
      commit
   endif
elseif N_AddRec()
   replace SEMAPHOR->s_label    with upper(cLabel),;
           SEMAPHOR->s_current  with 1,;
           SEMAPHOR->s_max      with nMax
   unlock
   commit
   is_ok := .T.
endif
select (oldarea)
return is_ok
```

ACCESSING THE SEMAPHORE .DBF FILE

Once you've created a semaphore and set its maximum value, an application must request the semaphore before it can use the resource the semaphore is controlling. If the program is allowed to access the semaphore, it can use the resource. If the current number of semaphore users is equal to the maximum allowed, then the program can wait until a user is done or it can abort and not allow the operation.

Listing 8.2 contains two functions, WAIT_SEMA() and FREE_SEMA(), that are used to control access to the semaphore file. The WAIT_SEMA() function can be used to ask permission to proceed. It expects the semaphore name as the first parameter and, optionally, can take a waiting time as a second parameter. It returns a logical value of TRUE if the semaphore is available or FALSE if not. If TRUE is returned, then the current count of the semaphore is also incremented by one.

The FREE_SEMA( ) function is called after your application has completed the process. It is used to reduce the number of current semaphore users by one. You need to pass the name of the semaphore to the function. If the semaphore is released, then a logical TRUE is returned. If a problem occurs, then FALSE is returned.

By using WAIT_SEMA() and FREE_SEMA(), you can easily control access to any resource or file on the network. The use of a semaphore .DBF allows you to use semaphore locking on any network.

Listing 8.2: WAIT_SEMA( ) and FREE_SEMA( ) Functions

```
*   Function:  Wait_Sema()
*   Authors:   Joseph D. Booth and Greg Lief
*   Purpose:   To wait for a semaphore before continuing
*******************************

function Wait_Sema( cLabel,nTime2Wait )
local oldarea := select()     // Save current area
local is_ok   := .F.
local nTime   := 0

if nTime2Wait == NIL
   nTime2Wait := 0
endif

if select("SEMAPHOR") = 0     // If not yet opened
   use SEMAPHOR shared new    // then open the file
   if file("SEMAPHOR.NTX")    // and see if an index
      set index to SEMAPHOR   // exists
   endif
endif
select SEMAPHOR
if indexord() == 0
   locate all for upper(SEMAPHOR->s_label) = upper(cLabel)
else
   seek upper(cLabel)
endif
if !eof()
   do while SEMAPHOR->s_current >= SEMAPHOR->s_max .and. ;
            nTime < nTime2Wait
      inkey(1)
      nTime++
   enddo
   if SEMAPHOR->s_current < SEMAPHOR->s_max
      if N_reclock()
         is_ok := .T.
         replace SEMAPHOR->s_current with ;
                 SEMAPHOR->s_current+1
         commit
```

Listing 8.2: WAIT_SEMA( ) and FREE_SEMA( ) Functions (Continued)

```
         unlock
      endif
   endif
endif
select (oldarea)
return is_ok

*  Function: Free_Sema()
*  Authors:  Joseph D. Booth and Greg Lief
*  Purpose:  To free a semaphore after a process
*            is complete
*******************************

function Free_Sema( cLabel )
local oldarea := select()      // Save current area
local is_ok   := .F.

if select("SEMAPHOR") = 0      // If not yet opened
   use SEMAPHOR shared new     // then open the file
   if file("SEMAPHOR.NTX")     // and see if an index
      set index to SEMAPHOR    // exists
   endif
endif
select SEMAPHOR
if indexord() == 0
   locate all for upper(SEMAPHOR->s_label) = upper(cLabel)
else
   seek upper(cLabel)
endif
if !eof() .and. SEMAPHOR->s_current > 0
   if N_RecLock()
      replace SEMAPHOR->s_current with ;
              SEMAPHOR->s_current -1
      commit
      unlock
      is_ok := .T.
   endif
endif
select (oldarea)
return is_ok
```

A SIMPLE SEMAPHORE EXAMPLE

To see how the semaphore system can work, let's return to our example of the CD-ROM device mentioned at the beginning of the chapter. Assume that you've just installed a new CD-ROM drive on your network. This drive has two active drive bays. You want to send a message to the operator to put the requested CD in either open bay. If both bays are being used, then the request should not be serviced.

The following code segment uses the semaphore functions from Listings 8.1 and 8.2 to control access to this CD-ROM device:

```
//
// First, set up the semaphore with a maximum of two users
//
UseSema( "CD_ROM",2 )
//
// Wait 10 seconds for the CD-ROM to become available
//
if Wait_Sema( "CD_ROM",10 )
   //
   // Send a message to the console using N_CONSOLE()
   // from Chapter 11.
   //
   N_Console("Please mount ZIP-code CD")
   //
   // Run the program to access the CD-ROM device
   //
   Free_Sema( "CD_ROM" )
else
   Alert("CD-ROM player is busy at this time...")
endif
```

This example shows how to control a simple network device by using a semaphore system. Some networks provide similar semaphore services. We will explore NetWare's semaphore services in the next section.

ACCESSING NETWARE'S SEMAPHORE SERVICES

Novell's NetWare provides semaphore services that you can use to control the behavior of your Clipper applications. If two Clipper programs agree on the use of the semaphore, any kind of control over network files and resources can be achieved.

There are five network services that deal with semaphores. The services are described in the following sections.

OPENING A SEMAPHORE

To use the semaphore system, you must first open the semaphore by specifying a name and an initial maximum value. If the semaphore name does not exist, one will be created and an initial maximum value will be assigned to it. If the semaphore already exists, then it will be opened and the initial value will be ignored.

The NetWare operating system allows semaphore names to be from 1 to 127 characters long. The maximum value must be positive and cannot be greater than 127 users. (Future versions of NetWare might increase this number.)

Once a semaphore is created, it is given a number known as a *handle*. This handle is used in any other semaphore services to refer to the semaphore.

Listing 8.3 contains a function called N_OPENSEM that is used to open a network semaphore. It expects two parameters: the semaphore name and the initial maximum value to assign if the semaphore does not exist. It returns a numeric handle that is passed to the other semaphore functions. Be sure to save this numeric handle, since other functions will need to refer to it.

Listing 8.3: N_OPENSEM Function

```
*     Program:  OpenSema.PRG
*     Authors:  Joseph D. Booth and Greg Lief
*     Function: N_OpenSem()
*     Purpose:  Opens a semaphore object and returns its
*               handle
*     Syntax:   nHandle := N_OpenSem( cLabel,nInitial )
**********************************

#define AX      1
#define BX      2
#define CX      3
#define DX      4
#define DI      6
#define DS      8

function N_OpenSem( cLabel,nInitial )
LOCAL nSize   := len(cLabel)
LOCAL nHandle := 0
LOCAL nReturn
LOCAL aRegs[ 10 ]
aRegs[ AX ] := 197 * 256           // Set AH to nService
```

Listing 8.3: N_OPENSEM Function (Continued)

```
aRegs[ DS ] := chr(nSize)+cLabel   // Request packet aRegs[ CX ] :=
nInitial            // Initial maximum
aRegs[ DX ] := .T.                 // Using a string

if ft_int86( 33, aRegs )
   nReturn := aRegs[AX] % 256  // Extract low byte
   if nReturn = 0
      nHandle := bin2l( i2bin( aRegs[CX] ) +;
                        i2bin( aRegs[DX] ) )
   endif
endif
  return nHandle
```

EXAMINING A SEMAPHORE

You can examine the current value of a semaphore without making any changes to it. If the value is greater than zero, then there are still semaphore slots available. If the value is less than zero, then the number indicates how many users are currently in the queue waiting for this semaphore.

Listing 8.4 contains the N_EXAMSEM() function, which takes as a parameter the handle returned from N_OPENSEM(). It returns the semaphore's value or –99 if an error occurs.

Listing 8.4: N_EXAMSEM Function

```
*    Program:   ExamSema.PRG
*    Authors:   Joseph D. Booth and Greg Lief
*    Function:  N_ExamSem()
*    Purpose:   Examines a semaphore handle and returns
*               the semaphore value
*    Syntax:    nValue := N_ExamSem( nHandle )
*********************************

#define AX         1
#define BX         2
#define CX         3
#define DX         4

function N_ExamSem( nHandle )
LOCAL nValue := -99
LOCAL nReturn
LOCAL aRegs[ 10 ]
aRegs[ AX ] := 197 * 256 +1        // Set AH to C5h, 01h
```

Listing 8.4: N_EXAMSEM Function (Continued)

```
aRegs[ CX ] := bin2i(substr(l2bin(nHandle),1,2))
aRegs[ DX ] := bin2i(substr(l2bin(nHandle),3,2))

if ft_int86( 33, aRegs )
   nReturn :=  aRegs[AX] % 256   // Extract low byte
   if nReturn = 0
      nValue := aRegs[CX] % 256
   endif
endif
return nValue
```

CLOSING A SEMAPHORE

Once you've finished using a semaphore, you should close it. Listing 8.5 contains the N_CLOSESEM() function. It expects the semaphore handle from N_OPENSEM() and returns a logical value indicating whether the semaphore has been closed.

Listing 8.5: N_CLOSESEM() Function

```
*    Program:   ClosSema.PRG
*    Authors:   Joseph D. Booth and Greg Lief
*    Function:  N_CloseSem()
*    Purpose:   Closes a semaphore handle
*    Syntax:    logical := N_CloseSem( nHandle )
**********************************

#define AX        1
#define BX        2
#define CX        3
#define DX        4

function N_CloseSem( nHandle )
LOCAL is_ok := .F.
LOCAL aRegs[ 10 ]
aRegs[ AX ] := 197 * 256 +4         // Service C5h, 04h
aRegs[ CX ] := bin2i(substr(l2bin(nHandle),1,2))
aRegs[ DX ] := bin2i(substr(l2bin(nHandle),3,2))

if ft_int86( 33, aRegs )
   is_ok  :=  (aRegs[AX] % 256) == 0
endif
return is_ok
```

This function decrements by one the count of the number of users who are using this semaphore. If this count equals zero as a result of the close semaphore call, then the semaphore will be deleted.

USING A SEMAPHORE

There are two services that are used to manage the semaphore counts. When you want to access a semaphore-controlled resource, you begin by waiting for that semaphore. If the semaphore is not fully used, you will be immediately allowed access and the count of available slots will decrease by one. If the semaphore is not available for use, the count will still decrease. The function will wait a specified amount of time to see if the semaphore becomes available. If the time passes and the semaphore is not free, then the count will be increased by one and access will be denied.

Once you've finished using the resource, you should signal the semaphore that you are done. This process increases the number of open semaphore slots by one, which allows other users access to the resource.

Listing 8.6 contains two functions. The first, N_WAITSEM(), should be used to check for access to a semaphore. It expects the semaphore handle and an optional number of seconds to wait. If the semaphore is available, TRUE is returned and the program can continue. If FALSE is returned, then the semaphore has no open slots and the program should inform the user that the resource is not available.

The second function, N_SIGNALSEM(), is used to inform the semaphore that you've finished using the resource. It increases the number of open semaphore slots. You should pass the handle from N_OPENSEM() to this function.

Listing 8.6: Two Functions for Network Semaphore Use

```
*    Program:  NET_SEMA.PRG
*    Authors:  Joseph D. Booth and Greg Lief
*    Function: N_WaitSem()
*    Purpose:  Wait for semaphore resource
*    Syntax:   logical := N_WaitSem( nHandle,nTimeOut )
********************************

#define AX        1
#define BX        2
#define CX        3
#define DX        4
#define BP        7

function N_WaitSem( nHandle,nTimeOut )
```

Listing 8.6: Two Functions for Network Semaphore Use (Continued)

```
LOCAL is_ok := .F.
LOCAL aRegs[ 10 ]
aRegs[ AX ] := 197 * 256 +2        // Service C5h, 02h
aRegs[ CX ] := bin2i(substr(l2bin(nHandle),1,2))
aRegs[ DX ] := bin2i(substr(l2bin(nHandle),3,2))
aRegs[ BP ] := nTimeOut * 18       // In clock ticks

if ft_int86( 33, aRegs )
   is_ok  := (aRegs[AX] % 256) == 0
endif
return isok

*  Function: N_SignalSem()
*  Purpose: Signal semaphore that we are done
*   Syntax: logical := N_SignalSem( nHandle )
***********************************

#define AX      1
#define BX      2
#define CX      3
#define DX      4

function N_SignalSem( nHandle )
LOCAL is_ok := .F.
LOCAL aRegs[ 10 ]
aRegs[ AX ] := 197 * 256 +3        // Service C5h, 02h
aRegs[ CX ] := bin2i(substr(l2bin(nHandle),1,2))
aRegs[ DX ] := bin2i(substr(l2bin(nHandle),3,2))

if ft_int86( 33, aRegs )
   is_ok  := (aRegs[AX] % 256) == 0
endif
return is_ok
```

Two semaphore examples

In this section, we will look at two examples in which semaphores are used to handle network problems. This should provide your imagination with many other ideas about possible uses for a signal system between two applications.

LIMITING THE NUMBER OF USERS

The semaphore system could be used to restrict the number of users who can simultaneously run your application. If your application is licensed to a maximum of three simultaneous users, you might want the program to detect when a fourth user attempts to access the program. This user could then be denied access to the program and would have to wait until another user finished.

Listing 8.7 contains a function called USE_APP() that returns a logical value indicating whether the maximum number of users has been exceeded. Your program can then determine the appropriate course of action.

Listing 8.7: USE_APP() Function

```
*   Program:   USE_APP.PRG
*   Authors:   Joseph D. Booth and Greg Lief
*   Function:  Use_App()
*   Purpose:   Check that the application's maximum number
*              of users has not been exceeded
*   Syntax:    logical := Use_App( nMaximum )
***********************

STATIC    nSemHandle := 0
STATIC    cAppName   := "LEDGER.EXE"

function Use_App( nMaxUsers )
nSemHandle := N_OpenSem( cAppName,nMaxUsers )
return N_WaitSem(nSemHandle,1)

function Close_App()
return n_CloseSem(nSemHandle)
The USE_APP() function should be placed at the beginning of the code, as shown
below:
#define MAX_USERS    3

if Use_App( MAX_USERS )    // Allow up to three users
   //
   // Call your program
   //
   Close_App()             // Close the semaphores
else
   Alert( "Too many users!" )
endif
```

Once the program is finished, be sure to call the CLOSE_APP() function to close the semaphore so someone else can access your program. You should place the call to CLOSE_APP() into your program's exit procedure and, optionally, into its error-handling routine. (Calling CLOSE_APP() during the error routine is especially necessary with releases of Clipper prior to release 5.2. These releases did not have an EXIT routine that would be called before the program returned to DOS).

A DIFFERENT APPROACH TO RECORD LOCKING

You could also use semaphores to handle an application in which multiple records in the same file must be locked to complete the transaction. Since Clipper allows only one lock per work area, we could use a semaphore system to communicate the records that must be locked. Once all the semaphores were obtained, the entire file would then be locked and the appropriate records would be updated. Once the transaction were done, the file would be unlocked and the semaphores would be closed.

Listing 8.8 contains a function called STARTLOCK() that takes an array of record numbers as the first parameter and an amount of time to wait, expressed in seconds, as the second parameter. The function creates a single semaphore for each record in the array. Each semaphore consists of the alias name and the record number.

If all semaphores are obtained before the specified time has elapsed, then the file is locked and TRUE is returned. If the semaphores cannot be obtained in the time allowed, FALSE is returned and the file is not locked.

Listing 8.8: STARTLOCK() Function

```
*    Program:   ST_LOCK.PRG
*    Authors:   Joseph D. Booth and Greg Lief
*    Function:  StartLock()
*    Purpose:   Try to lock multiple records in the file
*               using semaphores
*    Syntax:    logical := StartLock( aRecords,nTime )
**********************

STATIC   aSemHandle := {}

function StartLock( aRecords,nTime )
LOCAL cName := alias()
LOCAL x
```

Listing 8.8: STARTLOCK() Function (Continued)

```
LOCAL is_ok := .T.
LOCAL nSize := len(aRecords)

for x := 1 to nSize
   Aadd(aSemHandle,N_OpenSem(cName+str(aRecords[x],8),1))
next

nTime := (nTime * 18)

for x:= 1 to nSize
   if ! N_waitSem(aSemhandle,nTime)
      is_ok := .F.
   endif
next

if is_ok
   is_ok := Flock()
endif
return is_ok



* Function:  CloseLock()
* Purpose:   Closes all the semaphore locks opened
*            by the STARTLOCK function
*   Syntax:  <logical> := CloseLock()
***********************
function CloseLock()
LOCAL x
for x:= 1 to len(aSemhandle)
   n_CloseSem(aSemHandle[x])
next
aSemHandle := {}
unlock
return .T.
```

If the STARTLOCK() function returns TRUE, then the file is locked and all the records can be updated. As soon as the update is completed, you can call the CLOSELOCK() function, which closes all the semaphores and unlocks the file. The following code fragment shows an example.

```
//
// Update line items on an invoice
//
select LINEITEM

if StartLock( { 5,12,14 }, 10 }
   goto 5
   replace LINEITEM->quantity with LINEITEM->quantity -2
   goto 12
   replace LINEITEM->quantity with LINEITEM->quantity -2
   goto 14
   replace LINEITEM->quantity with LINEITEM->quantity -2
   CloseLock()
else
   Alert("Transaction couldn't be completed...")
endif
```

Although this approach requires more coordination between processes, it eliminates problems that can occur when only some records in a transaction obtain record locks. In this example, either all records or none are updated.

Summary

Semaphores are useful communication tools that can solve a large number of network problems. By designing applications that agree on the semaphores used, it is possible to have your program behave politely in a sometimes hostile network world.

The Novell Bindery: A Usable Database

WHAT IS THE BINDERY?

HOW THE BINDERY IS ORGANIZED

BINDERY OBJECT TYPES

UPDATING THE BINDERY FILES

TECHNICAL OVERVIEW OF THE BINDERY

Chapter 9

In this chapter, we will discuss how NetWare stores user information. We will also provide functions that allow you to use this information from within your Clipper applications. NetWare provides a very secure system for storing your information. Learning how to take advantage of it will help improve your Clipper application.

WHAT IS THE BINDERY?

Each NetWare file server contains a database with information about its users, groups, print queues, and more. This database is called the *bindery.* NetWare uses the bindery to provide extensive security and accounting for all users who have access to the network, and to keep track of all services such as print queues and remote bridges.

Using the bindery, the file server checks user ids, passwords, and authorization to queues and directories, and even controls the amount of disk space that each user can use. The bindery files contain the databases needed to provide these security and accounting services.

Each server running NetWare creates its own bindery files, which contain the names and attributes of all entities on the network. By using these files, the file server can allow or restrict access to all services available on the network.

WHY USE THE BINDERY?

If you've not yet developed a login and security system for your applications, consider the bindery: It is an excellent system and NetWare provides utility programs to update it. Even if you've already developed a system for security and login, you might want to use the bindery instead for the following benefits:

- The bindery is very secure. The network opens the bindery files when the network is started, and leaves them open and locked at all times. Only a supervisor user id (or a user with supervisor rights) can close the bindery. If you access the bindery via the Novell published API calls (as we do later in this chapter), each object has a read and write security automatically enforced by NetWare.
- NetWare comes with a program called SYSCON that allows update of bindery information in a very organized fashion. Network administrators and many users are comfortable working with SYSCON and other menu-driven NetWare utilities.

How the bindery is organized

The bindery is organized into a collection of objects. An object can be a *client* or a *server*. Client objects use services provided by server objects. Users are clients, for example, and the printer queues are servers.

Each object has a name, a type, and any number of properties. Each property can have a single value or multiple values associated with it. Figure 9.1 shows the bindery structure.

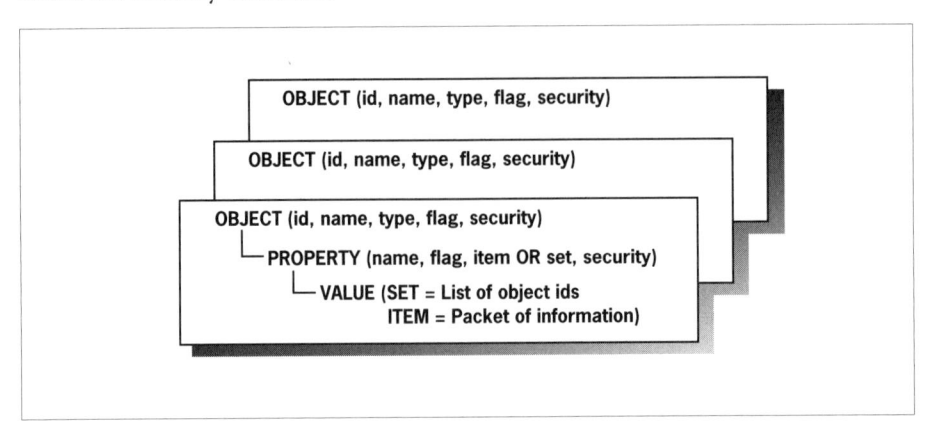

```
OBJECT (id, name, type, flag, security)
  OBJECT (id, name, type, flag, security)
    OBJECT (id, name, type, flag, security)
      └─ PROPERTY (name, flag, item OR set, security)
           └─ VALUE (SET = List of object ids
                     ITEM = Packet of information)
```

Figure 9.1: Bindery structure

OBJECTS

The bindery can hold up to 65,000 objects, although it should remain small (fewer than 1,000 objects) for performance reasons. An object may be a user, a group, or a resource. For example, TRACI might be a user in the PERSONNEL group who needs access to the LASER_PRINT_QUEUE. The network would use the bindery to determine if TRACI should be granted access and would also inform the other services that the LASER_PRINT_QUEUE is being used.

Each object has the following five pieces of information associated with it:

- Object id, a unique number assigned by NetWare to each object added to the network. This is a four-byte integer number.
- Object name, a character string representing the name of the object. For a user object, it might be the person's initials. The name can be up to 47 characters long.
- Object type, a numeric code indicating what type of object this is. The network expects certain characteristics based upon the object's type. The codes for the various object types are shown in Table 9.1.

Table 9.1: Object Types

Code	Type
1	User
2	Group of Users
3	Print Queue
4	File Server
5	Job Server
6	Gateway
7	Print Server
8	Archive Queue
9	Archive Server
10	Job Queue
11	Administration
33	NAS SNA Gateway
35	Async Gateway

Table 9.1: Object Types (Continued)

Code	Type
36	Remote Bridge Server
38	Async Bridge
40	X.25 Bridge
45	Time Synchronization Server
46	Archive Server
71	Advertising Print Server
80	Btrieve Value Added Process
83	Print Queue User
162	Bindery
163	Oracle DB Server
167	Rconsole

- Object flag, indicating whether this object is static or dynamic. Dynamic objects are temporary and will be deleted when the network is brought down. Static objects remain in the bindery until they are specifically removed.

- Object security, a read and write security associated with each object. This indicates which other objects have the ability to access this object. Security is a single byte; the first four bits indicate the write security and the last four are the read security. The values that the four bits can take on are

Code	Value
0	Anyone can access this object
1	Users logged in to the server
2	Only the current object
3	Supervisor only
4	NetWare operating system only

Objects are defined by both their name and type. Two objects may have the same name as long as their object types are different.

Finding objects NetWare provides an API function that can be used to obtain a list of all objects for a specified type. Listing 9.1 shows a function called N_SCANBINDERY() that takes an object type as a parameter and returns an array of all objects of that type.

Listing 9.1: N_SCANBINDERY() Function

```
*    Program:   SCANBIND.PRG
*    Authors:   Joseph D. Booth and Greg Lief
*    Function:  N_ScanBindery()
*    Purpose:   Scans the bindery for a given object type
*    Syntax:    aObjects := N_scanBindery( nType )
**********************************

#define MINUS_ONE   chr(255)+chr(255)+chr(255)+chr(255)

function N_ScanBindery( nType )
LOCAL cBuffer  := space(57)          // Reply buffer
LOCAL cRequest := chr(55)+ ;         // Novell API (55) - Scan Bindery
         MINUS_ONE+;                 // -1 in binary
         chr(0)+chr(nType)+;         // Byte swapped Object type
         Lstring("*",48)             // Scan for wildcard character
LOCAL arr_     := {}

do while NetWare( 227,cRequest,@cBuffer ) == 0
   // Extract the object name and save in array
   // ////////////////////////////////////////
   Aadd(arr_,CleanStr( substr(cBuffer,7,48) ) )
   //
   // Update the send buffer to get next member
   //
   cRequest := substr(cRequest,1,1)+substr(cBuffer,1,4)+;
            substr(cRequest,6)
enddo
return arr_
```

The N_SCANBINDERY() function works by performing a wildcard lookup from the bindery for the specified object type. The function loops around until a nonzero value is returned from NetWare, indicating the end of the list.

You can create a header file called BINDERY.CH containing the following preprocessor #XTRANSLATE() functions to access the N_SCANBINDERY() function without having to remember the object types.

```
#xtranslate   N_Users()     => N_ScanBindery( 1)
#xtranslate   N_Groups()    => N_ScanBindery( 2)
#xtranslate   N_PrintQs()   => N_ScanBindery( 3)
#xtranslate   N_Servers()   => N_ScanBindery( 4)
#xtranslate   N_Bridges()   => N_ScanBindery(36)
```

By using the list of object types provided earlier in the chapter, you can easily create your own set of customized preprocessor functions to return a list of objects.

Determine the security level   In addition to scanning the bindery, you can also determine the security level that the current workstation has to its logged object id. Listing 9.2 contains a function called N_BINDLEVEL() that returns a three-element array. The first two elements are read and write security bytes, respectively, and the third element is the bindery object id for the logged object.

Listing 9.2: N_BINDLEVEL() Function

```
*    Program:   BNDLEVEL.PRG
*    Authors:   Joseph D. Booth and Greg Lief
*    Function:  N_BindLevel()
*    Purpose:   Get workstation's access level to the bindery
*    Syntax:    aInfo := N_BindLevel()
**********************************

#define   SECURITY   "ALOSN"

function N_BindLevel
LOCAL cBuffer  := space(5)
LOCAL cRequest:= chr(70)           // Novell API (70) Bindery access level
LOCAL aInfo    := {}

if Netware(227,cRequest, @cBuffer) == 0
   aInfo := {substr(SECURITY,int(asc(cBuffer))%16+1,1),; // read
             substr(SECURITY,int(asc(cBuffer))/16+1,1),; // write
             Long2Clip(substr(cBuffer,2,4)) }            // user id
endif
return aInfo
```

The read and write security will consist of a letter that indicates the level for this object. Here are codes and their meanings:

Code	Meaning
A	Anyone can access this object
L	Users logged in to the server
O	Only the current object
S	Supervisor only
N	NetWare operating system only

Most information about the object can be updated by the workstation, although some properties of the object may be restricted to the supervisor or the NetWare operating system.

Identifying objects Once you have an object name or an object id, you can use this information to obtain additional information about the bindery object. Listing 9.3 contains a function called N_OBJECTNAME() that returns the object's name if passed a network object id. You could use this function along with the N_BINDLEVEL() function from Listing 9.2 to determine the name of the user currently logged in at the workstation.

Listing 9.3: N_OBJECTNAME() Function

```
*   Program:  OBJNAME.PRG
*   Authors:  Joseph D. Booth and Greg Lief
*   Function: N_ObjectName()
*   Purpose:  Returns the object name for a given object
*   Syntax:   cObject := N_ObjectName( <nObjectId> )
*******************************************

function N_ObjectName(nId)
LOCAL cBuffer  := Space(54)              // Set up Receive buffer
LOCAL cRequest := chr(54)+     ;         // Novell API (54) -Get object name
                 Clip2Long(nId)          // Object Id
LOCAL cName    := ""

if NetWare(227, cRequest, @cBuffer) == 0
   cName := CleanStr(substr(cBuffer,7))  // Object name
endif
return cName
```

You can also determine an object's id if you specify the object name and type. Listing 9.4 contains a function called N_OBJECTID() that takes the name and type as parameters and returns the bindery object id.

Listing 9.4: N_OBJECTID() Function

```
*   Program:   OBJID.PRG
*   Authors:   Joseph D. Booth and Greg Lief
*   Function:  N_ObjectId()
*   Purpose:   Returns the object id for a given object
*     Syntax:  nIdCode := N_ObjectId( <cObject>,<nObjType> )
****************************************
function N_ObjectId(cObject,nObjType)
LOCAL cBuffer   := space(54)              // Set up Receive Buffer
LOCAL nId       := 0
LOCAL cRequest  := chr(53)+;              // Novell API (53) -Get Object ID
                   chr(0)+chr(nObjType)+; // Object type
                   Lstring(cObject,48)    // Object Name

if Netware(227, cRequest, @cBuffer) == 0
   nId := Long2Clip(substr(cBuffer,1,4))  // Extract object id
endif
return nId
```

Determining user id   The N_BINDLEVEL() and N_OBJECTNAME() functions can be used together to produce a function that will return the user id of the user currently logged in. This function, called N_WHOAMI(), is illustrated in Listing 9.5.

Listing 9.5: N_WHOAMI() Function

```
*   Program:   WHOAMI.PRG
*   Authors:   Joseph D. Booth and Greg Lief
*   Function:  N_WhoAmI()
*   Purpose:   Returns the user name of the current connection
*     Syntax:  cUser := N_WhoAmI()
*******************************************

function N_WhoAmI()
LOCAL cUser := ""
LOCAL arr_  := N_BindLevel()
```

Listing 9.5: N_WHOAMI() Function (Continued)

```
if !empty(arr_)
   cUser := N_ObjectName( arr_[3] )
endif
return cUser
```

PROPERTIES

Each object may have any number of properties associated with it. The type of standard properties varies, depending upon the object type. For example, a user id object has a PASSWORD property, a GROUPS_I'M_IN property, and possibly an ACCOUNT_BALANCE property.

Each property has the following four pieces of information associated with it:

- Property name, a character string representing the name of the property. The name can be up to 15 characters long, and is stored in the bindery in uppercase.

- Property flag, indicating whether this property is static or dynamic. Dynamic properties are temporary and will be removed when the network is brought down. Static properties remain with the object until they are specifically removed.

- Item/set flag, an indicator of whether a property is an item or a set. An item property has a single value associated with it; a PASSWORD property, for example, contains the encrypted password for a user id object. A set property has multiple values; for example, a GROUP object has a property called GROUP_MEMBERS that lists the user objects belonging to the group.

- Security, an indicator of which other objects have the ability to access this property. Each property has both a read and write security associated with it. This byte is the same format as the security byte on the object, although it will not necessarily contain the same value.

Properties do not contain any data, but are merely the names of additional information attached to an object. This design allows for very flexible object creation and definition.

Standard NetWare properties   Table 9.2 lists the some of the more common standard NetWare properties. You can add your own properties as well. As more third-party products are developed for NetWare, this list is likely to expand.

Table 9.2: Standard NetWare Properties

Property Name	Type	Flag	Object(s)
ACCOUNT_BALANCE	Item	Static	Users
ACCOUNT_HOLDS	Item	Dynamic	Users
ACCOUNT_SERVERS	Set	Static	File Server
ACCOUNT_LOCKOUT	Item	Static	File Server
BLOCKS_READ	Item	Static	File Server
BLOCKS_WRITTEN	Item	Static	File Server
CONNECT_TIME	Item	Static	File Server
DISK_STORAGE	Item	Static	File Server
GROUP_MEMBERS	Set	Static	Group
GROUPS_I'M_IN	Set	Static	Users
IDENTIFICATION	Item	Static	Users, Groups
LOGIN_CONTROL	Item	Static	Users
MANAGERS	Set	Static	Groups
NET_ADDRESS	Item	Dynamic	File Server
NODE_CONTROL	Item	Static	User
OLD_PASSWORDS	Item	Static	User
OPERATORS	Set	Static	File Server
PASSWORD	Item	Static	Users
Q_DIRECTORY	Item	Static	Any Queue
Q_OPERATORS	Set	Static	Any Queue
Q_SERVER	Set	Static	Any Queue
Q_USERS	Set	Static	Any Queue
REQUESTS_MADE	Item	Static	File Server
SECURITY_EQUALS	Set	Static	User
USER_DEFAULTS	Item	Static	User

Accessing properties Once you know an object's name and its type, you can use this information to determine the properties attached to that object. Listing 9.6 contains a function called N_PROPERTIES() that takes an object name and its type as parameters. It returns an array containing the properties associated with this object.

Listing 9.6: N_PROPERTIES Function

```
*    Program:   PROPERTY.PRG
*    Authors:   Joseph D. Booth and Greg Lief
*    Function:  N_Properties()
*    Purpose:   Scans the bindery object for properties
*      Syntax:  aProperties := N_Properties( cObject,nType )
***********************************

#define MINUS_ONE   chr(255)+chr(255)+chr(255)+chr(255)

function N_Properties(cObject, nType)

LOCAL cBuffer     := space(24)
LOCAL aProperties := {}
LOCAL cRequest    := chr(60)+;        // Novell API (60) -Scan properties
        chr(0)+chr(nType)+;           // Object Type
        Lstring(cObject,48)+;         // Object Name
        MINUS_ONE+;
        Lstring("*",15)               // Property Name

do while ( Netware( 227, cRequest, @cBuffer) ) == 0

   Aadd(aProperties, Cleanstr(left(cBuffer,16)) )        // property name
   // replace sequence number with last one received
   cRequest := stuff(cRequest, 53, 4, Substr(cBuffer,19,4))

enddo
return aProperties
```

Keep in mind that the N_PROPERTIES() function returns only the properties and does not return any values for those properties. Listing 9.8 contains a function to determine the value for any property. If passwords are encrypted, however, you will not be able to determine an object's password through the bindery functions.

Expanding BINDERY.CH The property names can change between versions of NetWare, so we should allow for flexibility by using the preprocessor and defining the property names. This way, if a new release of NetWare changes any property names, you merely have to change the header file and recompile. Listing 9.7 contains some manifest constants that can be added to the BINDERY.CH file shown earlier in the chapter. Although many of the property names are the same as their values, MANAGERS is an example of one that has changed between NetWare versions. OBJ_SUPERVISORS is a property for NetWare 3.11 and MANAGERS is a property for NetWare 2.x.

Listing 9.7: More Preprocessor Directives for BINDERY.CH

```
#define    ACCOUNT_BALANCE    "ACCOUNT_BALANCE"
#define    ACCOUNT_HOLDS      "ACCOUNT_HOLDS"
#define    ACCOUNT_SERVERS    "ACCOUNT_SERVERS"
#define    ACCOUNT_LOCKOUT    "ACCOUNT_LOCKOUT"
#define    BLOCKS_READ        "BLOCKS_READ"
#define    BLOCKS_WRITTEN     "BLOCKS_WRITTEN"
#define    CONNECT_TIME       "CONNECT_TIME"
#define    DISK_STORAGE       "DISK_STORAGE"
#define    GROUP_FULL_NAME    "IDENTIFICATION"
#define    GROUP_MEMBERS      "GROUP_MEMBERS"
#define    GROUPS_IM_IN       "GROUPS_I'M_IN"
#define    GROUP_MEMBERSHIP   "GROUPS_I'M_IN"
#define    IDENTIFICATION     "IDENTIFICATION"
#define    LOGIN_CONTROL      "LOGIN_CONTROL"
#define    NET_ADDRESS        "NET_ADDRESS"
#define    NODE_CONTROL       "NODE_CONTROL"
#define    OLD_PASSWORDS      "OLD_PASSWORDS"
#define    OPERATORS          "OPERATORS"
#define    MANAGERS           "OBJ_SUPERVISORS"
#define    PASSWORD           "PASSWORD"
#define    Q_DIRECTORY        "Q_DIRECTORY"
#define    Q_OPERATORS        "Q_OPERATORS"
#define    Q_SERVER           "Q_SERVER"
#define    Q_USERS            "Q_USERS"
#define    REQUESTS_MADE      "REQUESTS_MADE"
#define    SECURITY_EQUALS    "SECURITY_EQUALS"
#define    USER_DEFAULTS      "USER_DEFAULTS"
#define    USER_FULL_NAME     "IDENTIFICATION"
```

PROPERTY VALUES

In addition to the properties themselves, the bindery also contains values for the properties. The value may be an item such as a character string or a set of objects ids. The property's item/set flag determines how the value is interpreted. A property value string can be up to 128 characters and can contain multiple strings, if needed, to represent the property. For set properties, 32 object ids, each four characters long, can be stored in one string of 128 characters.

Accessing property values   Listing 9.8 contains a function called N_PROPVAL that expects an object name, object type, and property name as parameters. It returns the value of that property. If the property is a set property, then an array of object ids is returned. If it is an item property, then a string containing the information for that item is returned. Some of these item-property strings contain structures holding multiple units of information. A good example is the ACCOUNT_BALANCE property, which contains both the account balance and the credit limit. The first four bytes of the string represent the account's balance, and the next four contain the credit limit. You will need to use the LONG2CLIP() function from Chapter 3 to convert this string into numeric values.

Listing 9.8: N_PROPVAL() Function

```
*    Program:    PROPVAL.PRG
*    Authors:    Joseph D. Booth and Greg Lief
*    Function:   N_PropVal()
*    Purpose:    Return value of a specified property
*    Syntax:     xValue := N_PropVal( cObject,;
*                                     ntype,;
*                                     cProperty )
***********************************

function N_PropVal(cObject, nType, cProperty,lClean )
LOCAL cBuffer   := space(130)
LOCAL xReturn   := ""
LOCAL nSegment  := 1
LOCAL nPos,nSet
LOCAL cName,nObjType
LOCAL nID
LOCAL cRequest := chr(61)+;            // Novell API (61) -Get Property value
        chr(0)+chr(nType)+;            // Object Type
        Lstring(cObject,48)+;          // Object Name
```

Listing 9.8: N_PROPVAL() Function (Continued)

```
         chr(nSegment)+;                  // Segment number
         Lstring(Upper(cProperty),16)     // Property Name String

if lClean == NIL
   lClean := .T.
endif

do while Netware(227, cRequest, @cBuffer) == 0
   nSet := asc(substr(cBuffer,130,1))
   if nSet <> 0
      if nSegment == 1
         xReturn := {}
      endif
      nPos := 1

      do while nPos < 128
         nId := Long2Clip(substr(cBuffer,nPos,4))  // Read bindery ID
         if nId == 0                               // Check for end
            exit
         endif
         cName := N_ObjectName(nId)    // Lookup Name & Type
         Aadd(xReturn, cName )         // and put in Return Array
         nPos += 4                     // then point to next ID
      enddo
   else
      if nSegment == 1
         xReturn := ""
      endif
      xReturn += left(cBuffer, 128)
   endif
   cRequest := Stuff(cRequest,53,1,chr(++nSegment))
enddo

if lClean .and. valtype(xReturn)="C"
   xReturn := CleanStr(xReturn)
endif

return (xReturn)
```

This function can be very handy for accessing the bindery when customizing your application. For example, if you wanted to determine a user's full name based upon his user id, you could use the following preprocessor directive:

```
#xtranslate N_UserName( <cId> ) =>  ;
    N_PropVal( <cId>,1,USER_FULL_NAME )
```

BINDERY OBJECT TYPES

The object type determines the behavior of the object. For example, a USER object must have a PASSWORD property to log in to the server, a file-server object needs an OPERATORS property, and so on. The following sections describe the four most common object types in more detail.

USERS

A user id object generally corresponds to a person using the network. The network administrator can grant rights to users individually or through their group membership. Users are generally clients of the network and request services, and they often have a network password associated with them.

The SUPERVISOR is a unique user object that is automatically created by NetWare. Its object id is always 1. The supervisor user id has access to many features of NetWare, and can manipulate the bindery. For this reason, you shouldn't allow every user to have supervisor equivalency.

User properties   Each user id object may contain any of the following properties:

- GROUPS_I'M_IN, a static set listing all groups of which this user is a member.
- IDENTIFICATION, a static item containing the user's full name.
- LOGIN_CONTROL, a static item that contains the login rules for this user, such as how long the password must be, whether unique passwords are required, and so on. The LOGIN_CONTROL property has the following structure:

Byte	Size	Contents
1	3	Account expiration date in *YYMMDD* format
4	1	0=account active, 1=disabled

Byte	Size	Contents
5	3	Password expiration date in *YYMMDD* format
8	1	Number of grace logins remaining
9	2	Number of days between passwords
11	1	Grace login reset value
12	1	Minimum password length
13	2	Maximum concurrent connections
15	42	Bitmap of allowed login times. Each group of six bytes contains 48 bits that represent half-slots of time
57	6	Last login date/time
63	1	Restriction flags
64	1	Not used
65	4	Maximum disk space allowed (in blocks)
69	2	Count of bad logins
71	4	Next login reset time
75	12	Bad login station address

- NODE_CONTROL, a static item that indicates stations the user can log in from.
- OLD_PASSWORD, a static item containing all prior passwords. This property exists only if unique passwords are required for this object. This object can usually be read only by the supervisor or the network operating system.
- PASSWORD, a static item containing the encrypted password string.
- SECURITY_EQUALS, a static set that contains the list of objects that this object is equivalent to in terms of security.

In addition, if accounting has been installed, each user id object will also have the following properties that are used by the accounting functions:

- ACCOUNT_BALANCE, a static item consisting of account balance and credit limit. The account balance property contains two four-byte numbers. The first four bytes are the actual balance and the second four bytes contain the credit limit.

- ACCOUNT_HOLDS, a dynamic item consisting of a string of services with holds against this account. This is a list of up to 16 objects. Each uses four bytes for the object id and another four bytes for the hold amount.

Figure 9.2 shows an example of a user-object structure on a server that has accounting installed.

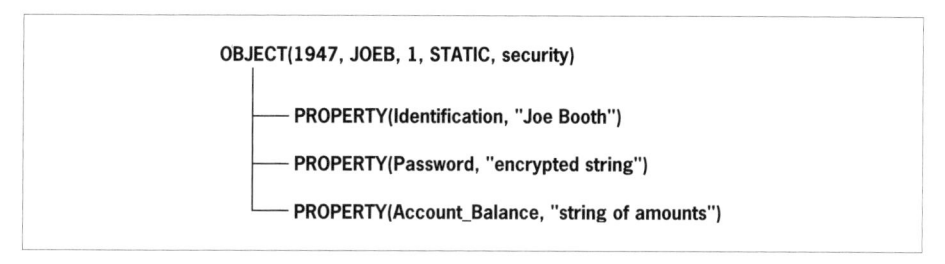

```
OBJECT(1947, JOEB, 1, STATIC, security)
    ├── PROPERTY(Identification, "Joe Booth")
    ├── PROPERTY(Password, "encrypted string")
    └── PROPERTY(Account_Balance, "string of amounts")
```

Figure 9.2: Example of a user-object structure

Functions for retrieving user information It would be useful to be able to interpret the information in the bindery for each user's properties and values. Using the functions we've created earlier in this chapter, we can create some additional functions to translate the user bindery information into a format that is usable by our Clipper application.

Table 9.3 lists a group of functions that will return information about the specified object name. The return value will vary, depending upon the property. All the functions listed in Table 9.3 appear in Listing 9.9, which follows.

Table 9.3: User Functions

Function	Returns
N_USERGROUPS()	List of groups the user is in
N_FULLNAME()	Full name of the user
N_ACCTEXPIRE()	Date the account will expire
N_BALANCE()	Account's balance
N_CREDLIMIT()	User's credit limit

Listing 9.9: User Bindery Functions

```
*   Program:  USERBIND.PRG
*   Authors:  Joseph D. Booth and Greg Lief
*   Purpose:  Various user information functions
***********************************
#include "BINDERY.CH"

function N_UserGroups( cUser )
return  N_PropVal(cUser,1,GROUPS_I'M_IN)
****************************************

function N_FullName( cUser )
return  N_PropVal(cUser,1,USER_FULL_NAME)
**************************************

function N_AcctExpire( cUser )
LOCAL cString := N_PropVal(cUser,1,LOGIN_CONTROL)
LOCAL yy      := 1900 + asc(substr(cString,1,1))
LOCAL mm      := asc(substr(cString,2,1))
LOCAL dd      := asc(substr(cString,3,1))
return if(mm=0,ctod("  /  /  "), ;
   ctod(str(mm,2)+"/"+str(dd,2)+"/"+str(yy,4)))


**********************************
//
// Returns the user's account balance
//
function N_Balance( cUser )
LOCAL cAmt := N_PropVal(cUser,1,ACCOUNT_BALANCE,.F.)
return Long2Clip(Substr(cAmt,1,4))
********************************

//
// Returns the user's credit limit.
//
function N_CredLimit( cUser )
LOCAL cAmt := N_PropVal(cUser,1,ACCOUNT_BALANCE,.F.)
return Long2Clip(Substr(cAmt,5,4))
************************************************************
```

These functions and the code in Listing 9.9 should give you enough examples to enable you to extract whatever information your application might need from the user's bindery object.

GROUPS

A group is a collection of users who share similar rights to the network. Group membership—that is, which groups an object belongs to—is one of the properties of user id objects. The network administrator can assign the users to a group and then grant services to the group. Each member can access the services of the group, allowing easier setup and maintenance.

We can also use the group membership to control the behavior of our application. For example, you could limit access to the PAYROLL option on a menu to only those users who are members of the PAYROLL group. In our EMAIL application at the end of this book, we allow mail to be sent to all members of a group by indicating the group's name.

Group properties   Each group object may contain any of the following properties:

- IDENTIFICATION, a static item usually containing the group's expanded name, such as "Finance Department"
- GROUP_MEMBERS, a static set containing a list of all user object ids who are members of this group
- OBJ_SUPERVISORS, a static set containing a list of all user object ids who are managers of this group

Clipper functions for groups   There are several functions that are useful when working with group objects. The primary information about a group is its name, its members, and its managers. You can add the following preprocessor command to BINDERY.CH to return a group name for a specified object id:

```
#xtranslate  N_GroupName( <nId> ) =>  ;
   N_PropVal( <nId>,2,GROUP_FULL_NAME )
```

The N_MEMBERS() and N_MANAGERS() functions in Listing 9.10 are used to return a list of user ids who are either members or managers for the selected group.

The final group functions, shown in Listing 9.11, are N_ISMEMBER() and N_ISMANAGER(). These functions can be used to determine if a user id is a member or a manager of the specified group. Both functions require the user object name and the name of the group. A logical value is returned, indicating membership in the group or that the id is a manager of the group.

Listing 9.10: Sample Group Functions

```
*   Program:  GRPUSERS.PRG
*   Authors:  Joseph D. Booth and Greg Lief
*   Function:
*   Purpose:
*     Syntax:
***********************************************************
#include "BINDERY.CH"

function N_Members( cGroup )
return N_PropVal( upper(cGroup), 2, GROUP_MEMBERS )

function N_Managers( cGroup )
return N_PropVal( upper(cGroup), 2, MANAGERS )
```

Listing 9.11: INGROUP Program

```
*   Program:  INGROUP.PRG
*   Authors:  Joseph D. Booth and Greg Lief
*   Function:
*   Purpose:
*     Syntax:
***********************************************************
#include "BINDERY.CH"

function N_IsMember( cUser,cGroup )
LOCAL cRequest := chr(67)+;                   // Novell API (67)-Object in Set?
       chr(0)+chr(1)+;                         // Object type
       Lstring(cUser,48)+;                     // User id Name
       Lstring(GROUP_MEMBERSHIP,16)+;          // Property Name
       chr(0)+chr(2)+;                         // Group Object type
       Lstring(cGroup,48)                      // Group to search for

return Netware(227,cRequest,"") == 0


function N_IsManager( cUser,cGroup )
LOCAL cRequest := chr(67)+;                   // Novell API (67) -Object in Set?
       chr(0)+chr(2)+;                         // Object type
       Lstring(cGroup,48)+;                    // Group Name
```

Listing 9.11: INGROUP Program (Continued)

```
        Lstring(MANAGER,16)+;          // Property Name
        chr(0)+chr(1)+;                // User Object type
        Lstring(cUser,48)              // User to search for

return Netware(227,cRequest,"") == 0
```

These functions can be very handy when you need to determine if access to a special portion of a menu is allowed. For example, the code fragment in Listing 9.12 allows only members in the FINANCE group to edit customer records and allows only the group manager to issue credit memorandums.

Listing 9.12: Using Group Functions to Control Access

```
#include "BINDERY.CH"

LOCAL cUser     := N_whoami()
LOCAL nChoice   :=1
LOCAL aOptions := { "Browse Customer file",;
                    "Enter invoices",;
                    "Edit customer address",;
                    "Issue Credit memos" }
LOCAL aAllowed := { .T.   ,;
                    .T.   ,;
                    N_IsMember( cUser,"FINANCE"),;
                    N_IsManager( cUser,"FINANCE") }

do while !empty( nChoice )
   nChoice := achoice( 2,15,6,35,aOptions,aAllowed )
   do case
      //
      // Menu options to call procedures
      //
      case nChoice == 1
         BrowCustomer()
      case nChoice == 2
         Invoices()
      case nChoice == 3
         EditCustomer()
```

Listing 9.12: Using Group Functions to Control Access (Continued)

```
   case nChoice == 4
      CredMemos()
   endcase
enddo
```

By taking advantage of the GROUP objects in NetWare, you allow your users to have one place to maintain security and user rights that can be used by many other applications, as well.

Checking membership   We can also make a general-purpose function called N_ISINSET() that indicates whether a particular object is within another object property set. Each object type has to be defined, so this function needs more parameters, but it can be used for many applications to determine allowable actions. It takes five parameters: the object name and type to check for membership, the object name and type for the object that owns the group, and the property name. It returns a logical value indicating whether the object is within the group. The N_ISINSET() function is shown in Listing 9.13.

Listing 9.13: N_ISINSET Function

```
*   Program:  ISINSET.PRG
*   Authors:  Joseph D. Booth and Greg Lief
*   Function:
*   Purpose:
*    Syntax:
***********************************************************
#include "BINDERY.CH"

function N_IsInSet( cObject1,nType1,cObject2,nType2,cProperty )
LOCAL cRequest := chr(67)+;            // Novell API (67) -Object in Set?
         chr(0)+chr(nType1)+;          // Object 1 type
         Lstring(cObject1,48)+;        // Object 1 Name
         Lstring(cProperty,16)+;       // Property Name
         chr(0)+chr(nType2)+;          // Object 2 type
         Lstring(cObject2,48)          // Object 2 name

return Netware(227,cRequest,"") == 0
```

PRINT QUEUES

A *print queue* is an object that offers printing services to network users. The print queue sets up a directory to hold the files to be printed until a printer is ready to service them.

Print queue properties   Each queue object may contain any of the following properties:

- Q_DIRECTORY, a static item containing the directory where files are stored until a printer can service the print request.
- Q_OPERATORS, a static set that lists the object ids of queue operators. A queue operator can directly manipulate the print queue.
- Q_SERVERS, a static set listing the object ids of servers that can service jobs in this queue.
- Q_USERS, a static set listing the object ids of users or groups that can submit jobs into this queue.

Clipper functions for print queues   There are several functions that are useful when working with print queues. The primary information about a print queue is its file storage directory, its operators, and its users. Using the functions we've developed thus far, we can add some useful preprocessor directives to BINDERY.CH to access print queue information. These directives are as follows:

```
#xtranslate  N_QDIR(<nId>)        => ;
             N_PropVal( <nId>,3,Q_QDIRECTORY )
#xtranslate  N_QOPERATORS(<nId>) => ;
             N_PropVal( <nId>,3,Q_OPERATORS )
#xtranslate  N_QUSERS(<nId>)      => ;
             N_PropVal( <nId>,3,Q_USERS )
```

By using our various functions and preprocessors, you could easily write a program to allow the user to contact the appropriate operator to get special forms mounted on the printer. Listing 9.14 illustrates such a program.

Listing 9.14: Q_OPER Program

```
*   Program:   Q_OPER.PRG
*   Authors:   Joseph D. Booth and Greg Lief
*   Function:
*   Purpose:
```

Listing 9.14: Q_OPER Program (Continued)

```
*    Syntax:
***********************************************************
#include "BINDERY.CH"

LOCAL arr_ := N_PrintQs()
LOCAL nChoice
LOCAL cName
LOCAL aOpers
LOCAL nId

if empty(arr_)
   Alert("No QUEUES are defined for this network")
   return .F.
endif

nChoice := achoice(8,20,8+len(arr_),40,arr_)
if nChoice > 0
   // Get selected print queue's object id
   nId    := N_ObjectId( arr_[nChoice],3 )
   // And the operators for that print queue
   aOpers := N_QOPERATORS( nId )
   if !empty(aOpers)
      cName := N_userName( aOpers[1] )   // Name of first operator
      Alert("Contact "+cName+" about special forms...")
   else
      Alert("There are no QUEUE operators...")
   endif
endif
```

FILE SERVERS

The file-server object is used to allow NetWare to control access to network resources and bindery rights. The object represents the actual computer being used as the file server.

File-server properties The file-server object may contain any of the following properties:

- NET_ADDRESS, a dynamic item that contains the 12-byte internet address of the file server

- OPERATORS, a static set that contains the object ids of an object authorized to operate the file console
- USER_DEFAULTS, a static item that holds the default LOGIN_CONTROL value that should be applied to all new user objects created

In addition, if accounting has been installed, the server object will also have the following properties that are used by the accounting functions:

- ACCOUNT_SERVERS, a static set of all server object ids that are allowed to charge a user for services if accounting is installed
- ACCOUNT_LOCKOUT, a static item that lists the object ids of locked-out accounts
- BLOCKS_READ, a static item that contains the amount to charge users for blocks read since they've logged on
- BLOCKS_WRITTEN, a static item that contains the amount to charge users for blocks written since they've logged on
- CONNECT_TIME, a static item that contains the amount the server will charge for connect time (from when the object logged in until it logs out)
- DISK_STORAGE, a static item that contains the amount to charge users for disk storage
- REQUESTS_MADE, a static item that indicates what the system charges for requests made by a user

Clipper functions for file servers There are several functions that are useful when trying to get information from the file server. A lot of information is available, but some of it needs to be extracted from the property values.

Listing 9.15 contains some sample Clipper functions to read the information from the file-server object.

Listing 9.15: FILESERV Program

```
*   Program:  FILESERV.PRG
*   Authors:  Joseph D. Booth and Greg Lief
*   Function:
*   Purpose:
*     Syntax:
************************************************************
#include "BINDERY.CH"
```

Listing 9.15: FILESERV Program (Continued)

```
function N_IsOperator( cUser,cServer )
//
// This function returns .T. if the requested USER is
// allowed to access the FILE CONSOLE.
//
return N_IsInSet( cUser,2,cServer,4,OPERATORS )


*******************************
function N_DefExpire( cServer )

//
// This function returns the default USER expiration
// date that will be assigned to new users.
//
LOCAL cString := N_PropVal(cServer,4,USER_DEFAULTS)
LOCAL yy      := 1900 + asc(substr(cString,1,1))
LOCAL mm      := asc(substr(cString,2,1))
LOCAL dd      := asc(substr(cString,3,1))
return if(mm=0,ctod("  /  /  "),;
ctod(str(mm,2)+"/"+str(dd,2)+"/"+str(yy,4)))
****************************************************************** **
```

Some of the information from the file server may not be readable, depending upon the security level the user has on the network.

OTHER OBJECT TYPES

Although the first four object types are the ones most commonly used, NetWare also supports many other object types.

Novell reserves object types up to 65,536 for well-known object types. Developers may use object types above that number for their applications, if needed. If a common object type is needed, contact Novell to request that they assign an object type for you.

The functions we've developed in this chapter should provide you with the ability to read any bindery information from any object. You can customize your applications to utilitize the bindery much more fully.

Updating the bindery files

Since the bindery API is accessible directly from Clipper, you can read and query the bindery, as well as update it. Although your application can add information to the bindery, it is best not to overload the bindery files. If the bindery is large, network performance will deteriorate. If you need user-specific information, you should create a file in the user's mail directory. The mail directory is SYS:MAIL\ [User objectid].

Keep in mind that while the bindery can be updated from Clipper, most bindery update rights are limited to the supervisor. The functions in this chapter can be used to update bindery information, but NetWare will restrict most rights according to the security information. Unless you possess supervisor rights, you will probably be able to update only your current object. If you have supervisor rights, then you'll be able to use these functions on almost any object in the bindery.

BINDERY OBJECT FUNCTIONS

The following group of functions allow you to add, delete, and rename bindery objects. Keep in mind that the bindery should remain small, so don't allow your users to populate the bindery with information that could be stored elsewhere on the network.

Adding an object to the bindery   Listing 9.16 contains a function called N_ADDOBJECT() that allows you to place an object into the bindery. It takes the object name and type as the first two required parameters. The next parameter is the static/dynamic flag, which is either (S)tatic or (D)ynamic. The default value is static. The next two parameters indicate the security and can be (A)nyone, (L)ogged, (O)bject, (S)upervisor, and (N)etWare. The default is object.

Listing 9.16: N_ADDOBJECT() Function

```
*    Program:   ADDOBJ.PRG
*    Authors:   Joseph D. Booth and Greg Lief
*    Function:  N_AddObject()
*    Purpose:   Adds an object into the bindery
*     Syntax:   <logical> := N_AddObject(cObject,;
*                                        nType,;
*                                        cFlag,;
*                                        cRead,;
*                                        cWrite )
```

Listing 9.16: N_ADDOBJECT() Function (Continued)

```
************************************
#include "BINDERY.CH"

#define   SECURITY  "ALOSN"

function N_AddObject(cObject, nType, cFlag, cRead, cWrite)

LOCAL cRequest := chr(50)              // Novell API (50) -Add object
LOCAL nRead
LOCAL nWrite

if cFlag = NIL .or. ! cFlag$"SD"
   cFlag := "S"
end
if cRead = NIL .or. ! cRead$SECURITY
   cRead := "O"
endif
if cWrite = NIL .or. ! cWrite$SECURITY
   cWrite := "O"
endif
nWrite := at(cWrite,SECURITY)-1
nRead  := at(cRead ,SECURITY)-1

cRequest+= chr(if(cFlag="D", 1, 0))+;    // Set Dynamic/Static bit
           chr((nWrite * 16) + nRead)+;  // Security Level
           chr(0)+chr(nType) +;          // Object type
           Lstring(cObject,48)           // Object Name

return Netware(227,cRequest,"") == 0
```

Removing an object from the bindery Listing 9.17 contains a function called N_DELOBJECT() that allows you to remove an object from the bindery. It takes the object name and type as parameters and returns a logical value indicating whether the object was removed.

Listing 9.17: N_DELOBJECT() Function

```
*   Program:  DELOBJ.PRG
*   Authors:  Joseph D. Booth and Greg Lief
*   Function: N_DelObject()
*   Purpose:  Removes an object from the bindery
```

Listing 9.17: N_DELOBJECT() Function (Continued)

```
*    Syntax:    <logical> := N_DelObject( cOject,nType )
***********************************
#include "BINDERY.CH"

function N_DelObject(cObject, nType)
LOCAL cRequest := chr(51)+;                // Novell API (51) -Remove object
               chr(0)+chr(nType)+;         // Object type
               Lstring(cObject,48)         // Object name

return Netware(227,cRequest,"") == 0
```

Changing an object's name   Listing 9.18 contains a function called N_RENOBJECT() that allows you to change the name of an object. It takes three parameters and returns a logical value indicating whether the object name was changed. The parameters are the current object name and type, followed by the new name you wish to assign to the object.

Listing 9.18: N_RENOBJECT() Function

```
*    Program:   RENOBJ.PRG
*    Authors:   Joseph D. Booth and Greg Lief
*    Function:  N_RenObject()
*    Purpose:   Renames a bindery object
*    Syntax:    <logical> := N_RenObject( cOld,nType,cNew )
***********************************
#include "BINDERY.CH"

function N_RenObject(cOld, nType, cNew)
LOCAL cRequest := chr(52)+;                // Novell API (52) -Rename Object
         chr(0)+chr(nType)+;               // Object type
         Lstring(cOld,48)+;                // Current Object Name
         Lstring(cNew,48)                  // New Object Name

return Netware(227,cSend,"") == 0
```

Keep in mind that the functions to manipulate the bindery objects are subject to NetWare's bindery security. If your user id does not have enough security, the function call will return a FALSE.

OBJECT PROPERTY FUNCTIONS

The following functions allow you to add and delete properties from bindery objects. In addition, you can change the values of properties and add new object ids to set properties.

Adding a property to an object Listing 9.19 contains a function called N_ADDPROPERTY() that adds the specified property to an object. It takes seven parameters and returns a logical value indicating whether the property was added.

Listing 9.19: N_ADDPROPERTY() Function

```
*    Program:   ADDPROP.PRG
*    Authors:   Joseph D. Booth and Greg Lief
*    Function:  N_AddProperty()
*    Purpose:   Adds a property to a bindery object
*    Syntax:    <logical> := N_AddProperty( cObject,;
*                                           nType,;
*                                           cProperty,;
*                                           cFlag,;
*                                           cItemSet,;
*                                           cRead,;
*                                           cWrite )
*********************************
#include "BINDERY.CH"

#define   SECURITY   "ALOSN"

function N_AddProperty(cObject,nType,cProperty,cFlag,;
          cItemSet,cRead,cWrite)
LOCAL cRequest := chr(57)+;                // Novell API (57) -Add Property
     chr(0)+chr(nType)+;                   // Object type
     Lstring(cObject,48)                   // Object Name
LOCAL nRead
LOCAL nWrite

if cFlag = NIL .or. ! cFlag$"SD"
   cFlag := "S"
end
if cItemSet = NIL .or. ! cItemSet$"SI"
   cItemSet := "I"
end
if cRead = NIL .or. ! cRead$SECURITY
```

Listing 9.19: N_ADDPROPERTY() Function (Continued)

```
   cRead := "O"
endif
if cWrite = NIL .or. ! cWrite$SECURITY
   cWrite := "O"
endif
nWrite := at(cWrite,SECURITY)-1
nRead  := at(cRead ,SECURITY)-1

cRequest += chr(if(cFlag="D", 1, 0))+;       // Duration flag
            chr(if(cItemSet="S",2,0))+;      // Property SET or ITEM
            chr((nWrite*16)+nRead)+;         // Security Level
            Lstring(Upper(cProperty),16)     // Property Name

return Netware(227,cRequest,"") == 0
```

The required parameters are the current object name and type, followed by the property you wish to add to the object. The fourth parameter is either (S)tatic or (D)ynamic to indicate the duration of the property. The fifth parameter is either (I)tem or (S)et, indicating if this is an item property or a set of object ids. The final two parameters indicate the security and can be (A)nyone, (L)ogged, (O)bject, (S)upervisor, and (N)etWare. The default is object.

Deleting a property from an object Listing 9.20 contains a function called N_DELPROPERTY() that removes the specified property from an object. It takes three parameters and returns a logical value indicating whether the property was removed. The parameters are the current object name and type, followed by the property you wish to remove from the object.

Listing 9.20: N_DELPROPERTY() Function

```
*    Program:    DELPROP.PRG
*    Authors:    Joseph D. Booth and Greg Lief
*    Function:   N_DelProperty()
*    Purpose:    Removes a property from a bindery object
*    Syntax:     <logical> := N_DelProperty( cObject,nType,cProperty )
*********************************

function N_DelProperty(cObject, nType, cProperty)
```

Listing 9.20: N_DELPROPERTY() Function (Continued)

```
LOCAL cRequest := chr(58)+ ;            // Novell API (58) -Delete property
       chr(0)+chr(nType)+;              // Object type
       Lstring(cObject,48)+;            // Owner Name
       Lstring(Upper(cProperty),16)     // Property Name

return Netware(227,cRequest,"") == 0    // Request to remove property
```

Changing a property's value   Listing 9.21 contains a function called N_CHGVALUE() that allows you to change the value of a property. It takes four parameters and returns a logical value indicating whether the property's value was changed. The parameters are the current object name and type, followed by the property you wish to change and the new value to change the property to.

Listing 9.21: N_CHGVALUE() Function

```
*    Program:   CHGVALUE.PRG
*    Authors:   Joseph D. Booth and Greg Lief
*    Function:  N_ChgValue()
*    Purpose:   Changes a property's value
*    Syntax:    <logical> := N_ChgValue( cObject,nType,cProperty,xValue )
**********************************

function N_ChgValue(cObject, nType, cProperty, xValue)
LOCAL cRequest := chr(62)+;              // Novell API (62) -Write value
        chr(0)+chr(nType)+;              // Object Type
        Lstring(cObject,48)+;            // Object Name
        chr(1)+chr(255)+;                    // Segment
        Lstring(upper(cProperty,16))+;   // Property name
        Substr(xValue,1,128)             // This segments value

return Netware(227,cRequest,"")  == 0
```

This function should be used only to change ITEM properties. It does not check if the property is an item, but merely changes it. It also cannot make an item larger than 128 characters.

WORKING WITH SET PROPERTIES

A set property contains a list of object ids within that property. For example, each group has a set property called GROUP_MEMBERS that contains the object ids for all users within the group. In this section, we will present functions to allow you to add and delete objects from set properties.

Adding an object to a set   Listing 9.22 contains a function called N_ADD2SET() that allows you to add more object ids to a set property. It takes five parameters and returns a logical value indicating whether the object was added. The parameters are the current object name and type, followed by the object id and type of the object you wish to add and the property to add the object into.

Listing 9.22: N_ADD2SET() Function

```
*    Program:   ADD2SET.PRG
*    Authors:   Joseph D. Booth and Greg Lief
*    Function:  N_Add2Set()
*    Purpose:   Adds an object to a set
*      Syntax:  <logical> := N_Add2Set( cOwner,nOwnType,;
*                                       cObject,nType,cProperty )
**********************************

function N_Add2Set( cOwner, nOwnType, cObject, nType, cProperty)

LOCAL cRequest :=chr(65)+;                    // Novell API (65) -Add
            chr(0)+chr(nOwnType)+;            // Owner object type
            Lstring(cOwner,48)+;              // Owner name
            Lstring(Upper(cProperty),16)+;    // Property Name
            chr(0)+chr(nType)+;               // Member object type
            Lstring(cObject,48)               // Member name

return Netware(227,cRequest,"") == 0
```

Removing an object from a set   Listing 9.23 contains a function called N_DELFROMSET() that allows you to remove an object id from a set property. It takes five parameters and returns a logical value indicating whether the object was removed. The parameters are the current object name and type, followed by the object id and type of the object you wish to remove and the property to remove the object from.

Listing 9.23: N_DELFROMSET() Function

```
*   Program:    REMOVSET.PRG
*   Authors:    Joseph D. Booth and Greg Lief
*   Function:   N_DelFromSet()
*   Purpose:    Removes an object from a set
*     Syntax:   <logical> := N_DelFromSet( cOwner,nOwnType,;
*                                          cObject,nType,cProperty )
**********************************
function N_DelFromSet(cOwner, nOwnType, cObject, nType, cProperty)

LOCAL cRequest := chr(66)+;                         // Novell API (66) -Remove
                  chr(0)+chr(nOwnType)+;            // Owner Object type
                  Lstring(cOwner,48)+;              // Owner Object Name
                  Lstring(Upper(cProperty),16)+;    // Property Name
                  chr(0)+chr(nType)+;               // Member Object type
                  Lstring(cObject,48)               // Member Object's Name

return Netware(227,cRequest,"") == 0
```

TECHNICAL OVERVIEW OF THE BINDERY

This section discusses the technical details of bindery files and record formats. You may skip this section if this does not concern you; since the bindery is always open and always locked, it would be very difficult for you to access the bindery at the record level anyway.

BINDERY FILES

In Novell NetWare 2.x there are two files that contain the bindery information: NET$BIND.SYS and NET$BVAL.SYS. In NetWare 3.x, three files are used: NET$OBJ.SYS, NET$PROP.SYS, and NET$VAL.SYS. Table 9.4 shows where the data is stored.

Table 9.4: Bindery Files

File Name	Contents
NetWare 2.x	
NET$BIND.SYS	Objects, properties
NET$BVAL.SYS	Property values
NetWare 3.x	
NET$OBJ.SYS	Objects
NET$PROP.SYS	Properties
NET$VAL.SYS	Property values

The files are stored in the SYS:SYSTEM directory with attributes set to hidden and system. The most important thing to know about these files is that the NetWare operating system opens them and keeps them locked as long as the network is up and running. This makes data stored in the bindery very secure. The information in the bindery can be obtained only through a series of NetWare API calls. The bindery itself can be closed only by the SUPERVISOR or a user with the same rights as the SUPERVISOR. Of course, when the bindery is closed, the network does not do very much.

BINDERY RECORD FORMATS

The structure for the bindery objects is shown in Table 9.5.

Table 9.5: Bindery Record Formats

Object records structure

Object id	4 bytes
Object name	1–48 bytes (first byte is object-name length)
Object type	1 byte
Static/dynamic flag	1 byte (0 for static and 1 for dynamic)
Security flag	1 byte

Table 9.5: Bindery Record Formats (Continued)

Property records structure

Property name	1–16 bytes (first byte is property-name length)
Static/dynamic flag	Combined into 1 byte
Item/set flag	Bit 0 is set to 1 for a dynamic property and 0 for a static one. Bit 4 is set to 1 for a set property and 0 for an item property
Security flag	1 byte

The security flag indicates who can read or write this bindery object. It consists of two four-bit fields placed into a single byte. Bits 1–4 are the write security and bits 5–8 are the read security. Table 9.6 shows the security levels.

Table 9.6: Bindery Security Levels

Level	Who	Explanation
0	ANYONE	Everyone, even users not yet logged in
1	LOGGED	Any object logged in to the server
2	OBJECT	Only objects logged in with the same object name, type, and password
3	SUPERVISOR	Supervisor or objects with supervisor equivalence
4	NETWARE	Only the NetWare operating system

Summary

In this chapter, we explored NetWare's bindery and provided functions to allow our applications to access the information contained within. We also discussed how the bindery is organized and how bindery records are stored within the bindery files.

If you are looking for a secure environment for user information or just want to take advantage of what NetWare offers, then use the bindery. With the functions provided in this chapter, your application can access the bindery fairly easily. Many of these functions will be used in the electronic-mail program at the end of this book.

Printing on a Network

Accessing a network printer

Print queues

DOS printing

All together now: functions for printer management

Chapter 10

One of the benefits of a network is that it allows users to share a variety of peripheral devices. In this chapter, we will discuss how the network handles print requests and directs them to the network printers. After reading this chapter, you will be able to send print jobs directly from your Clipper application to the file server's printers. The user will be able to place jobs into the queue and to remove them. Finally, at the end of the chapter we will present functions to handle printing from within your Clipper program.

ACCESSING A NETWORK PRINTER

When the network shell is loaded on a workstation, it redirects several of DOS's interrupts for its own use. One of these is the printer service interrupt (17H). When the workstation tries to print something, DOS gives control to the printer service interrupt (and, therefore, the network shell). The network shell can then pass the print request to a local printer or redirect it to the network.

NetWare provides a command called CAPTURE that instructs the shell to send print requests to the network. When CAPTURE is installed, all data sent to the specified printer is sent to the network. The network operating system then takes the data and writes it into a file called the capture file. NetWare assigns the file to a *printer queue*, a bindery object that stores files and directs them to the specified printer. All subsequent printing is written to this capture file.

The application program can at some point direct the network to start printing the capture file on a printer. This can be done by closing the capture or by flushing the capture. A flush command instructs the network to print the contents of the file, but does not release the printer capture. Closing the capture first flushes the file, and then releases the printer capture. Once released, subsequent print requests will be handled by the local printer.

The capture system allows any program to print on a network printer. Since the program just turns the request over to DOS for processing, it has no idea where the information is being printed. However, this presents a slight problem, since the application program probably won't send the instruction to the network to print the capture file.

CAPTURE solves the problem by allowing a time-out value to be specified. If no new data is received within the specified amount of time, then the network assumes that the print request is complete and will start to print the capture file.

USING CAPTURE

Although it is possible to load CAPTURE at the DOS command prompt and then run your Clipper application, doing so may present two problems: First, someone might forget to load CAPTURE and accidentally start printing on the local printer; and second, once CAPTURE is loaded, that printer port is no longer available for local printing. If you will want to use both a network and a local printer, loading CAPTURE before your program starts is not a viable solution.

We can use the FT_INT86() function from Chapter 3 to access the CAPTURE services from within our Clipper application. If you want to print on a network, you can start CAPTURE before your print routine and turn it off when your print routine is done. This allows the user to print locally from within your application.

Starting a capture   Listing 10.1 contains a function called N_STARTCAP() that starts a capture on the default local printer (usually LPT1). When we discuss capture flags a little bit later in the chapter, you will see that you can change which local printer is captured.

Flushing the capture   Listing 10.2 contains a function called N_FLUSHCAP() that flushes the current capture file to a network printer. It does not stop the capture, but merely asks the network to print the capture file and start another one. If the function is successful, it will return TRUE. If not, FALSE will be returned.

Listing 10.1: N_START() Function

```
*   Program:   N_STARTCAP
*   Authors:   Joseph D. Booth and Greg Lief
*   Purpose:   To allow capture of local printers
*              from within a CA-Clipper program
***************************************************

#define AX      1
#define BX      2
#define CX      3
#define DX      4

function N_StartCap(nPrinter)
LOCAL aRegs[ 10 ]
LOCAL is_ok  := .F.
if valtype(nPrinter) <> "N"
   aRegs[ AX ] := 223 * 256            // DFh 00h -Capture specific
   aRegs[ DX ] := 0
else
   aRegs[ AX ] := 223 * 256            // DFh 04h -Capture
   aRegs[ DX ] := (nPrinter-1)*256 +4
endif

if ft_int86( 33, aRegs )
   is_ok := (aRegs[AX] % 256)==0  // Extract low byte
endif
return is_ok
```

Listing 10.2: N_FLUSHCAP() Function

```
*   Program:   N_FLUSHCAP
*   Authors:   Joseph D. Booth and Greg Lief
*   Purpose:   To force the network to print the
*              current capture file.
*     Syntax:  <nJob> := N_FLUSHCAP( [<nPrinter>] )
*
* Arguments:   nPrinter  - Optional captured printer to flush
*
*    Returns:  Job number for print queue handling printing, or
*              zero if a problem occurs.
*
*      Notes:  This function is used to send a capture file to
*              the network printer. The capture will not be
```

Listing 10.2: N_FLUSHCAP() Function (Continued)

```
*               stopped and all subsequent output will be
*               redirected as well.
*
*   Example:    if N_FlushCap( 1 )
*               endif
*
****************************************************

#define AX           1
#define BX           2
#define CX           3
#define DX           4

#define PRINT_JOB    9

function N_FlushCap(nPrinter)
LOCAL aRegs[ 10 ]
LOCAL is_ok := .F.
LOCAL arr_  := {}
LOCAL nJob  := 0
if valtype(nPrinter) <> "N"
   aRegs[ AX ] := 223 * 256        // DFh 03h -Flush default
   aRegs[ DX ] := 3
else
   aRegs[ AX ] := 223 * 256        // DFh 07h -Flush specific
   aRegs[ DX ] := (nPrinter-1)*256 +07
endif

if ft_int86( 33, aRegs )
   is_ok := (aRegs[AX] % 256)==0  // Extract low byte
endif
if is_ok
   arr_ := N_CapFlags()
   if !empty(arr_)
      nJob := arr_[PRINT_JOB]
   endif
endif
return nJob
```

The N_FLUSHCAP() function could be called after each report if you were running several to the printer at once. If you want to return control to your user after printing, you should probably use N_CLOSECAP(), discussed next, to print the file and return control to the local printer.

Closing the capture   Listing 10.3 contains the function N_CLOSECAP(), which closes the current capture and returns control to the local printer. It also requests that the network print the contents of the capture file.

Listing 10.3: N_CLOSECAP() Function

```
*    Program:  N_CLOSECAP
*    Authors:  Joseph D. Booth and Greg Lief
*    Purpose:  To close the capture and return control
*              to the local printer
*     Syntax:  <nJob> := N_CLOSECAP( [<nPrinter>] )
*
*  Arguments:  nPrinter  - Optional captured printer to close
*
*    Returns:  Job number for print queue handling printing, or
*              zero if a problem occurs.
*
*      Notes:  This function is used to close a capture being
*              run on a printer. The output will be set to the
*              network printer.
*
*    Example:  if N_CloseCap( 1 )
*                  Alert("Output redirected to your local printer!")
*              endif
*

************************************************

#define AX           1
#define BX           2
#define CX           3
#define DX           4

#define PRINT_JOB    9

function N_CloseCap(nPrinter)
LOCAL aRegs[ 10 ]
LOCAL is_ok    := .F.
LOCAL arr_     := {}
LOCAL nJob     := 0

if valtype(nPrinter) <> "N"
   aRegs[ AX ] := 223 * 256         // DFh 01h -Close default capture
   aRegs[ DX ] := 1
else
```

Listing 10.3: N_CLOSECAP() Function (Continued)

```
   aRegs[ AX ] := 223 * 256           // DFh 05h -Close specific capture
   aRegs[ DX ] := (nPrinter-1)*256 +5
endif

if ft_int86( 33, aRegs )
   is_ok := (aRegs[AX] % 256)==0   // Extract low byte
endif
if is_ok
   arr_ := N_CapFlags()
   if !empty(arr_)
      nJob := arr_[PRINT_JOB]
   endif
endif
return nJob
```

Both the N_FLUSHCAP() and the N_CLOSECAP() functions place a job into the print queue for printing and return a job number. This job number must be used later with the queue-management system to determine information about the job. Be sure to save the job number to a variable if you will want to be able to check on the job's status.

Canceling the capture Listing 10.4 contains the function N_CANCELCAP(), which cancels the current capture and returns control to the local printer. Unlike N_CLOSECAP(), it does not request that the network print the contents of the capture file. The contents of the capture file will be lost after N_CANCELCAP() is performed.

Listing 10.4: N_CANCELCAP() Function

```
*   Program:   N_CANCELCAP()
*   Authors:   Joseph D. Booth and Greg Lief
*   Purpose:   To cancel the capture and return control
*              to the local printer. The file is not printed.
*    Syntax:   <logical> := N_CANCELCAP( [<nPrinter>] )
*
* Arguments:   nPrinter  - Optional captured printer to cancel
*
*   Returns:   TRUE if canceled, FALSE otherwise
*
```

Listing 10.4: N_CANCELCAP() Function (Continued)

```
*      Notes:   This function is used to cancel a capture being
*               run on a printer. No output will be set to the
*               network printer, it will all be discarded if the
*               function returns TRUE.
*
*      Example: if N_CancelCap( 1 )
*                  Alert("All output to printer LPT1 is canceled!")
*               endif
*
*
***************************************************

#define AX        1
#define BX        2
#define CX        3
#define DX        4

function N_CancelCap(nPrinter)
LOCAL aRegs[ 10 ]
LOCAL is_ok   := .F.
if valtype(nPrinter) <> "N"
   aRegs[ AX ]   := 223 * 256          // DFh 02h -Cancel default Capture
   aRegs[ DX ]   := 2
else
   aRegs[ AX ]   := 223 * 256          // DFh 06h -Cancel specific Capture
   aRegs[ DX ]   := (nPrinter-1)*256 +6
endif

if ft_int86( 33, aRegs )
   is_ok := (aRegs[AX] % 256)==0  // Extract low byte
endif
return is_ok
```

SETTING PRINTER FLAGS

The CAPTURE command operates on the default LPT. Although this is usually LPT1, it can be changed. In addition to capturing the printer, there are a number of flags that can be set to control the printing. In this section, we will discuss some of these flags.

- *Local printers* The local printer ports to be captured can be LPT1, LPT2, or LPT3. These are referred to by number, starting with zero, as listed here:

Number	Printer
0	LPT1
1	LPT2
2	LPT3

    Serial ports (COM1, COM2, and so on) cannot be captured by the network, since these are two-way communication ports. The network operating system does not communicate to the port when it is capturing a file.

- *Network printers* There can be five printers attached to a network file server. These are referred to by number, starting with zero: The first printer is 0, the second printer is 1, and so on. Although you can specify which network printer to use, the network operating system will still place your print requests into a print queue for servicing. It will not send data directly to a network printer from a workstation.

- *Queue to use* You can specify the print queue to which the capture file should be sent. The queue flag must contain the bindery id of the print queue to which you want to print. Using the N_QUEUES() function and the N_OBJECTID() functions from Chapter 9, you can print the capture file from any valid queue.

- *Number of copies* You can specify the number of copies of your capture file to print. This can be a number between 0 and 255. The default is one copy.

- *Print form names* If you need to print on special paper, you can specify a print form number. If you specify a nonzero number, then the network will send a message to the server instructing the operator to mount the form specified by that number. Until the print form is changed, only jobs matching the currently loaded form will print. You can also specify a form name for the convenience of the person operating the printer. The form number alone, however, determines whether the system can print.

- *Banners* A banner is a page that is printed prior to your print job. This page usually contains your user id and other information that allows the printouts to be identified easily. If this is not necessary, you can instruct the CAPTURE command to not print a banner page (and save a few trees).

- *Job number*   When a capture file is closed or flushed to the printer, the network assigns a job number to the request. This job number will be used by the queue functions, which are discussed later in this chapter.

The N_CAPFLAGS() function   Listing 10.5 contains a function called N_CAPFLAGS() that is a get/set block for setting some of the common flags. It takes an optional array of parameters. If this array is passed, then the appropriate flags are set to new values. The function returns an array containing the current settings. Table 10.1 lists the contents of the array.

Table 10.1: Capture Flags Array Structure

Element	Type	Contents
1	Logical	Print banner pages
2	Char	Banner heading to use
3	Numeric	Local printer to capture
4	Numeric	Network printer to use
5	Numeric	Bindery id of print queue
6	Numeric	Number of copies
7	Numeric	Form number to mount before printing
8	Char	Form name
9	Numeric	Job number
10	Numeric	Maximum lines per page; defaults to 66
11	Numeric	Maximum characters per line; defaults to 132
12	Numeric	Time-out value in seconds

You can set any of the capture flags by updating the appropriate element in the array and passing the array to the N_CAPFLAGS() function. The function will return an array containing the original flags for the default capture.

Listing 10.5: N_CAPFLAGS() Function

```
*    Program:   N_CAPFLAGS
*    Authors:   Joseph D. Booth and Greg Lief
*    Purpose:   To set the network capture flags
*     Syntax:   <aOldFlags> := N_CapFlags( [<aNewFlags>] )
*
*  Arguments:   aNewFlags - Optional array of new capture flags to set
*
*    Returns:   aOldFlags - Current capture flags
*
*      Notes:   This function is a get/set block to set the capture
*               flags for the default printer. The array consists of
*               twelve elements as defined below:
*
*               1  Logical   Should banners be printed?
*               2  Char      Text of the banner
*               3  Numeric   Which local printer is captured?
*               4  Numeric   Which network printer is serving it?
*               5  Numeric   Bindery print queue object id
*               6  Numeric   Number of copies to print
*               7  Numeric   Form number
*               8  Char      Name of the form to load in printer
*               9  Numeric   Job number
*              10  Numeric   Maximum lines down
*              11  Numeric   Maximum characters across
*              12  Numeric   Timeout value in seconds
*
*    Example:   LOCAL arr_ := CapFlags()    // Get current flags
*               arr_[ 6] := 2                // Make two copies
*               CapFlags( arr_ )             // Reset the capture flags
*               N_StartCap()                 // Start a CAPTURE process
*
**********************************************

#define    PRINT_BANNERS        1
#define    BANNER_TEXT          2
#define    LOCAL_PRINTER        3
#define    NETWORK_PRINTER      4
#define    PRINT_QUEUE_ID       5
#define    NUMBER_OF_COPIES     6
#define    FORM_NUMBER          7
#define    FORM_NAME            8
#define    JOB_NUMBER           9
#define    MAX_LINES           10
#define    MAX_CHARACTERS      11
```

Listing 10.5: N_CAPFLAGS() Function (Continued)

```
#define    TIMEOUT_VALUE      12

#define AX          1
#define BX          2
#define CX          3
#define DX          4
#define DI          6
#define ES          9

function N_CapFlags( aFlags )
LOCAL aRegs[ 10 ]
LOCAL aOld     := array(12)
LOCAL is_ok    := .F.
LOCAL x,y
LOCAL cReply   := space(63)
aRegs[ AX ]    := 184 * 256            // B8h 00h -Get Flags
aRegs[ BX ]    := .F.
aRegs[ CX ]    := 63
aRegs[ ES ]    := cReply


if ft_int86( 33, aRegs )
   is_ok := (aRegs[AX] % 256)==0  // Extract low byte
   if is_ok
      cReply := aRegs[ES]
      aOld[PRINT_BANNERS]    := asc(substr(cReply,2,1))>127
      aOld[BANNER_TEXT]      := CleanStr(substr(cReply,8,13))
      aOld[LOCAL_PRINTER]    := asc(substr(cReply,22,1))
      aOld[NETWORK_PRINTER]  := asc(substr(cReply,4,1))
      aOld[PRINT_QUEUE_ID]   := long2clip(substr(cReply,58,4))
      aOld[NUMBER_OF_COPIES]:= asc(substr(cReply,5,1))
      aOld[FORM_NUMBER]      := asc(substr(cReply,6,1))
      aOld[FORM_NAME]        := CleanStr(substr(cReply,30,13))
      aOld[JOB_NUMBER]       := int2clip(substr(cReply,62,2))
      aOld[MAX_LINES]        := int2clip(substr(cReply,26,2))
      aOld[MAX_CHARACTERS]   := int2clip(substr(cReply,28,2))
      aOld[TIMEOUT_VALUE]    := int2clip(substr(cReply,23,2))
   endif
endif
if !empty(aFlags) .and. is_ok
   for x:= 1 to len(aFlags)
      if aFlags[x] <> NIL
         do case
         case x == PRINT_BANNERS
```

Listing 10.5: N_CAPFLAGS() Function (Continued)

```
            if aFlags[x] <> aOld[x]
                if aFlags[x]
                    y := asc(substr(cReply,2,1)) +128
                else
                    y := asc(substr(cReply,2,1)) +128
                endif
                cReply := stuff(cReply,2,1,chr(y))
            endif
        case x == BANNER_TEXT
            cReply := stuff(cReply,8,13,padr(aFlags[x],13,chr(0)))
        case x == LOCAL_PRINTER
            cReply := stuff(cReply,22,1,chr(aFlags[x]))
        case x == NETWORK_PRINTER
            cReply := stuff(cReply,4,1,chr(aFlags[x]))
        case x == PRINT_QUEUE_ID
            cReply := stuff(cReply,58,4,clip2long(aFlags[x]))
        case x == NUMBER_OF_COPIES
            cReply := stuff(cReply,5,1,chr(aFlags[x]))
        case x == FORM_NUMBER
            cReply := stuff(cReply,6,1,chr(aFlags[x]))
        case x == FORM_NAME
            cReply := stuff(cReply,31,13,padr(aFlags[x],13,chr(0)))
        case x == MAX_LINES
            cReply := stuff(cReply,26,2,clip2int(aFlags[x]))
        case x == MAX_CHARACTERS
            cReply := stuff(cReply,28,2,clip2int(aFlags[x]))
        case x == TIMEOUT_VALUE
            cReply := stuff(cReply,23,2,clip2int(aFlags[x]))
        endcase
    endif
next
cReply       := substr(cReply,1,53)
aRegs[ AX ]  := 184 * 256  +1   // B8h 01h -Set Flags
aRegs[ BX ]  := .F.
aRegs[ CX ]  := 53
aRegs[ ES ]  := cReply

if ft_int86( 33, aRegs )
    is_ok := (aRegs[AX] % 256)==0   // Extract low byte
endif
endif
return aOld
```

Using N_CAPFLAGS(), the following code shows how you could change to printer 2 and request three copies of the report you are about to print.

```
#define    LOCAL_PRINTER       3
#define    NUMBER_OF_COPIES    6

LOCAL aFlags := array(12)
LOCAL aOld   := {}

aFlags[ LOCAL_PRINTER ]     := 2
aFlags[ NUMBER_OF_COPIES ]  := 3

aOld := N_CapFlags(aFlags)

N_StartCap()
//
// Printing the report
//
N_EndCap()
N_CapFlags( aOld )       // Restore original flags
```

The P_START() function shown later in the chapter also provides an example of using the CAPTURE functions.

PRINT QUEUES

The network does not allow a program direct access to the printers, but rather places all print requests into a directory. It then prints the files from this directory one at a time. This process is known as *queuing*.

The network provides services to manage the print queues collectively called *queue-management services* (QMS). These services allow you to control what gets printed and when, what forms must be mounted when printing, and so on.

DETERMINING THE AVAILABLE PRINT QUEUES

In Chapter 9, we discussed a function called N_PRINTQS() that returned a list of print queues available on the network. For your convenience, its syntax is repeated here.

```
aQueues := N_QUEUES()
```

The function returns a list of queue names that are available for use. You will also need the N_OBJECTID() function from Chapter 9, which gives you the bindery object id number for a specified object and type. Print queues are object type 4, so the following syntax will return the bindery id for a queue name.

```
nId := N_ObjectId( aQueues[x],4 )
```

All the QMS functions refer to a queue by its bindery id number.

WHERE IS THE JOB BEING PRINTED?

When N_FLUSHFCAP() or N_CLOSECAP() is called to print the capture file, a job number is assigned and returned. This job number is used in conjunction with the queue bindery id number to determine information about the print job. You can use the N_CAPFLAGS() function discussed earlier to determine the queue from which the job is being printed. Here is an example:

```
nJob      := N_FLUSHCAP()
nQueueId  := N_CAPFLAGS()[5]
```

GETTING A LIST OF JOBS IN A PRINT QUEUE

Once you know the queue id, you can use the N_QJOBLIST() function shown in Listing 10.6 to return an array of jobs within that print queue. The function takes the queue's bindery id number as a parameter and returns an array of job descriptions for each queue job. This description consists of the job's position in the queue and the text string describing the job.

Listing 10.6: N_QJOBLIST() Function

```
*    Program:   QJOBLIST.PRG
*    Authors:   Joseph D. Booth and Greg Lief
*    Function:  N_QJOBLIST()
*    Purpose:   Get the list of jobs within the queue
*    Syntax:    <aJobs> := N_QjobList()
**********************************

function N_QJobList(nQueue)
LOCAL cReply   := space(506)        // Reply buffer
LOCAL cRequest := chr(107)+;        // E3h 6Bh
                  clip2long(nQueue)
LOCAL aJobs    := {}
LOCAL cList    := ""
LOCAL nCount
LOCAL x
LOCAL nJob

if NetWare( 243,cRequest,@cReply ) == 0
   nCount := int2clip(substr(cReply,1,2))
```

Listing 10.6: N_QJOBLIST() Function (Continued)

```
   cList    := substr(cReply,3)
   for x:= 1 to nCount
      nJob := long2clip(substr(cList,(x-1)+1,4))
      if nJob > 0
         cReply   := space(258)
         cRequest := chr(108)+clip2long(nQueue)+;
                     clip2int(nJob)
         if NetWare(243,cRequest,@cReply) == 0
            Aadd(aJobs, str(asc(substr(cReply,29,1)))+;
                        CleanStr(substr(cReply,57,50)) )
         endif
      endif
   next
endif
return aJobs
```

CHANGING A JOB'S QUEUE POSITION

When your print job is placed into the queue, it is assigned the next queue position and waits its turn. You can request that the network change your position in the queue if you need to rush your job. The N_QPOSITION function shown in Listing 10.7 is a get/set function. If you pass it a position parameter, it will attempt to change the job's position in the queue to the new position. The function returns the current position. If you need to determine the current position, just pass the queue id number and the job number and leave the third parameter blank.

Listing 10.7: N_QPOSITION() Function

```
*    Program:   QPOSIT.PRG
*    Authors:   Joseph D. Booth and Greg Lief
*    Function:  N_QPOSITION()
*    Purpose:   Queries/Changes a job's print position
*     Syntax:   <logical> := N_QPOSITION(nQueue,nJob,nPosition)
**********************************

function N_QPOSITION(nQueue,nJob,nPos)
LOCAL cReply   := space(258)
LOCAL cRequest := chr(108)+clip2long(nQueue)+;
                  clip2int(nJob)
LOCAL nOld     := 0

if NetWare(243,cRequest,@cReply) == 0
```

Listing 10.7: N_QPOSITION() Function (Continued)

```
   nOld := asc(substr(cReply,29,1))
endif

if nPos <> NIL
   cReply   := space(2)           // Reply buffer
   cRequest := chr(110)+;         // E3h 6Eh
               clip2long(nQueue)+;
               clip2int(nJob)+;
               chr(nPos)
   NetWare( 243,cRequest,@cReply )
endif
return nOld
```

REMOVING A JOB FROM THE PRINT QUEUE

If you need to cancel your print job, you can use the N_QREMOVE() function shown in Listing 10.8. This function takes the queue id and the job number as a parameter. If the job can be successfully removed from the queue, a TRUE value will be returned. If the job cannot be removed, then the function returns FALSE. If the job has already been printed, the function returns FALSE, since printed jobs are no longer present in the print queue.

Listing 10.8: N_QREMOVE() Function

```
*   Program:  QREMOVE.PRG
*   Authors:  Joseph D. Booth and Greg Lief
*   Function: N_QREMOVE()
*   Purpose:  Remove a job from the print queue
*     Syntax: <logical> := N_QREMOVE(nQueue,nJob)
*********************************furnace

function N_QREMOVE(nQueue,nJob)
LOCAL cReply   := space(2)           // Reply buffer
LOCAL cRequest := chr(106)+;         // E3h 6Ah
                  clip2long(nQueue)+;
                  clip2int(nJob)
LOCAL is_ok    := .F.

if NetWare( 243,cRequest,@cReply ) == 0
   is_ok := .T.
endif
return is_ok
```

DOS PRINTING

The DOS operating system also contains a print-queue program called PRINT.EXE. This service allows you to print files in the background while your application is running. We can use the FT_INT86() function from Chapter 2 to allow our Clipper program access to these DOS services.

However, even with a function to access an interrupt, we still need to find the appropriate interrupts. According to the trusty *MS-DOS Programmer's Reference Manual,* the DOS interrupts needed to handle the print queue are as follows:

Hex	Decimal	Purpose
0100	256	Find out if PRINT.EXE is installed
0101	257	Add a file to the printer queue
0102	258	Remove a file from the print queue
0103	259	Cancel all files in the print queue

CHECKING IF PRINT.EXE IS INSTALLED

The Q_INSTALLED() function in Listing 10.9 is used to check if the user has installed the DOS print queue. (The print queue is installed by typing **PRINT** at the DOS prompt). If the print queue has not been installed, then—obviously—Clipper cannot use it.

Listing 10.9: Q_INSTALLED() Function

```
*   Program:   QINSTALL.PRG
*   Authors:   Joseph D. Booth and Greg Lief
*   Function:  Q_installed()
*   Purpose:   To check installed state of PRINT.EXE
*   Returns:   lInstalled  - TRUE if installed, FALSE otherwise
*********************
#define     AX    1

function Q_installed
* 100h - Get PRINT.EXE installed state
LOCAL aRegs := {256,0,0,0,0,;
                0,0,0,0,0}          // Save registers
Ft_int86(47,aRegs)                  // Execute multiplex interrupt
return (aRegs[AX]%256)==255    // AL is 255 if installed
```

Of course, many astute readers are going to ask, Why not install the print queue like this:

```
if .not. Q_installed()
    run PRINT/D:prn            // Run PRINT
endif
Q_add( cFilename )
```

After all, if the user forgot to install the print queue, shouldn't our program do it for them? The answer is a resounding NO! In the example above, PRINT is installed as a memory-resident program, above the Clipper program in memory. When you leave your Clipper application, PRINT.EXE will be occupying memory above your Clipper program. We ran a memory map prior to executing the program and it showed 591,200 bytes free. We then loaded the Clipper program, ran PRINT from within it (installing it as a TSR), and exited the Clipper program. Memory now showed 264,256 bytes free. Since memory-resident programs are installed at the lowest free memory spot, PRINT was installed right after the Clipper program, effectively reducing our free memory by over 60 percent. It is best to install PRINT via the AUTOEXEC.BAT file if you plan on using the DOS print-queue functions. This ensures that PRINT is loaded as low as possible in memory.

ADDING A FILE TO THE PRINT QUEUE

You can use the Q_ADD() function shown in Listing 10.10 to add a file to the DOS print queue. It takes the file name as the parameter and returns TRUE if the file was added to the print queue or FALSE if not.

Listing 10.10: Q_ADD() Function

```
*   Program:   QADD.PRG
*   Authors:   Joseph D. Booth and Greg Lief
*   Purpose:   To add a file to the print queue
*    Syntax:   Q_add( cFilename )
* Parameter:   cFilename
*   Returns:   lSuccess  - TRUE if file added, FALSE otherwise
***************************
#define     DS         8
#define     DX         4
#define     REG_DS     .T.
#define     FLAGS      10

function Q_add( cFilename )
* 101h - Add a file to the queue
```

Listing 10.10: Q_ADD() Function (Continued)

```
LOCAL aRegs:= {257,0,0,0,0,0,0,0,0,0}   // Save registers
LOCAL nAddr:= Bufalloc( cFilename )     // Allocate memory buffer
aRegs[ DS ] := chr(0)+l2bin(nAddr)      // Pass level/address
aRegs[ DX ] := REG_DS                   // Tell interrupt we are
Ft_int86(47,aRegs)                      // using a string
BufFree(nAddr)                          // Unallocate buffer
return (aRegs[FLAGS] % 2 ) == 0         // Check carry flag
```

Note that both BUFFREE() and BUFALLOC() functions used in Listing 10.10 are also on the disk accompanying this book. These were written by Ted Means, the author of the FT_INT86() function from the Nanforum Toolkit.

REMOVING A FILE FROM THE PRINT QUEUE

The Q_REMOVE() function in Listing 10.11 is used to remove a file from DOS's print queue. It takes a file name as the parameter and returns TRUE if the file was removed, or FALSE if not.

Listing 10.11: Q_REMOVE() Function

```
*   Program:     QDELETE.PRG
*   Authors:     Joseph D. Booth and Greg Lief
*   Purpose:     To remove a file from the print queue
*    Syntax:     Q_remove( cFilename )
* Parameter:     cFilename
*   Returns:     lSuccess  - TRUE if removed, FALSE otherwise
***************************

#define     DS         8
#define     DX         4
#define     REG_DS     .T.
#define     FLAGS      10

function Q_remove( cFilename )
* 102h - Remove a file to the queue
LOCAL aRegs:= { 258,0,0,0,0,;
                0,0,0,0,0 }         // Save registers
aRegs[ DS ] := cFilename            // File name
aRegs[ DX ] := REG_DS               // Tell interrupt we
Ft_int86(47,aRegs)                  // are using a string
return (aRegs[FLAGS] % 2)==0        // Check carry flag
```

CANCELING ALL FILES IN THE PRINT QUEUE

You can also erase the entire print queue by using DOS interrupts, which is exactly what Q_CANCEL() in Listing 10.12 does.

Listing 10.12: Q_CANCEL() Function

```
*     Program:   QCANCEL.PRG
*     Authors:   Joseph D. Booth and Greg Lief
*     Purpose:   To cancel all jobs in the print queue
*      Syntax:   Q_cancel()
*   Parameter:   NONE
*     Returns:   lSuccess  - TRUE if all jobs were canceled
*                            FALSE otherwise
***************************
function Q_cancel()
* 103h - Cancel all jobs in the print queue
LOCAL aRegs:= {259,0,0,0,0,0,0,0,0,0}  // Save registers
return Ft_int86(47,aRegs)              // Execute interrupt
```

All together now: functions for printer management

Now that we have discussed the various printing options available to a workstation on a network, let's write some functions to handle printer management. Specifically, we'd like to be able to allow the user to select where to print, and to have the ability to start the printing process, to cancel it, and to end printing. The functions to accomplish these tasks are as follows:

- P_WHERE() determines where the printing should take place. The options include the screen, a text file, a local printer, or a network printer. The function returns a logical TRUE if the user selects somewhere to print or FALSE if he or she presses the Escape key.

- P_START() performs the necessary setup to start printing at the location specified by the user. Its action will vary, depending upon what the user selects during the P_WHERE() function call.

- P_CANCEL() optionally cancels the printing and will cancel the job from the network print queue, if appropriate. You should call this function frequently while printing, to check if the Escape key has been pressed. If it has, then the user is given the option to cancel or continue. If cancel is selected, the function returns TRUE; otherwise, it returns FALSE.

- P_END() is called when the printing is completed. It will clean up the printing environment and print the report at the selected printer (or screen display).

The following code fragment shows how to use these print functions to control your application's printing needs.

```
//
// Using the printer functions
//

if P_Where()            // select where to print
   if P_start()         // Able to start printing
      do while !P_Cancel()
         //
         // Print a line of the report
         //
      enddo
      P_end()
   endif
endif
```

If the user selects to print to the screen, then the entire file is created and a function is called to display the file. This function is called FT_DISPFILE().

Listing 10.13 contains the P_ printing functions. The FT_DISPFILE() function is part of the Nanforum Toolkit and is included on the disk that accompanies this book.

Listing 10.13: Printing Functions

```
*    Program:   PSTUFF.PRG
*    Authors:   Joseph D. Booth and Greg Lief
*    Purpose:   Various printing functions
*************************

#include "INKEY.CH"
#include "BINDERY.CH"

STATIC     cPrt
STATIC     cFIle
STATIC     nBindery
STATIC     cSave
STATIC     lCancel        := .F.
STATIC     aOld           := {,,,,,,,,,,,}
```

Listing 10.13: Printing Functions (Continued)

```
*  Function:  P_Where()
*   Purpose:  Selects where to print a report
*   Returns:  TRUE if printer select,
*             FALSE if the escape key pressed
************************************
function P_Where()
LOCAL getlist   := {}
LOCAL aQueues   := N_PrintQs()
LOCAL arr_      := { "Display to screen   ",;
                     "Text file...        ",;
                     "Local Printer       ",;
                     "--------------------" }
LOCAL cOld

LOCAL aFlags    := { .T.,.T.,.T.,.F. }
LOCAL x

for x :=  1 to len(aQueues)
   Aadd(aFlags,.T.)
   Aadd(arr_,aQueues[x])
next

cSave := savescreen( 8,30,16,52 )
cOld  := setcolor("W+/R")
DispBox(8,30,16,52,2,"W+/R")
@ 9,31 clear to 15,51
x := achoice(9,31,15,51,arr_,aFlags)
do case
case x == 1
   cPrt := "D"
case x == 2
   cPrt  := "T"
   cFile := space(12)
   DispBox(10,35,13,50,1)
   @ 11,36 clear to 12,49
   @ 11,36 say "File Name:"
   @ 12,36 get cFIle   picture "@!"
   read
   if lastkey() == K_ESC
      x := 0
   elseif .not. "."$cFile
      cFile := trim(cFile)+".TXT"
   endif
case x == 3
```

Listing 10.13: Printing Functions (Continued)

```
   cPrt := "L"
case x > 4
   cPrt     := "N"
   nBindery := N_ObjectId( aQueues[x-4],3 )
endcase
restscreen( 8,30,16,52,cSave)
setcolor(cOld)
cSave := ""
return x > 0
*************************************************************************
*****

*  Function:  P_Start()
*  Purpose:   Sets the environment up to print
************************************
function P_Start()
LOCAL aFlags := array(12)
LOCAL is_ok  := .T.
lCancel      := .F.
do case
case cPrt == "D"
   cFile := N_Unique()
   cSave := savescreen(0,0,maxrow(),maxcol())
case cPrt == "L"
   if Q_installed()           // If DOS print queue is
      cFile := N_Unique()     // installed, print to a file
   else
      cFile := "LPT1"         // Else, directly to the printer
   endif
case cPrt == "N"
   N_StartCap()
   aFlags[ 5 ] := nBindery
   aOld        := N_CapFlags( aFlags )
   cFile       := "LPT"+alltrim(str(aOld[3]+1))

endcase
set printer to (cFile)
set printer on
set console off
return is_ok

*  Function:  P_Cancel()
*  Purpose:   Check to see if ESCAPE was pressed
*  Returns:   FALSE to continue printing
```

Listing 10.13: Printing Functions (Continued)

```
*              TRUE if the escape key pressed
***********************************
function P_Cancel()
lCancel := (inkey()==K_ESC)
return ! lCancel


*  Function:  P_End()
*   Purpose:  Finishes the report and prints it
***********************************
function P_End()

set printer off
set printer to
set console off
do case
case cPrt == "D"
   @ maxrow(),00
   @ maxrow(),00 say "Press <ESCAPE> when done viewing "+;
                "the report..."
   FT_DfSetup( cFile,0,0,maxrow()-1,maxcol(),;
               1,23,31,chr(27),.F.,1,255,4096)
   FT_DispFile()
   FT_Dfclose()
   restscreen(0,0,maxrow(),maxcol(),cSave)
   cSave := ""
   erase(cFile)
case cPrt == "L"
   if !lCancel
      if Q_Installed()
         Q_add(cFile)
      endif
   endif
case cPrt == "N"
   if !lCancel
      N_CloseCap()
   else
      N_CancelCap()
   endif
   N_CapFlags(aOld)      // Restore original flags
endcase
return NIL
```

Summary

After reading this chapter, you should be able to give your user the option of printing just about anywhere on the network. By using the print-queue information from the bindery, we can use these routines on any NetWare configuration that has printers.

Sending Messages across the Network

COMMUNICATING BETWEEN CLIPPER APPLICATIONS

NETWARE MESSAGING

Chapter 11

Workstations often need to communicate between themselves and/or the file console. Clipper allows you to communicate between applications and to access NetWare's messaging system. In this chapter, we will discuss how to use Clipper to provide workstation communications.

COMMUNICATING BETWEEN CLIPPER APPLICATIONS

It is possible to design your Clipper programs in such a way that they use a common file that serves as a communications buffer. If two workstations were each running such a Clipper application, each program would check this common file during Clipper's wait states to see if any messages had been added and not yet read. If a message were found, the program could display the message and mark it as received. It could then continue from where the wait state left off.

THE MESSAGE FILE STRUCTURE

The structure of the message file, MESSAGES.DBF, is shown below.

Field	Type	Size
USER_ID	Char	12
FROM_USER	Char	12
MESSAGE	Char	60
RECEIVED	Logical	1

If you anticipate a large number of messages in the file, you might want to consider keeping an index on the user id as well. This would allow better performance during message lookups. The key would be

```
UPPER(user_id)+IF(received,"Y","N")
```

This key allows one seek to determine if there are any unread messages for a user.

RETRIEVING A MESSAGE FROM THE MESSAGE FILE

The GETAMSG() function is used to check the message file for messages that have not yet been received. If one is found, it is displayed on the screen and the record in the file is flagged as received. Listing 11.1 contains the source code for the GETAMSG() function.

Listing 11.1: GETAMSG() Function

```
*   Program:  GETAMSG.PRG
*   Authors:  Joseph D. Booth and Greg Lief
*   Function: GetaMsg()
*   Purpose:  Retrieve a message from the message file
*   Syntax:   GetaMsg()
*********************************

#define MESSAGE_ROW        24

function GetaMsg()
local oldarea  := select()
local oldrow   := row()
local oldcol   := col()
local cUser    := N_whoami()      // From chapter 9
local cSave    := savescreen(MESSAGE_ROW,0,MESSAGE_ROW,80)

if select("MESSAGES") = 0         // If not yet opened
   use MESSAGES shared new        // then open the file
   if file("MESSAGES.NTX")        // and see if an index
      set index to MESSAGES       // exists
   endif
endif
select MESSAGES
if indexord() == 0
   locate all for upper(MESSAGES->user_id) = upper(cUser) ;
          .and. !MESSAGES->received
else
   seek upper(cUser) + "N"
```

Listing 11.1: GETAMSG() Function (Continued)

```
endif
if found() .and. !MESSAGES->received
   @ MESSAGE_ROW,0 say padr(MESSAGES->message,79)
   if N_reclock()
      replace MESSAGES->received with .T.
      commit
      unlock
   endif
   inkey(500)
endif
select (oldarea)
setpos(oldrow,oldcol)
restscreen(MESSAGE_ROW,0,MESSAGE_ROW,80,cSave)
return NIL
```

The GETAMSG() function checks to see if there is an index file called MESSAGE.NTX. If it exists, it is used to speed up message checks. If the index file does not exist, the program will resort to using the LOCATE command instead.

WAIT STATES

The GETAMSG() function call should be performed at every Clipper wait state. Clipper's wait states occur during those commands that expect user input before continuing: TBROWSE(), MEMOEDIT(), ACHOICE(), and the GET/READ commands.

Using GETAMSG() in TBROWSE() In a TBROWSE loop, the GETAMSG() call would be made after the stabilization loop and before the keystrokes are processed.

The following code fragment illustrates where to place the GETAMSG() function call.

```
do while .T.
   do while !brow:stabilize()
   enddo
   //
   // After stabilizing the loop, but before checking
   // for keystrokes, we check for any pending messages
   //
   GetaMsg()
```

```
//
// Now process the keystrokes
//
key := inkey(500)
do case
case key == K_ESC
case key == K_ENTER
//
// etc...
//
endcase
enddo
```

You can review Chapter 6 if you need more information about using TBROWSE(). In particular, look at the REFRESH.PRG program that causes TBROWSE() to refresh after a certain period of time.

Using GETAMSG() with MEMOEDIT() and ACHOICE()   In MEMOEDIT() and ACHOICE(), the GETAMSG() function would be called from within the user-defined keystroke-handling function. Although the parameters and return values are different in each function, the placement of the GETAMSG() function call is the same—immediately after the function is called, and before the keys are processed.

The following code fragments show sample key-handling functions for ACHOICE() and MEMOEDIT(), with the GETAMSG() function added.

```
#include "INKEY.CH"
#include "ACHOICE.CH"

//
// Achoice keystroke handler
//
function AC_UDF(nMode,nElement,nPosition)
*
* This checks for a message constantly, not just at
* keystrokes.  Remove the AC_IDLE if you want to check
* only during keystroke exceptions.
*
LOCAL nLast    := lastkey()    // Save lastkey
LOCAL nAction  := AC_CONT
if nMode == AC_IDLE .or. nMode == AC_EXCEPT
   GetAmsg()
endif
```

```
if nMode == AC_EXCEPT
   do case
   case nLast == K_ENTER
      nAction := AC_SELECT
   case nLast == K_ESC
      nAction := AC_ABORT
   endcase
endif
return nAction
*************************************************************

#include "INKEY.CH"
#include "MEMOEDIT.CH"

//
// MemoEdit keystroke handler
//
function ME_UDF(nMode,nRow,nColumn)
*
*
LOCAL nLast    := lastkey()    // Save lastkey
LOCAL nAction  := ME_DEFAULT
if nMode == ME_IDLE
   GetAmsg()
   nAction := ME_IGNORE
endif
return nAction
```

You might also want to provide some mechanism to allow the user to disable messages during MEMOEDIT(). It could be a bit disconcerting to have messages popping up on the screen frequently during a text-entry session.

Using GETAMSG() in the GET system Since Clipper includes the source code for the GET system (in the GETSYS.PRG), it is possible to modify the function to call GETAMSG(). However, if you take that approach, you will most likely get stung by version changes. Every time a new version of Clipper is released, you will have to modify the GETSYS.PRG file all over again.

Clipper allows you to specify an alternate reader program to handle each GET. This reader can call the components of the default GET reader, so you can add the functionality you need without rewriting the entire GET system.

Listing 11.2 shows an alternate GET reader that calls the GETAMSG() function as part of its behavior.

Listing 11.2: GET Reader with GETAMSG() Function

```
*    Program:   GETREADR.PRG
*    Authors:   Joseph D. Booth and Greg Lief
*    Function:  GetaMsg()
*    Purpose:   Retrieve a message from the message file
*    Syntax:    GetaMsg()
***********************************
#include "getexit.ch"

function MsgGReader( get )
// read the GET if the WHEN condition is satisfied
if ( GetPreValidate(get) )
   // Check the message stack
   GetaMsg()
   // activate the GET for reading
   get:SetFocus()
   do while ( get:exitState == GE_NOEXIT )
      // check for initial typeout (no editable positions)
      if ( get:typeOut )
         get:exitState := GE_ENTER
      endif
      // apply keystrokes until exit
      do while ( get:exitState == GE_NOEXIT )
         GetApplyKey( get, Inkey(0) )
      enddo
      // disallow exit if the VALID condition is not satisfied
      if ( !GetPostValidate(get) )
         get:exitState := GE_NOEXIT
      endif
   enddo
   // de-activate the GET
   get:KillFocus()
endif
return nil
```

PLACING A MESSAGE INTO THE MESSAGE FILE

The function that puts a message onto the message stack is simply a database update program that has been augmented to make sure that the user id belongs to a valid network user. Listing 11.3 illustrates the function PUTAMSG(), which writes an entry in the MESSAGE.DBF file.

Listing 11.3: PUTAMSG() Function

```
*    Program:   PUTAMSG.PRG
*    Authors:   Joseph D. Booth and Greg Lief
*    Function:  PutaMsg()
*    Purpose:   Places a message into the message file
*     Syntax:   PutaMsg()
**********************************

function PutaMsg( cToUser,cMessage )
local oldarea := select()
local cUser   := N_whoami()        // From Chapter 9
local is_ok   := .F.
if select("MESSAGES") = 0           // If not yet opened
   use MESSAGES shared new          // then open the file
   if file("MESSAGES.NTX")          // and see if an index
      set index to MESSAGES         // exists
   endif
endif
select MESSAGES
if N_addrec()
   replace MESSAGES->user_id    with cToUser,;
           MESSAGES->message    with cMessage,;
           MESSAGES->from_user  with cUser,;
           MESSAGES->received   with .F.
   commit
   unlock
   is_ok := .T.
endif
select (oldarea)
return is_ok
```

Using Clipper, it is easy to allow for communication between two network workstations, provided they are both running a Clipper program. If you want to allow messages to be sent between stations regardless of the applications being run, you will need to explore the messaging services provided by NetWare.

NetWare messaging

There are two kinds of messaging services available on NetWare file servers: broadcast and pipe. Broadcast messages are transmitted through the server and are used for brief communications between workstations and with the file console. Pipe messages use the IPX software shell and do not rely upon the server's resources. They are sent between workstations and can contain up to six lines of message text. Note that Novell has indicated that broadcast messages will not be supported in future NetWare releases, beginning with version 4.0. Since the IPX software allows communication without using the server's resources, the use of pipe messages for communication frees the file server to perform more tasks.

Broadcast messages

Broadcast messages are one-line messages that are limited to 55 characters. They should be used for short, quick messages, such as "Please turn on the laser printer." Each user has the ability to accept broadcast messages or to turn them off.

In this section, we will provide the Clipper code to control the user's broadcast mode and to send and receive broadcast messages. Later in this chapter, we will discuss pipe messages, which require a bit more work to set up and use.

Setting the broadcast mode A workstation can specify to either accept or reject broadcast messages from other stations. The funtion MSGMODE() in Listing 11.4 is used to control the setting. If you pass MSGMODE() a TRUE value, then broadcast messages will be accepted. If you pass FALSE, then broadcast messages will be rejected when other stations attempt to send them.

Listing 11.4: MSGMODE() Function

```
*   Program:   MSGMODE.PRG
*   Authors:   Joseph D. Booth and Greg Lief
*   Function:  MsgMode()
*   Purpose:   Toggle whether or not messages will be accepted
*   Syntax:    <logical> := MsgMode( <logical> )
**********************************

function MsgMode( lAccept )
LOCAL cReply   := space(2)              // Reply buffer
LOCAL cRequest := chr(if(lAccept,3,2))  // 2==Reject
LOCAL is_ok    := .F.                   // 3==Accept
```

Listing 11.4: MSGMODE() Function (Continued)

```
if NetWare( 225,cRequest,@cReply ) == 0
   is_ok := .T.
endif
return is_ok
```

Sending messages between workstations   You can use the N_SENDMSG() function in Listing 11.5 to send a message to another workstation. It takes the text of the message as the first parameter. The second parameter is the workstation number. The function returns a logical value indicating TRUE if the message was sent, FALSE otherwise.

Listing 11.5: N_SENDMSG() Function

```
*   Program:   NMESSAGE.PRG
*   Authors:   Joseph D. Booth and Greg Lief
*   Function:  N_SendMsg()
*   Purpose:   Sends a message to another workstation
*     Syntax:  <logical> := N_SendMsg( cMessage,nStation )
**********************************

function N_SendMsg( cMessage, nStation )
LOCAL cReply    := space(2)         // Reply buffer
LOCAL cRequest  := chr(0)+;         // E1h 00h - Send Message
                   chr(1)+;         // Number of stations
                   chr(nStation)+;  // Station number
                   chr(len(cMessage))+;
                   cMessage
LOCAL is_ok     := .F.

if NetWare( 225,cRequest,@cReply ) == 0
   is_ok := (asc(substr(cReply,2,1)) == 0)
endif
return is_ok
```

Getting a broadcast message   If a workstation has set its broadcast mode above zero, then messages will not be automatically displayed by the shell software. In this case, it is necessary to check for messages and have your application take care of displaying them. Listing 11.6 contains a function called N_GETMSG() that will return the text of any pending messages.

Listing 11.6: N_GETMSG() Function

```
*    Program:   NGETMSG.PRG
*    Authors:   Joseph D. Booth and Greg Lief
*    Function:  N_GetMsg()
*    Purpose:   Get the next pending message
*     Syntax:   <cMessage> := N_GetMsg()
**********************************

function N_GetMsg()
LOCAL cReply   := space(58)        // Reply buffer
LOCAL cRequest := chr(1)           // E1h 01h - Get Message
LOCAL cMessage := ""

if NetWare( 225,cRequest,@cReply ) == 0
   cMessage := substr(cReply,2)
endif
return cMessage
```

Keep in mind that new messages will overwrite older ones, so this function should be called frequently to ensure that messages are received.

Sending broadcast messages to the console   You can instruct the workstation to send a message to be broadcast on the file console. Listing 11.7 shows a function called N_CONSOLE() that can be used to send the message. It expects the message text as a parameter and returns TRUE or FALSE, depending upon whether the message was sent. Keep in mind that NetWare will not confirm whether the message has been received, so a TRUE return does not guarantee that someone actually read the message.

Listing 11.7: N_CONSOLE() Function

```
*    Program:   NCONSOLE.PRG
*    Authors:   Joseph D. Booth and Greg Lief
*    Function:  N_Console()
*    Purpose:   Sends a message to the file server console
*     Syntax:   <logical> := N_Console( cMessage )
**********************************

function N_Console( cMsg )
LOCAL cReply   := space(2)              // Reply buffer
LOCAL cRequest := chr(09)+ ;            // Novell API (09)
                 chr(len(cMsg))+;       // Message text
                 cMsg
```

Listing 11.7: N_CONSOLE() Function (Continued)

```
LOCAL is_ok      := .F.

if NetWare( 225,cRequest,@cReply ) == 0
   is_ok := .T.
endif
return is_ok
```

This function can fail if the server's message queue is already filled or if an I/O error occurs. When the message is received, it will appear on the server preceded by the colon prompt.

PIPE MESSAGES

Pipe messages require more work on the part of the programmer than broadcast messages, but allow up to six lines of message text, with up to 126 characters in each line. In addition, pipe messages do not use the file server, but communicate directly through the IPX software.

While broadcast messages are used to send short, one-line communications to any workstation, pipe messages are better suited for chatting between workstations. Before such communication can start, the two workstations must connect and open a pipe between them.

Opening message pipes The first step is to open the pipe. Each workstation that is going to communicate needs to open a pipe to the other station. This is done through the N_OPENPIPE() function in Listing 11.8.

Listing 11.8: N_OPENPIPE() Function

```
*    Program:   OPENPIPE.PRG
*    Authors:   Joseph D. Booth and Greg Lief
*    Function:  N_OpenPipe()
*    Purpose:   Opens a message pipe between stations
*     Syntax:   <logical> := N_OpenPipe( nStation )
**********************************

STATIC  nPipeStation

function N_OpenPipe( nStation )
LOCAL cReply   := space(2)       // Reply buffer
LOCAL cRequest := chr(06)+ ;     // Novell API (06)
                  chr(1) +;
```

Listing 11.8: N_OPENPIPE() Function (Continued)

```
            chr(nStation)
LOCAL is_ok    := .F.

nPipeStation   := 0

if NetWare( 241,cRequest,@cReply ) == 0
   is_ok := asc(substr(cReply,2,1))=0
   nPipeStation := nStation
endif
return is_ok
```

N_OPENPIPE() can be used to open a single pipe from one workstation to another station. The function returns a logical value indicating whether the pipe was opened. The STATIC variable *nPipeStation* contains the station number if the connection was made. The remaining pipe functions are stored in the same program file as the N_OPENPIPE() function so they can access the STATIC *nPipeStation* variable.

Sending pipe messages Once the pipe connections are opened, the next step is to send the message. This is done through the N_SENDPIPE() function in Listing 11.9. It takes the message text as a parameter and returns a logical value of TRUE if the message was sent, or FALSE otherwise.

Listing 11.9: N_SENDPIPE() Function

```
*  Function:  N_SendPipe()
*   Purpose:  Sends a message text between stations
*    Syntax:  <logical> := N_SendPipe( cMessage )
**********************************

function N_SendPipe( cMessage )
LOCAL cReply   := space(103)       // Reply buffer
LOCAL cRequest := chr(04)+ ;       // Novell API (04)
                  chr(1) +;
                  chr(nPipeStation)+;
                  len(cMessage)+;
                  cMessage
LOCAL is_ok    := .F.
```

Listing 11.9: N_SENDPIPE() Function (Continued)

```
if NetWare( 241,cRequest,@cReply ) == 0
   is_ok := asc(substr(cReply,2,1))=0
endif
return is_ok
```

Getting pipe messages The N_GETPIPE() function in Listing 11.10 is used to get up to six messages from the pipe buffer. It concatenates the six messages into a single string, which it then returns. If a workstation sends messages to a pipe that is filled, the messages will be rejected. By getting the pipe messages frequently, you can empty the pipe queue and allow more messages to be sent.

Listing 11.10: N_GETPIPE() Function

```
*  Function:  N_GetPipe()
*   Purpose:  Gets the messages from the pipe
*    Syntax:  <cMessage> := N_GetPipe()
***********************************

function N_GetPipe()
LOCAL cReply   := space(130)     // Reply buffer
LOCAL cRequest := chr(05)        // Novell API (05)
LOCAL cMessage := ""
LOCAL x

for x := 1 to 6
   if NetWare( 241,cRequest,@cReply ) == 0
      cMessage += substr(cReply,3)
   else
      exit
   endif
next
return cMessage
```

Closing the pipe Once you are finished using the pipe, you should close the connection. This is done by the N_CLOSEPIPE() function in Listing 11.11. All pending pipe messages will be discarded, so you might want to get the messages before closing the pipe.

Listing 11.11: N_CLOSEPIPE() Function

```
*  Function:  N_ClosePipe()
*   Purpose:  Closes a message pipe between stations
*    Syntax:  <logical> := N_ClosePipe()
**********************************

function N_ClosePipe()
LOCAL cReply    := space(103)        // Reply buffer
LOCAL cRequest  := chr(07)+ ;        // Novell API (07)
                   chr(1) +;
                   chr(nPipeStation)
LOCAL is_ok     := .F.

if NetWare( 241,cRequest,@cReply ) == 0
   is_ok := asc(substr(cReply,2,1))=0
   nPipeStation := -99
endif
return is_ok
```

Pipes are a handy mechanism for chatting between two workstations on a network. Since they do not use the server's resources, they are the preferred communications method. They also operate very quickly, since the IPX communications shell is designed for good performance.

CHAT program: an example of pipe usage As an example of pipe usage, Listing 11.12 contains a function called LETS_CHAT(). This function is an interactive chat program that allows communication between two stations on a network. It expects as a parameter the station you wish to chat with. If the station is available for chatting, then a box will appear and you may type messages to that station. Messages sent to you from the other station will appear in the upper half of the box. You can continue chatting until you press the Escape key, which will close the pipe and prevent more messages from being sent between stations.

Listing 11.12: LETS_CHAT() Function

```
*  Program:   LETSCHAT.PRG
*  Authors:   Joseph D. Booth and Greg Lief
*  Function:  Lets_Chat()
*   Purpose:  Interactive chat between two stations
*    Syntax:  <logical> := Lets_Chat( nStation )
**********************************
```

Listing 11.12: LETS_CHAT() Function (Continued)

```
#include "INKEY.CH"

function Lets_chat(nStation)
LOCAL cSave    := savescreen(4,10,22,70)
LOCAL is_ok    := .F.
LOCAL nKey     := K_ENTER
LOCAL cMessage
LOCAL cReply   := space(736)

if N_openPipe(nStation)
   DispBox(4,10,22,70,2)
   @ 13,11 say replicate(chr(196),59)
   do while nKey <> K_ESC
      **
      ** Check for messages and display them
      **
      cMessage := N_GetPipe()
      @ 7,11 clear to 12,79
      memoedit(cMessage,5,11,12,79,.F.,.F.)
      **
      ** Enter a messages and send it
      **
      cReply := memoedit(cReply,14,11,21,79,.T.)
      nKey := lastkey()
      if nKey <> K_ESC
         N_SendPipe(cReply)
         cReply := space(736)
      endif
   enddo
   is_ok := .T.
endif
restscreen(4,10,22,70,cSave)
return is_ok
```

It would be easy to set up the LETS_CHAT program to allow a user to access it from a hot key while your application is running. You can even use the broadcast functions discussed earlier and the bindery functions from Chapter 9 to handle chat requests across the network. Those exercises are left to the reader.

Summary

Communication between workstations on a network has a variety of uses. In our electronic-mail program at the end of the book, we will use the message broadcast functions to inform the user when new mail is received. The functions presented in this chapter should allow your users to talk amongst themselves without leaving their workstations.

System Information

MAKING CONTACT WITH A FILE SERVER

WORKSTATION INFORMATION

DETERMINING THE NETWORK SHELL VERSION

FILE-SERVER INFORMATION

CONSOLE OPERATIONS

Chapter 12

The network operating system maintains quite a bit of information about the network and the workstations connected to it. These settings can be used for a wide variety of purposes. For example, you might restrict your application to run only on a specific server, or have it confirm that a drive letter is a valid network drive.

In this chapter, we will discuss how a workstation connects to the network and what information is available from the workstation. We also will discuss the type of information available from the file server. Finally, we will provide Clipper code to access this information.

MAKING CONTACT WITH A FILE SERVER

When a user attempts to connect a workstation to a network, two programs are loaded into memory. The first, usually called NETX.COM or EMSNETX.COM, is the network shell. This program is responsible for receiving DOS requests and either delegating them to DOS to handle or routing them to the network.

The network shell program does not directly communicate with the file server, but rather uses another program—typically IPX or SPX—to handle the messaging.

When the shell program (NETX) starts, the workstation requests a connection with the nearest server. It places the server name into a table and sends a request for connection to the IPX program, which passes the request to the file server. If a connection is granted, the server returns a connection number.

The version of NetWare determines the maximum number of connections a file server may have. NetWare 2.x allows up to 100 connections, while NetWare 386 allows 250. Newer versions of NetWare will undoubtedly increase this number.

CONNECTION TABLES

When a connection is made, the shell updates two tables: the connection id table and the file-server name table. The connection id table contains status information about each connection. Its contents are shown below:

Position	Size	Contents
1	1	255 if attached server, 0 otherwise
2	1	Connection number
3	1	Network node-order number
4	4	Server's network address (4 bytes)
8	6	Server's node address (6 bytes)
14	2	Socket number for server requests
16	2	Receive time-out, in clock ticks
18	6	Bridge node (if remote network)
24	1	Packet sequence number
25	1	Connection number at file server
26	1	255 when connection is active, 0 otherwise
27	2	Maximum time-out, in clock ticks

The file-server name table is a list of the eight workstation slots available for server connection. Each time a connection is made to a server, the server's name is updated in the table.

The N_CONTABLE() function in Listing 12.1 returns an array containing the information from both tables. The array will contain eight elements. Each element will have the following structure:

Element	Type	Contents
1	Char	File-server name
2	Logical	Attached to a server?
3	Numeric	Connection number

Element	Type	Contents
4	Numeric	Network node number
5	Numeric	Server network address
6	Numeric	Server node address
7	Numeric	Socket number
8	Numeric	Receive time-out, in seconds
9	Numeric	Bridge node address
10	Numeric	Packet sequence number
11	Numeric	Connection number at server
12	Logical	Is connection active?
13	Numeric	Maximum time-out, in seconds

Listing 12.1: N_CONTABLE() Function

```
*   Program:    NCTABLE.PRG
*   Authors:    Joseph D. Booth and Greg Lief
*   Function:   N_Contable()
*   Purpose:    Retrieves an array of connection information
*    Syntax:    arr_ := N_Contable()
* Arguments:    <NONE>
*
*   Returns:    Array of connection information or an empty array
*               if the user is not connected to a file server.
*
*     Notes:    The connection table is a two dimensional array.
*               There are eight connections, each of which has the
*               following x pieces of information associated with it.
*
*               Element   Type      Contents
*                     1   Char      File Server name
*                     2   Logical   Attached to a server?
*                     3   Numeric   Slot number
*                     4   Numeric   Network node number
*                     5   Numeric   Server network address
*                     6   Numeric   Server node address
*                     7   Numeric   Socket number
*                     8   Numeric   Receive time-out in seconds
*                     9   Numeric   Bridge node address
*                    10   Numeric   Packet sequence number
*                    12   Numeric   Connection number at server
*                    12   Logical   Is connection active?
*                    13   Numeric   Maximum time-out in seconds
```

Listing 12.1: N_CONTABLE() Function (Continued)

```
*
*
*
*    Example:  LOCAL aConnect := N_ConTable()
*              LOCAL x
*              LOCAL nSize := len(aConnect)
*              ? "You are connected to the following servers..."
*              for x := 1 to nSize
*                 ? aConnect[x,1]
*              next
*
**************************************************************************
function N_ConTable()

#define AX       1
#define SI       5
#define ES       9

LOCAL aRegs[10]
LOCAL aReply := array(8)
LOCAL aNames := array(8)
LOCAL jj, nSeg, nOff

aRegs[ AX ] := 239 * 256 +4         // Get file server names

if ft_int86( 33, aRegs )
   nSeg := aRegs[ ES ]
   nOff := aRegs[ SI ]
   for jj := 1 to 8
      aNames[jj] := alltrim(CleanStr(PeekStr(nSeg,@nOff,48)))
   next
else
   return {}
endif

aRegs[ AX ] := 239 *256 + 3    // EFh, 03h
if ft_int86( 33, aRegs )
   nSeg := aRegs[ ES ]
   nOff := aRegs[ SI ]

   for jj := 1 to 8               // fill sub-arrays with tables
      aReply[jj] := { aNames[jj],;
         (ft_Peek(nSeg,nOff++)<>0 ),;          // Slot in Use?
          ft_Peek(nSeg,nOff++),;               // Connection Number
          Long2Clip(PeekStr(nSeg,@nOff,4)),;   // Server's network addr
          Six2Clip(PeekStr(nSeg,@nOff,6)),;    // Server's node addr
          Int2Clip(PeekStr(nSeg,@nOff,2)),;    // Socket #
          Int2Clip(PeekStr(nSeg,@nOff,2))/18,; // Time-Out
```

Listing 12.1: N_CONTABLE() Function (Continued)

```
            Six2Clip(PeekStr(nSeg,@nOff,6)),;    // Bridge node address
            ft_Peek( nSeg, nOff++),;              // Packet sequence number
            ft_Peek( nSeg, nOff++),;              // Connection number
            ft_Peek( nSeg, nOff++)==255,;         // Is Connected
            Int2Clip(PeekStr(nSeg,@nOff,2))/18 }  // Maximum timeout
        nOff +=5
    next
endif
return( aReply )

STATIC function PeekStr( nSegment, nOffset, nBytes )
LOCAL cReturn := ""
LOCAL jj
for jj := 1 to nBytes
    cReturn += chr(ft_Peek(nSegment,nOffset++))
next
return cReturn
```

The FT_PEEK() function is from the Nanforum Toolkit included on the disk accompanying this book. It was written by Ted Means, the author of the FT_INT86() function discussed earlier in the book.

ATTACHING TO OTHER SERVERS

Once you've attached a workstation to a file server, you can attach the workstation to up to seven additional servers. The N_ATTACH() function in Listing 12.2 takes a server name as a parameter and attempts to connect to it. If the connection is made or if you are already attached to the requested server, the function will return TRUE. If you are already attached to eight servers, or if the server does not exist, then the function will return FALSE.

Keep in mind that connecting to a file server is not the same as logging in to the server. You will still need to log in before you can send or receive any information from the server.

Listing 12.2: N_ATTACH() Function

```
*    Program:    ATTACH.PRG
*    Authors:    Joseph D. Booth and Greg Lief
*    Function:   N_Attach()
*    Purpose:    Attempt to connect to a server
*    Syntax:     <logical> := N_Attach(cServer)
*  Arguments:    cServer  - Server name to attempt to attach to
*    Returns:    TRUE - if attached to specified server
```

Listing 12.2: N_ATTACH() Function (Continued)

```
*                FALSE - if cannot attach for some reason
*       Notes:   Attaching to a server is not the same as logging in
*                to the server. After you successfully attach to the
*                server, you still need to call the login function to
*                be able to use the server's resources.
******************************************************************

function N_attach( cServer )

#define     AX      1
#define     DX      4
#define     SI      5
#define     ES      9

LOCAL aRegs[ 10 ]
LOCAL is_ok := .F.
LOCAL cAddress
LOCAL aTable
LOCAL nSlot
LOCAL nNetNo
LOCAL nNodeAddr
LOCAL nSocketNo
LOCAL jj
LOCAL nSeg,nOff
LOCAL cTmp
LOCAL x,y

cServer := upper( cServer )
if N_ObjectID(cServer,4) == 0
   return is_ok
endif

cAddress := N_PropVal( cServer, 4, "NET_ADDRESS",.F. )

if empty( cAddress )
   return is_ok
endif

nNetNo    := Long2Clip(substr(cAddress,1,4))
nNodeAddr := Six2Clip(substr(cAddress,5,6))
nSocketNo := Int2Clip(substr(cAddress,11,2))

aTable    := N_ConTable()
```

Listing 12.2: N_ATTACH() Function (Continued)

```
if ( ascan( aTable, {|a| ( (a[4]==nNetNo) .and. ;
                           (a[5]==nNodeAddr) ) } ) <> 0 )
   return .T.
endif

if ( nSlot := ascan( aTable, {|a| !a[2]})) == 0
   return is_ok
endif

aTable[ nSlot,1 ] := cServer
aTable[ nSlot,2 ] := .T.
aTable[ nSlot,3 ] := nSlot
aTable[ nSlot,4 ] := nNetNo
aTable[ nSlot,5 ] := nNodeAddr
aTable[ nSlot,6 ] := nSocketNo

aRegs[ AX ] := 239 * 256 +4
if ft_int86( 33, aRegs )
   nSeg := aRegs[ ES ]
   nOff := aRegs[ SI ]
   for jj := 1 to 8
       PokeStr(nSeg,@nOff,padr(aTable[jj,1],48))
   next
else
   return .F.
endif

aRegs[ AX ] := 239 * 256 +3
if ft_int86( 33, aRegs )
   nSeg := aRegs[ ES ]
   nOff := aRegs[ SI ]
   for jj := 1 to 8
       x    := aTable[jj,4]

       cTmp := chr(255)+chr(jj)+Clip2Long( aTable[jj,3] )+;
              Clip2Six(aTable[jj,4])+;
              Clip2Int(aTable[jj,5])+;
              Clip2Int(aTable[jj,6]*18)+;
              Clip2Six(aTable[jj,7])+;
              Chr( aTable[jj,8] )+;
              Chr( aTable[jj,9] )+;
              Chr( 0 )+;
              Clip2Int(aTable[jj,11]*18)
```

Listing 12.2: N_ATTACH() Function (Continued)

```
      PokeStr(nSeg,@nOff,cTmp,48)
   next
else
   return .F.
endif
/* attempt to attach to the server */

aRegs[ AX ] := 241 * 256
aRegs[ DX ] := nSlot

is_ok := ft_int86( 33, aRegs )

if ( !is_ok .or. LowByte(aRegs[AX]) <> 0  )
   return .F.
endif
return is_ok

STATIC function PokeStr( nSegment, nOffset, cString )
LOCAL jj
for jj := 1 to len(cString)
   ft_Poke(nSegment,nOffset++,asc(substr(cString,jj,1)))
next
return NIL
```

DETACHING FROM A FILE SERVER

You can also detach from a server if you no longer need to keep the connection. This prevents you from using that server and frees up one connection slot on the workstation.

The N_DETACH() function shown in Listing 12.3 will detach a workstation from one server. If you pass it a numeric parameter between 1 and 8, it will attempt to detach the server at the specified connection. You may also specify a server name as the parameter. If you detach your workstation from all servers, the network will no longer be available to you.

Listing 12.3: N_DETACH() Function

```
*    Program:  DETACH.PRG
*    Authors:  Joseph D. Booth and Greg Lief
*    Function: N_Detach()
*    Purpose:  Attempt to disconnect from a server
*    Syntax:   <logical> := N_Detach(cServer|nConnection)
*********************************
```

Listing 12.3: N_DETACH() Function (Continued)

```
#define AX            1
#define DX            4
#define MAX_CONNECTS  8

function N_Detach( xServer )
LOCAL aRegs[10]
LOCAL is_done := .F.
LOCAL arr_    := N_ConTable()
LOCAL x
if valtype(xServer)=="C"
   x := ascan(arr_, {|zz|upper(zz[1])=upper(xServer)})
else
   x := xServer
endif
if x >0 .and. x <= MAX_CONNECTS
   aRegs[AX] := 241 *256 + 1
   aRegs[DX] := x
   is_done   := ft_int86(33,aRegs)
endif
return is_done
```

LOGGING IN AND OUT

Once you've attached to a server, you must log in as a valid user of that server. To log in to a server, you must supply a valid object name and password. Listing 12.4 contains the N_LOGIN() function, which takes a user id and a password. It returns TRUE if the login was successful, or FALSE if not.

Listing 12.4: N_LOGIN() Function

```
*   Program:   LOGIN.PRG
*   Authors:   Joseph D. Booth and Greg Lief
*   Function:  N_Login()
*   Purpose:   Attempt to log in to a server
*    Syntax:   <logical> := N_Login(cUser,cPassword)
*********************************
function N_login( cUser, cPassword )
LOCAL cRequest    := chr(14)+;
                     Clip2Long(1)+;
                     Lstring(upper(cUser),48)+;
```

Listing 12.4: N_LOGIN() Function (Continued)

```
                        Lstring(upper(cPassword))
LOCAL cReply       := space(2)

return ( Netware( 227, cRequest, @cReply ) == 0 )
```

You can log out from attached servers one at a time or all at once by using the N_LOGOUT() function shown in Listing 12.5. If you specify a server name or a connection number, the function will attempt to log out that connection. If you do not pass any parameter, then all connections will be logged out from their respective servers.

If you successfully log out from the requested server or servers, the function will return TRUE. Logging out does not disconnect you from the server. Your connection table still contains a list of attached servers. However, some networks might be configured to disconnect your workstation if you don't log in within a certain period of time.

Listing 12.5: N_LOGOUT() Function

```
*    Program:  LOGOUT.PRG
*    Authors:  Joseph D. Booth and Greg Lief
*    Function: N_Logout()
*    Purpose:  Attempt to log out from one or more servers
*    Syntax:   <logical> := N_Logout(cServer|nConnection)
***********************************

#define AX              1
#define DX              4
#define MAX_CONNECTS    8

function N_Logout( xServer )
LOCAL aRegs[10]
LOCAL is_gone := .F.
LOCAL arr_    := N_ConTable()
LOCAL x

if xServer == NIL
   aRegs[AX] := 215 * 256
   is_gone   := FT_Int86(33,aRegs)
else
   if valtype(xServer)=="C"
      x := ascan(arr_, {|zz|upper(zz[1])=upper(xServer)})
```

Listing 12.5: N_LOGOUT() Function (Continued)

```
   else
      x := xServer
   endif
   if x >0 .and. x <= MAX_CONNECTS
      aRegs[AX] := 241 *256 + 2
      aRegs[DX] := x
      is_gone   := ft_int86(33,aRegs)
   endif
endif

return is_gone
```

Workstation information

Once you have connected and logged in to a server, you can obtain connection information such as bindery and drive-mapping settings. In this section, we will discuss this information and how you can use it.

SERVER HIERARCHY

When you make a connection to a network, the shell program must decide which server gets the information about the connection. In addition, if there are multiple servers available, the shell program must decide which one to connect to first. NetWare has a hierarchy of server designations that control how servers are selected in a multiple-server network.

Preferred server   The *preferred server* is the server that the shell will attempt to connect to first. The preferred server's name is specified in the shell configuration file, called SHELL.CFG. All shell requests are sent to the preferred server.

  The N_PREFSERVER() function in Listing 12.6 contains a get/set block that will return the current preferred server's name and allow you to change it. If you pass as a parameter the name of a server to which you are already connected, then that server becomes the preferred server. The function will always return the previous preferred server name. Keep in mind that you must already be connected to the server to specify it as the preferred server.

Default server   The *default server* is the server that is mapped to a particular drive. When a connection is established, the workstation creates a table that contains each drive letter and the server on which it resides. When you set your default drive, the associated server becomes the default server.

Listing 12.6: N_PREFSERVER() Function

```
*    Program:   SERVERS.PRG
*    Authors:   Joseph D. Booth and Greg Lief
*    Function:  N_PrefServer()
*    Purpose:   Get/set block for the preferred server
*    Syntax:    <cServer> := N_PrefServer(cServer|nConnection)
**********************************

#define AX            1
#define DX            4
#define MAX_CONNECTS  8

function N_PrefServer( xServer )
LOCAL aRegs[ 10 ]
LOCAL cReturn := ""
LOCAL arr_    := N_ConTable()    // Get server info
LOCAL x

aRegs[ AX ] := 240 *256 + 1      // Get preferred server
if ft_int86( 33, aRegs )
   x := LowByte(aRegs[AX])
   if x > 0 .and. x <= MAX_CONNECTS
      cReturn := arr_[x,1]
      if xServer <> NIL
         if valtype(xServer)=="C"
            x := ascan(arr_,{|zz|zz[1]=xServer})
         else
            x := xServer
         endif
         if x > 0 .and. x <= MAX_CONNECTS
            aRegs[AX] := 240 * 256 +0
            aRegs[DX] := x
            ft_int86(33,aRegs)
         endif
      endif
   endif
endif
return cReturn
```

The N_DEFSERVER() function in Listing 12.7 returns the name of the default server. Since you cannot change the default server, N_DEFSERVER() does not take any parameters.

Listing 12.7: N_DEFSERVER() Function

```
*    Program:   SERVERS.PRG
*    Authors:   Joseph D. Booth and Greg Lief
*    Function:  N_DefServer()
*    Purpose:   Get the default server
*      Syntax:  <cServer> := N_DefServer()
*********************************

#define AX              1
#define DX              4
#define MAX_CONNECTS    8

function N_DefServer()
LOCAL aRegs[ 10 ]
LOCAL cReturn := ""
LOCAL arr_    := N_ConTable()    // Get server info
LOCAL x

aRegs[ AX ] := 240 *256 + 2      // Get default server
if ft_int86( 33, aRegs )
   x := LowByte(aRegs[AX])
   if x > 0 .and. x <= MAX_CONNECTS
      cReturn := arr_[x,1]
   endif
endif
return cReturn
```

Primary server The *primary server* is the lowest server-connection priority in the connection table. The primary server is used only if the default drive is set to a local drive and there is no preferred server specified.

The N_PRIMSERVER() function in Listing 12.8 contains a get/set block that will return the primary server's name and allow you to change it. If no parameters are passed, the name of the primary server will be returned. If you pass as a parameter the name of a server to which you are already connected, then that server becomes the primary server. The function will return the previous primary server name.

Listing 12.8: N_PRIMSERVER() Function

```
*   Program:    SERVERS.PRG
*   Authors:    Joseph D. Booth and Greg Lief
*   Function:   N_PrimServer()
*   Purpose:    Get/set block for the primary server
*   Syntax:     <cServer> := N_PrimServer(cServer|nConnection)
**********************************

#define AX              1
#define DX              4
#define MAX_CONNECTS    8

function N_PrimServer( xServer )
LOCAL aRegs[ 10 ]
LOCAL cReturn := ""
LOCAL arr_    := N_ConTable()    // Get server info
LOCAL x

aRegs[ AX ] := 240 *256 + 5       // Get primary server
if ft_int86( 33, aRegs )
   x := LowByte(aRegs[AX])
   if x > 0 .and. x <= MAX_CONNECTS
      cReturn := arr_[x,1]
      if xServer <> NIL
         if valtype(xServer)=="C"
            x := ascan(arr_,{|zz|zz[1]=xServer})
         else
            x := xServer
         endif
         if x > 0 .and. x <= MAX_CONNECTS
            aRegs[AX] := 240 * 256 +4
            aRegs[DX] := x
            ft_int86(33,aRegs)
         endif
      endif
   endif
endif
return cReturn
```

INFORMATION ABOUT THIS CONNECTION

Once you log in to a specified server, the shell keeps track of the object id and the login time for each connection. A single workstation might have three users logged in to different servers. You can use the N_CONINFO() function in Listing 12.9 to determine the id and login time for any connection on the workstation.

N_CONINFO() takes a connection number between 1 and 8 or the server name as a parameter. It returns an array consisting of the object id's information, the login date, and the login time. If the connection does not exist or is not logged in, an empty array is returned. The structure of the array is as follows:

Element	Type	Contents
1	Numeric	Connection's bindery id
2	Numeric	Connection's object type
3	Char	Object name
4	Date	Last login date
5	Char	Last login time

Listing 12.9: N_CONINFO() Function

```
*    Program:  CONINFO.PRG
*    Authors:  Joseph D. Booth and Greg Lief
*    Function: N_ConInfo()
*    Purpose:  Get array of connection information
*    Syntax:   <aInfo> := N_ConInfo(cServer|nConnection)
**********************************

#define AX              1
#define DX              4
#define MAX_CONNECTS    8

#include "SET.CH"

function N_ConInfo( xServer )
LOCAL aRegs[ 10 ]
LOCAL aReturn := {}
LOCAL arr_    := N_ConTable()    // Get server info
LOCAL x
LOCAL dLogDate
LOCAL cLogTime
LOCAL nOld    := SET( _SET_EPOCH )
LOCAL cRequest
LOCAL cReply
set epoch to 1979
```

Listing 12.9: N_CONINFO() Function (Continued)

```
if valtype(xServer)=="C"
   x := ascan(arr_,{|zz|zz[1]=xServer})
else
   x := xServer
endif
if x > 0 .and. x <= MAX_CONNECTS
   cRequest := chr(22)+chr( arr_[x,10] )
   cReply   := space(63)
   if Netware(227,cRequest,@cReply) == 0

      Aadd( aReturn,long2Clip(substr(cReply,1,4)) )
      Aadd( aReturn,int2Clip(substr(cReply,5,2)) )
      Aadd( aReturn,cleanstr(substr(cReply,7,48)) )
      dLogDate:=ctod( str(asc(substr(cReply,56,1)),2)+"/"+;
                      str(asc(substr(cReply,57,1)),2)+"/"+;
                      str(asc(substr(cReply,55,1)),2) )
      Aadd( aReturn,dLogDate )
      cLogTime := str(asc(substr(cReply,58,1)),2)+":"+;
                  str(asc(substr(cReply,59,1)),2)+":"+;
                  str(asc(substr(cReply,60,1)),2)
      Aadd( aReturn,cLogTime )
   endif
endif
set epoch to (nOld)
return aReturn
```

DETERMINING THE NETWORK SHELL VERSION

You can also ask the shell software to identify itself. The N_SHELLVER() function in Listing 12.10 returns a character string that represents the current shell version.

Listing 12.10: N_SHELLVER() Function

```
*   Program:   SHELLVER.PRG
*   Authors:   Joseph D. Booth and Greg Lief
*   Function:  N_ShellVer()
*   Purpose:   Retrieves network shell information
*   Syntax:    arr_ := N_ShellVer()
**********************************

#define      AX      1
#define      BX      2
#define      CX      3
```

Listing 12.10: N_SHELLVER() Function (Continued)

```
function N_ShellVer()
LOCAL x
LOCAL aRegs[ 10 ]
LOCAL cVersion := ""
aRegs[ AX ] := 234 * 256

if Ft_Int86(33,aRegs)
   if aRegs[ AX ] >= 0
      cVersion := alltrim(str(int(aRegs[BX]/256)))+"."+;
                  alltrim(str(int(aRegs[BX]%256)))+;
                  chr(65+(aRegs[CX]%256))
      if substr(cVersion,1,1)>="3"
         x := aRegs[CX]/256
         if x > 0
            cVersion += if(x=1,"e","x")
         endif
      endif
   endif
endif
return cVersion
```

FILE-SERVER INFORMATION

The file server itself maintains a large amount of information about the network, although much of this is available only to the supervisor id or an equivalent user. This section contains a sampling of some of the information available to you from the file server if you have supervisor privileges.

CHECKING CONSOLE PRIVILEGES

In order to perform some processes on the file server, the user must have console privileges. Almost all options that can be performed at the file-server console can also be done through the NetWare API if the user has sufficient security and privileges.

The N_CONSPRIV() function in Listing 12.11 returns TRUE if the user has console privileges and FALSE if not. Note that this function makes use of the N_ISINSET() function from Chapter 9.

Listing 12.11: N_CONSPRIV() Function

```
*   Program:   HASCONS.PRG
*   Authors:   Joseph D. Booth and Greg Lief
*   Function:  N_ConsPriv()
*   Purpose:   Determines if user has console privileges
*    Syntax:   <logical> := N_ConsPriv()
*********************************
function N_ConsPriv()
LOCAL arr_  := N_ConTable()
LOCAL x     := N_PrefServer()
LOCAL arr2_ := N_ConInfo(x)
return N_IsInSet( arr2_[3],arr2_[2],;
                  arr_[x,1],4,"OPERATORS" )
```

DETERMINING THE CURRENT LOGIN STATUS

You can enable or disable login capabilities on a server. If disabled, no additional users can log in to the server, although current users are not affected. The N_SERVLOGIN() function in Listing 12.12 is a get/set function that allows you to get the current status of logins (TRUE if allowed, FALSE if not). You can also pass a parameter to determine whether logins are allowed. If the optional parameter is TRUE, then additional logins will be permitted. If FALSE, then no other users will be able to log in to the server.

Listing 12.12: N_SERVLOGIN() Function

```
*   Program:   SERVER.PRG
*   Authors:   Joseph D. Booth and Greg Lief
*   Function:  N_ServLogin()
*   Purpose:   Get/set block for server logins allowed
*    Syntax:   <logical> := N_ServLogin( [lSetting] )
*********************************
function N_ServLogin( lSetting )
LOCAL is_allowed := .T.
LOCAL cReply     := space(1)

if NetWare(227,chr(205),@cReply) == 0
   is_allowed := .not. (asc(cRep)==0)
   if valtype(lSetting) == "L"
      cReply := space(2)
```

Listing 12.12: N_SERVLOGIN() Function (Continued)

```
      NetWare( 227, chr(if(lSetting,204,203)),@cReply )
   endif
endif
return is_allowed
```

RETRIEVING THE SERVER DATE AND TIME

You can also get the file server's date and time from within your Clipper application. The FSDATETIME() function in Listing 12.13 returns a two-element array. The first element is the date from the file server, and the second is the time. If a problem occurs, then an empty array is returned.

Listing 12.13: FSDATETIME() Function

```
*     Program:   SERVDT.PRG
*     Authors:   Joseph D. Booth and Greg Lief
*     Function:  FsDateTime()
*     Purpose:   Get the file server date and time
*     Syntax:    <array> := FSDateTime()
**********************************
#define     AX      1
#define     DX      4
#define     DS      8

function FsDateTime()
LOCAL aRegs[ 10 ]
LOCAL cReply   := space(7)
LOCAL arr_     := {}
LOCAL dDate
LOCAL cTime

aRegs[AX]     := 231 * 256
aRegs[DS]     := cReply
aRegs[DX]     := .T.

if ft_int86( 33, aRegs )
   dDate := ctod( str(asc(substr(aRegs[DS],2,1)),2)+"/"+;
                  str(asc(substr(aRegs[DS],3,1)),2)+"/"+;
                  str(asc(substr(aRegs[DS],1,1)),2) )
   cTime :=     str(asc(substr(aRegs[DS],4,1)),2)+":"+;
                str(asc(substr(aRegs[DS],5,1)),2)+":"+;
                str(asc(substr(aRegs[DS],6,1)),2)
```

Listing 12.13: FSDATETIME() Function (Continued)

```
   arr_ := { dDate,cTime }
endif

return arr_
```

RETRIEVING NETWORK INSTALLATION INFORMATION

One tidbit of information buried in the file server is the name of the NetWare distributor for this server, along with the version number and revision date, and the copyright notice. You can obtain this information by using the N_WHO2BLAME() function in Listing 12.14. The function returns an array of four elements with the following structure:

Element	Type	Contents
1	Char	Name of company that installed network
2	Char	NetWare version and revision
3	Date	NetWare revision date
4	Char	NetWare copyright notice

Listing 12.14: WHO2BLAME() Function

```
*   Program:   WHOBLAME.PRG
*   Authors:   Joseph D. Booth and Greg Lief
*   Function:  N_Who2Blame()
*   Purpose:   Get the file-server installation array
*   Syntax:    <array> := N_Who2Blame()
*********************************

function N_Who2Blame()

LOCAL cRequest := chr(201)
LOCAL cReply   := space(512)
LOCAL aInfo    := {}
LOCAL x,jj

if Netware( 227, cRequest, @cReply ) == 0
   aInfo := array(4)
   for jj := 1 to 4
      x          := at(chr(0),cReply)
      if x > 0
         if jj = 3
```

Listing 12.14: WHO2BLAME() Function (Continued)

```
            aInfo[jj] := ctod(substr(cReply,1,x-1))
         else
            aInfo[jj] := substr(cReply,1,x-1)
         endif
         cReply    := substr(cReply,x+1)
      endif
   next
endif
return aInfo
```

MISCELLANEOUS SERVER INFORMATION

There is a NetWare API that returns miscellaneous information about the server, such as its name, the NetWare version, number of connections, and so on. Listing 12.15 contains a function called N_MISCINFO() that returns an array of miscellaneous server information. If no server is found, then the array will be empty. The contents of the returned array are as follows:

Element	Type	Contents
1	Char	File-server name
2	Numeric	NetWare major version number
3	Numeric	NetWare minor version number
4	Numeric	Maximum connections allowed
5	Numeric	Connections currently in use
6	Numeric	Maximum connected volumes
7	Numeric	OS revision number
8	Numeric	SFT level
9	Numeric	TTS level
10	Numeric	Peak connections used
11	Numeric	Accounting version number
12	Numeric	VAP version number
13	Numeric	Queuing version number

Element	Type	Contents
14	Numeric	Print-server version number
15	Numeric	Virtual-console version number
16	Numeric	Security restrictions level
17	Numeric	Internetwork-bridge version number

Listing 12.15 contains the source to the N_MISCINFO() function.

Listing 12.15: N_MISCINFO() Function

```
*   Program:  MISCINFO.PRG
*   Authors:  Joseph D. Booth and Greg Lief
*   Function: N_MiscInfo()
*   Purpose:  Get an array of miscellaneous server information
*   Syntax:   <array> := N_MiscInfo()
**********************************

function MiscInfo()
LOCAL cRequest := chr(17)
LOCAL cReply   := space(130)
LOCAL aInfo    := {}

if Netware( 227, cRequest, @cReply ) == 0
   aInfo     := array(17)
   aInfo[ 1] := CleanStr(substr(cReply,1,48))
   aInfo[ 2] := asc(substr(cReply,49,1))
   aInfo[ 3] := asc(substr(cReply,50,1))
   aInfo[ 4] := Int2Clip(substr(cReply,51,2))
   aInfo[ 5] := Int2Clip(substr(cReply,53,2))
   aInfo[ 6] := Int2Clip(substr(cReply,55,2))
   aInfo[ 7] := asc(substr(cReply,57,1))
   aInfo[ 8] := asc(substr(cReply,58,1))
   aInfo[ 9] := asc(substr(cReply,59,1))
   aInfo[10] := Int2Clip(substr(cReply,60,2))
   aInfo[11] := asc(substr(cReply,62,1))
   aInfo[12] := asc(substr(cReply,63,1))
   aInfo[13] := asc(substr(cReply,64,1))
   aInfo[14] := asc(substr(cReply,65,1))
   aInfo[15] := asc(substr(cReply,66,1))
   aInfo[16] := asc(substr(cReply,67,1))
   aInfo[17] := asc(substr(cReply,68,1))
endif
return aInfo
```

Console operations

If your user id has console privileges and supervisor rights, you can perform some console tasks from within your Clipper application. Normally these tasks would be performed from the file server's keyboard, but you could do them from within your program if need be. Use discretion when experimenting with bringing the server down or clearing someone's connection.

Downing the file server

The N_DOWN function shown in Listing 12.16 brings the server down. Normally, the server will not be brought down if there are currently open files on it. However, you can pass a TRUE to the N_DOWN() function to bring the server down regardless of whether open files are detected.

Listing 12.16: N_DOWN() Function

```
*     Program:  DOWN.PRG
*     Authors:  Joseph D. Booth and Greg Lief
*     Function: N_Down()
*     Purpose:  Brings down the file server
*      Syntax:  N_Down( lForceDown )
*********************************

function N_Down( lForceDown )
LOCAL cRequest := chr(211)+if(lForceDown,1,0)
LOCAL cReply   := space(2)
return NetWare(227,cRequest,@cReply)
```

Clearing a connection

There may be times when a connection gets hung on the server. Using the N_CLEARCON() function in Listing 12.17, you can clear a workstation's connection to the server. If the workstation needs to get back onto the server, the user will need to reattach the workstation and log on again. If the connection exists and was cleared, the function will return TRUE. If a problem occurs, FALSE will be returned.

Listing 12.17: N_CLEARCON() Function

```
*     Program:  NCLEAR.PRG
*     Authors:  Joseph D. Booth and Greg Lief
*     Function: N_ClearCon()
*     Purpose:  Clear an individual connection
```

Listing 12.17: N_CLEARCON() Function (Continued)

```
*      Syntax:   N_ClearCon( nConnect )
**********************************

function N_ClearCon( nConnect )
LOCAL cRequest := chr(210)+chr(nConnect)
LOCAL cReply   := space(2)
return NetWare(227,cRequest,@cReply)
```

SETTING THE SERVER DATE AND TIME

You can set the server's date and time from within your Clipper program by using the N_SETDATE() function in Listing 12.18. N_SETDATE() expects two parameters: the date and time to which to set the file server. If the call was successful, TRUE will be returned. If a problem occurred, the function will return FALSE.

Listing 12.18: N_SETDATE() Function

```
*    Program:   NSETDT.PRG
*    Authors:   Joseph D. Booth and Greg Lief
*    Function:  N_SetDate()
*    Purpose:   Sets the server's date and time
*      Syntax:  N_SetDate( dDate,cTime )
**********************************

function N_SetDate( dDate,cTime)
LOCAL cRequest := chr(202)+;
                  chr(year(dDate)-1900)+;
                  chr(month(dDate))+;
                  chr(day(dDate))+;
                  chr(val(substr(cTime,1,2)))+;
                  chr(val(substr(cTime,4,2)))+;
                  chr(val(substr(cTime,7,2)))
LOCAL cReply    := space(2)
return NetWare(227,cRequest,@cReply)
```

Summary

In this chapter, we touched upon some of the information available from the workstation and the file server. This information can be used for a variety of purposes, depending upon the needs of your application.

These functions should give you an idea of the kind of information available and how it can be accessed. Additional network information is listed in Appendix C.

EMAIL Program User Reference

WHAT IS ELECTRONIC MAIL?

EMAIL PROGRAM COMPONENTS

EMAIL AND THE NETWORK

THE EMAIL PROGRAM

USING THE MAIL SYSTEM

Chapter 13

In this chapter, we will discuss a sample application that can be written in Clipper for a network environment. Chapter 14 provides the complete source code and data structures for the program. This example uses many of the functions and much of the information found in this book.

WHAT IS ELECTRONIC MAIL?

Electronic mail is part of a new category of software called *groupware*. Groupware is software that helps members of a group to communicate and work as a team.

Electronic mail, or e-mail for short, can be thought of as electronic Post-it notes. It allows you to send a message or letter via computer to another user or group of users.

The mail program included in this book is designed to provide basic mail services on a Novell network. Because this program is a Clipper-based system, it provides the added benefit of permitting other Clipper applications to send mail to network users. For example, many companies run reports during the nighttime hours. If these reports were programmed in Clipper, summarized versions could be sent to various network users via our e-mail system. When the users arrived the next morning, they would just check their e-mail to view the reports. By incorporating the SENDMAIL component into your error-handling program, you can ensure that critical errors requiring intervention will be directed to the network administrator or some other user capable of fixing the problem.

EMAIL PROGRAM COMPONENTS

There are three main parts to our electronic-mail system. These components probably reflect how you handle your traditional mail: You check to see if you have any unopened mail; if you do, you probably read and might respond to it; and you send mail to other individuals or groups.

In this section, we will briefly cover these three components.

CHECKING YOUR MAIL

The CHKMAIL component checks your user id for unread mail. Generally, this program is called in the system start-file, either AUTOEXEC.BAT or the login script.

If any unread mail is found, a message is displayed so that you can choose whether to read the mail. The DOS ErrorLevel is set also, so you can have a batch file call the mail program directly if mail is found.

SENDING MAIL

The SENDMAIL component is a program that allows you to send mail to another user or a group of network users. It requires you to specify the user name and a brief subject, along with the actual mail text. This information is recorded in the central mail repository until the user to whom the mail was sent next accesses the mail system.

READING YOUR MAIL

The READMAIL component is the module that allows you to read any mail you have received. It displays a list of current mail and lets you scroll through your mail messages. You might forward, reply to, or discard any message. The READMAIL program handles all these functions.

Now that we have briefly described what the component pieces do, let's explore them in more detail to see how the system works and how it will interface with the network.

EMAIL AND THE NETWORK

Figure 13.1 shows how the mail system is organized on the network. The file called POSTBOX is the central repository for all mail in the system. Each record in this file represents one item of mail and is addressed to either a single user or a group of users.

In addition to the POSTBOX central file, each user has his or her own personal file called MAILBOX. This file contains any mail sent to the user.

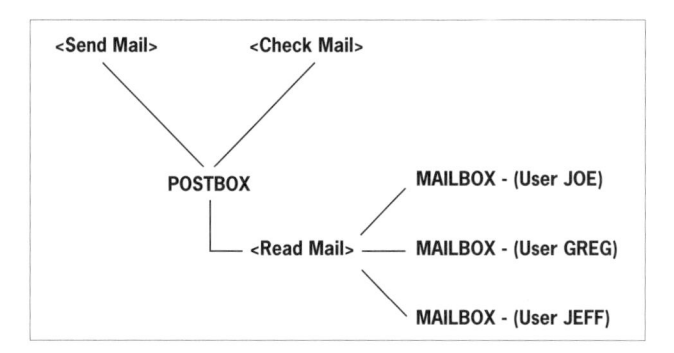

Figure 13.1: Mail file structure

DIRECTORY STRUCTURE

The mail program places POSTBOX in the F:\MAIL directory (you can easily change this in the source code, if you like). This directory should be set up so that all network users have read/write access to it.

Within this directory, each user will have a subdirectory that is given the user's bindery id as a name. Each user will have read/write access to his or her own directory only. This allows the network to enforce security and protect the privacy of the individual's mail.

THE EMAIL PROGRAM

The EMAIL program consists of a main menu with five options. Figure 13.2 shows the main menu for the program.

From this main menu, the user may read or send mail, discard any old mail, update system colors and directories, and pack the file (remove deleted mail). The user selects an option by moving the highlight bar to the desired task and pressing the Enter key. Each of these options is described in the following sections.

READING MAIL

If you select the Read option, the program checks to see if any mail has been sent to you. If you don't have any mail, a message to this effect is shown and you are returned to the main menu.

If mail is found, the screen in Figure 13.3 is displayed.

```
Electronic MAIL                                          01/27/93
┌─────────┐
│Read...  │
│Send...  │
│Erase... │
│Options..│
│Pack/Index│
└─────────┘
```

Figure 13.2: EMAIL main menu

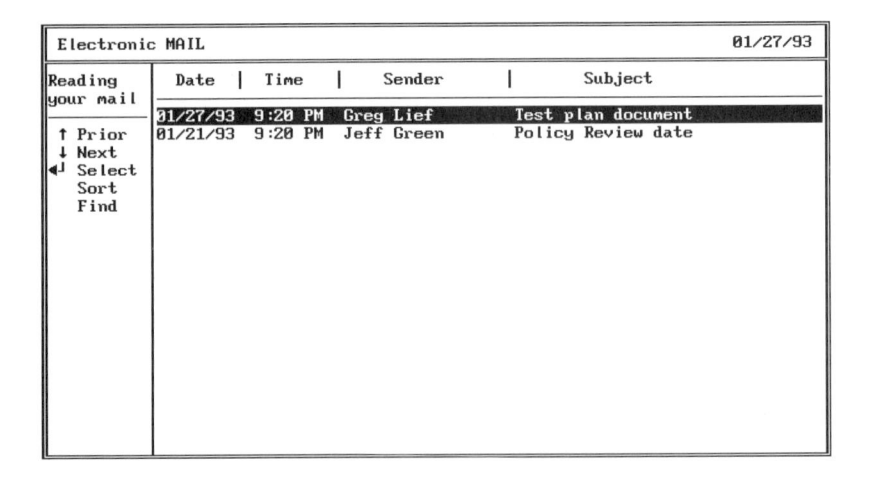

```
Electronic MAIL                                          01/27/93
Reading    Date    |  Time   |   Sender     |   Subject
your mail
           01/27/93  9:20 PM   Greg Lief       Test plan document
 ↑ Prior   01/21/93  9:20 PM   Jeff Green      Policy Review date
 ↓ Next
 ↵ Select
   Sort
   Find
```

Figure 13.3: Read Mail screen

From this screen, you can move up and down through your mail messages. The mail is sorted so that the newest messages are at the top of the list and the oldest are at the bottom. Unread mail is shown in a different color than mail you've already read.

Sorting mail You can also change the sort order of the mail. This change is "sticky," meaning that the new order will be used until you change it to something different. If you press S to select the Sort option, a check box will appear under each column. You would then enter Y in the column you wish to sort on. The contents of your MAILBOX file will then be sorted and redisplayed in the correct order.

Finding mail   You can use the Find option to scan the subject and/or sender of your mail messages for a particular keyword. This feature does not check the mail text, only the subject information or sender name. If mail that contains the keyword is found, the highlight bar will be positioned on that piece of mail. If the keyword is not found, you will receive an error message and the highlight bar will stay in its original position.

Reading the message   Once you've positioned the highlight bar on the mail you want to read, you can press the Enter key to read the message. The mail will be displayed as shown in Figure 13.4. When mail is displayed on the screen, you may discard it, forward it to another user, send a reply, or print it.

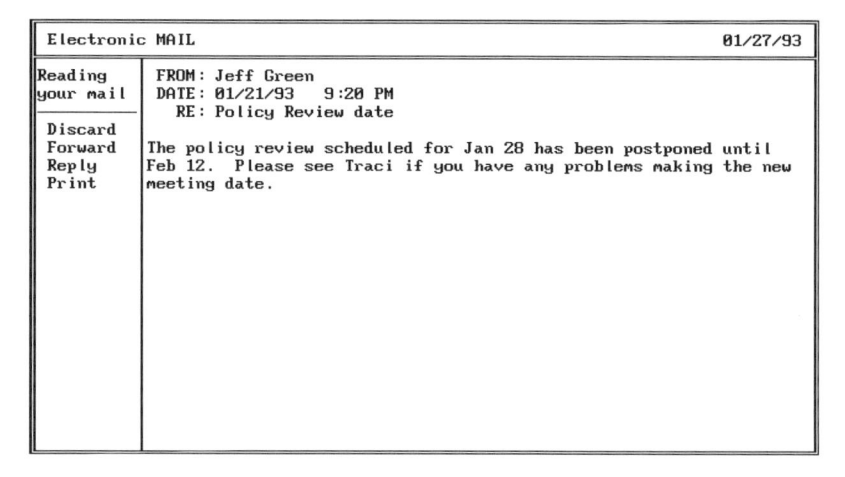

```
 Electronic MAIL                                              01/27/93
┌──────────┬─────────────────────────────────────────────────────────┐
│Reading   │ FROM: Jeff Green                                        │
│your mail │ DATE: 01/21/93   9:20 PM                                │
│──────────│   RE: Policy Review date                                │
│Discard   │                                                         │
│Forward   │ The policy review scheduled for Jan 28 has been postponed until │
│Reply     │ Feb 12.  Please see Traci if you have any problems making the new │
│Print     │ meeting date.                                           │
│          │                                                         │
```

Figure 13.4: Reading a message

- *Discarding the message*   If you press D, the message currently displayed will be marked for deletion. You should get in the habit of deleting mail you don't need, rather than letting it accumulate in your MAILBOX file. If you delete a message but haven't packed the file, you can still recall the message and its text. Once you've packed the file, however, the message is gone forever.

- *Forwarding the message*   If you press F, the message currently displayed will be forwarded to another user and then deleted from your MAILBOX file. You will be prompted for the recipient's user id. If you don't know the user's network id, press the F4 key and a list will appear from which you can select a person or group.

- *Replying to the message*   If you press R to reply to a message, the Send Mail screen will appear. The To: field will automatically contain the user id of the person who sent you the original mail message. In addition, the text of the original mail message will be copied into your edit area. This way, you can respond to particular parts of the original message. Once you've written your reply, you can press Enter to send the mail to the requested user.

- *Printing the message*   If you press P, the message currently displayed will be printed. A list box of available printers will be displayed. You may select any printer, the screen, or a text file. The mail will be formatted and printed accordingly.

SENDING MAIL

If you elect to send mail to another user, the window shown in Figure 13.5 is displayed. You can then specify the user or group name to send the mail to. Press F4 to display a list of users and group ids.

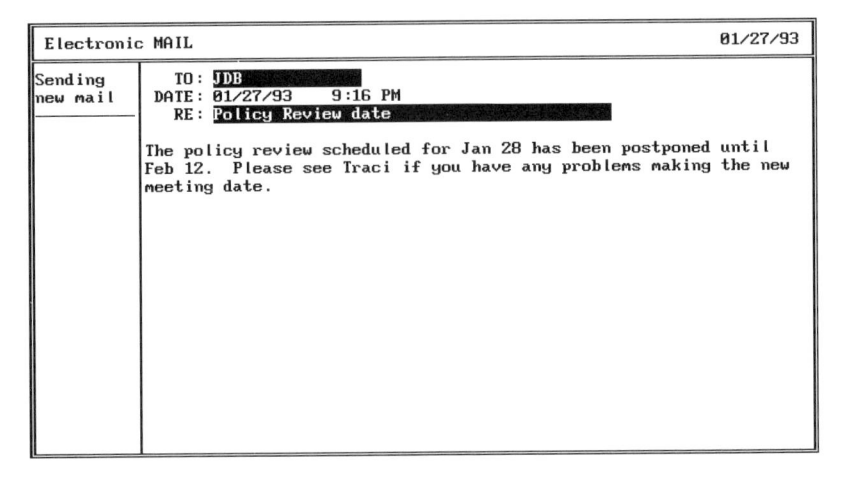

```
┌─────────────────────────────────────────────────────────────────────┐
│ Electronic MAIL                                            01/27/93 │
├──────────┬──────────────────────────────────────────────────────────┤
│Sending   │   TO: JDB                                                │
│new mail  │ DATE: 01/27/93      9:16 PM                              │
│          │   RE: Policy Review date                                 │
│          │                                                          │
│          │ The policy review scheduled for Jan 28 has been postponed until │
│          │ Feb 12.  Please see Traci if you have any problems making the new │
│          │ meeting date.                                            │
│          │                                                          │
└──────────┴──────────────────────────────────────────────────────────┘
```

Figure 13.5: Sending a message

Once you specify the mail recipient, you can enter the subject and the actual text of the mail message. When done, you can look over your message, and if it looks OK, just press the Enter key to send the mail.

ERASING MAIL

Since mail tends to accumulate, you need an option to flag messages for deletion. This is the function of the Erase option. When you select this option, a list of all current messages is displayed. To discard or save a message, press the Spacebar to toggle the setting. When you have marked the desired messages to delete, you can return to the main menu by pressing the Escape key. From there, select Pack/Index to remove the deleted mail permanently.

Figure 13.6 shows the screen for flagging mail to be erased.

```
 Electronic MAIL                                          01/27/93
┌──────────┬────────┬─────────┬──────────────┬─────────────────────┐
│Erasing   │  Date  │  Time   │   Sender     │      Subject        │
│old mail  ├────────┼─────────┼──────────────┼─────────────────────┤
│          │01/27/93│ 9:20 PM │ Greg Lief    │ Test plan document  │
│Space to  │01/21/93│ 9:20 PM │ Jeff Green   │ Policy Review date  │
│tag <ESC> │
│when done │
```

Figure 13.6: Erasing mail messages

CONFIGURING THE MAIL SYSTEM

The mail system's screen colors and formats, as well as the location of the central mail directory, are all configurable. Selecting O from the main menu will display the screen shown in Figure 13.7. You may change the options as required and press Enter when done. If you press Escape, the original options will be restored.

You can change the various colors of the mail system using the normal Clipper color syntax. The color consists of a foreground setting, the slash character, and a background setting. The following chart shows the colors you can use. Only the colors in the left column can be used for the background setting; the colors in either column can be used for the foreground.

Color	Setting	Color	Setting
Black	N	Gray	N+
Blue	B	Bright Blue	B+
Green	G	Bright Green	G+
Cyan	BG	Bright Cyan	BG+
Red	R	Bright Red	R+
Magenta	RB	Bright Magenta	RB+
Brown	GR	Yellow	GR+
White	W	Bright White	W+

In addition to the colors, you can also change the background fill character and the frame style. Finally, you can set a data path where the central mailbox can be found. When entering a path name, be sure to place a slash as the last character.

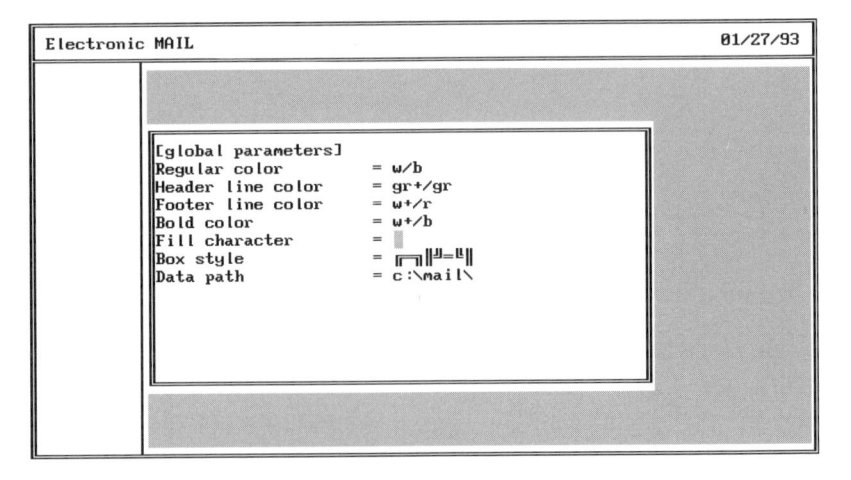

```
Electronic MAIL                                      01/27/93

    [global parameters]
    Regular color           = w/b
    Header line color       = gr+/gr
    Footer line color       = w+/r
    Bold color              = w+/b
    Fill character          = 
    Box style               = ┌─┐║=║
    Data path               = c:\mail\
```

Figure 13.7: Configuration options

THE PACK/INDEX OPTION

This option removes all records that are marked for deletion from your personal MAILBOX file. You should pack periodically to keep your file size to a minimum. Once the MAILBOX file is packed, there is no way to restore any deleted messages.

This option also reindexes the MAILBOX file. If the index files should become corrupted, you can run this option to recreate them. Because the MAILBOX file will typically be small, the pack and index are performed together to keep the files up-to-date.

Using the mail system

One of the benefits of a Clipper-based mail system is that it allows your other Clipper applications to send mail to the appropriate user if some condition occurs. For example, let's consider a company that runs several reports each night. These reports update a log indicating the start and end time for each report. Here is the log file's structure:

Field	Type	Size
RPT_NAME	Char	25
STARTED	Date	8
S_TIME	Char	5
ENDED	Date	8
E_TIME	Char	5

As each reports starts, it erases the end time and records when it started. The next morning, one user comes in and browses the log to see if all the reports were run satisfactorily.

Instead of manually checking the report-completion log, however, you can easily automate this process. Listing 13.1 shows a program that reads the log file. If a report has not run completely, a message to that effect is sent via e-mail to Betty, who is in charge of report distribution.

Listing 13.1: CHECKLOG Program

```
*  Program:  CheckLog
*  Authors:  Joseph D. Booth and Greg Lief
*  Purpose:  A sample Clipper program to send messages
*            via the e-mail system
******************************************
#define CRLF chr(13)+chr(10)
function CheckLog()
LOCAL aFailedRpts := {}
LOCAL cText,x
```

Listing 13.1: CHECKLOG Program (Continued)

```
use RPT_LOG new shared
if !Net_Err()
   go top
   do while !eof()
      if empty(RPT_LOG->ended)
         Aadd(aFailedRpts,RPT_LOG->rpt_name)
      endif
      skip +1
   enddo
   use
   if !empty(aFailedRpts)
      cText := "The following reports did not "+;
               "finish running last night."+CRLF+CRLF
      for x:= 1 to len(aFailedRpts)-1
         cText += trim(aFailedRpts[x])+", "
      next
      cText += trim(aFailedRpts[len(aFailedRpts)])
      SendMail("BETTY","Some Reports Failed,cText)
   endif
endif
return nil
```

Summary

The EMAIL program is an example of the type of Clipper application that can be run on a network. Chapter 14 provides the complete source code to the system. Play with the code and explore it—it should provide you with some idea of the potential created by combining Clipper and NetWare. We hope that the functions in this book serve as a good starting place.

EMAIL Program Source Code

DATABASES

PROGRAM SOURCE CODE

Chapter 14

In this chapter, we present the source code for the complete electronic-mail system introduced in Chapter 13. In its own right, it is a useful program for your applications; it should also serve to demonstrate how to use some of the functions presented in this book. To compile and link the program, use the following commands:

```
Clipper EMAIL -n -m -w -l
RTLINK FI EMAIL LIB BLNET
```

The code is written in Clipper, so you can also set up overlay structures to place the code and the book library into an overlay area to reduce memory requirements.

The BLNET.LIB file is on the disk accompanying this book and should be placed into the directory with your other Clipper libraries.

DATABASES

The EMAIL application requires two databases. The first one, called POST-BOX, is a central repository for all messages. Its structure is as follows:

Field Name	Type	Size	Contents
FOR_USER	Numeric	12	User/group bindery id
BEEN_READ	Logical	1	Has user read this mail?
DATE_SENT	Date	8	When was the mail sent?

Field Name	Type	Size	Contents
TIME_SENT	Numeric	5	Time sent, in seconds
FROM_USER	Character	15	User who sent the message
DISCARD	Date	8	Date after which to discard the message
RECEIPT	Logical	1	Acknowledge receipt of mail?
SUBJECT	Character	25	One-line subject
MESSAGE	Memo	10	Actual mail text

The second database is called MAILBOX and is used to hold each user's personal mail. Its structure is as follows:

Field Name	Type	Size	Contents
DATE	Date	8	When was the mail received?
TIME	Numeric	5	Time sent, in seconds
SENDER	Character	15	User who sent the message
SUBJECT	Character	25	One-line subject
READ	Logical	1	Has mail been read?
TEXT	Memo	10	Actual mail text

The program will create any missing databases and/or indexes. The index keys are as follows:

POSTBOX   `if(been_read,[N],[Y])+str(for_user,12)`

MAILBOX   `descend(date)*100000+descend(time)`

Program source code

We will now walk you through all the source code for the EMAIL program. The code is included on the disk, as well.

```
* Program:  EMAIL.PRG
* Authors:  Joseph D. Booth and Greg Lief
* Purpose:  An e-mail application to demonstrate the
*           functions and techniques included in
*           Network Programming in CA-Clipper 5.2,
*           published by Ziff-Davis Press
*
```

```
*   --------------------------------------------------
*   The source code to the MEMOGET function is hereby
*   donated to the public domain by:
*
*   Darren J. Forcier
*   Forcier Computer Services
*   253 Main Street
*   Cherry Valley, MA 01611
*   CIS ID 72117,1632
*
*   It is provided solely on an as-is basis for
*   instructional purposes. It may be used in any
*   programming development effort, be it commercial
*   or personal. No warranties are expressed or implied
*   as to its fitness for use.  Questions or comments
*   may be addressed to the author at the above address
*   or CompuServe ID.
*   --------------------------------------------------
*
************************************************************

#include    "INKEY.CH"
#include    "MEMOEDIT.CH"
#include    "GETEXIT.CH"
```

Header files   The Clipper 5.2 release has made the DEFAULT TO preprocessor directive part of the language. It is stored in a file called COMMON.CH. The Clipper 5.01 version of the DEFAULT TO command is stored in a file called CL501.CH, which is included on the disk accompanying this book. Be sure to comment out the appropriate #include statement.

```
*   #include    "CL501.CH"          // Clipper 5.01
#include    "COMMON.CH"         // Clipper 5.2
```

Memo get   Clipper's flexibility makes it possible to design a GET command that acts like a memo entry. The #XCOMMAND below provides just such a command. This version was contributed by Darren Forcier.

```
#xcommand @ <nT>,<nL>,<nB>,<nR> GET MEMO <mVar> ;
    [PICTURE <pic>] [<ro: READONLY>] [COLOR <cColor>]    ;
                                                 => ;
    MEMOEDIT(<mVar>,<nT>,<nL>,<nB>,<nR>,.F.,.F.) ;       ;
    AADD(GetList, GETNEW(<nT>, <nL>,                     ;
      {|val| iif(val==NIL,<mVar>,<mVar> := val)},        ;
      <(mVar)>,<pic>,<cColor>))                  ;       ;
```

```
ATAIL(getlist):Reader:={|oget|MemoReader(oGet,<nT>, ;
            <nL>,<nB>,<nR>,!<.ro.>,<cColor>) }
```

Additional preprocessor commands The following section contains some additional preprocessor definitions that are used by the program.

```
#xtranslate NeedDir(<cDir>)   => ;
        empty( directory(<cDir>,"D") )

#define    K_SPACE                         32
#define    TEXT_SIZE                       2048
#define    NUMBER_OF_USERS                 50

#define    USER_LIST           N_ScanBindery(1)
#define    GROUP_LIST          N_ScanBindery(2)

#define    SYS_COLOR             What_Is( 1)
#define    SYS_HEADER            What_Is( 2)
#define    SYS_FOOTER            What_Is( 3)
#define    SYS_BOLD              What_Is( 4)
#define    SYS_HIGHLIGHT         What_Is( 5)
#define    SYS_FILLCHAR          What_Is( 6)
#define    SYS_BOXSTYLE          What_Is( 7)
#define    SYS_DATAPATH          What_Is( 8)

#define    AX                    1
#define    DX                    4
#define    DS                    8
#define    FLAGS                 10
```

Now the actual code The code to the program begins here. The program confirms that the directory and files exist. If everything appears to be correct, then the main mail loop can begin.

Note that this code calls the N_BINDLEVEL() function from Chapter 9 to get the user's bindery object number. In addition, the configuration files discussed in Chapter 7 are used to control how the application operates. Finally, the NET_USE() and VALIDNTX() functions from Chapter 3 are used to handle the opening of the files and their indexes.

```
STATIC     cLastOption            := ""

procedure main( cArg )

LOCAL getlist   := {}
LOCAL nOption   := 1
```

```
LOCAL cSave
LOCAL aOptions := N_BindLevel()
LOCAL arr_
LOCAL cTemp
LOCAL nId     := if(!empty(aOptions),aOptions[3],0)

ReadConfig("MAIL.INI")    // Get options from MAIL.INI
N_Init()                  // Initialize locks file
**************************************************
** Check to see if the data directory exists   **
**************************************************
if NeedDir( SYS_DATAPATH+alltrim(str(nId)) )
   if !MkDir( SYS_DATAPATH+alltrim(str(nId)) )
      Alert("Couldn't create a data directory...")
      quit
   endif
endif


****************************************
* Does the central mailbox exist?      *
****************************************
if !file( SYS_DATAPATH+"POSTBOX.DBF" )
    MkFile("POSTBOX",SYS_DATAPATH)
endif

if Net_Use(SYS_DATAPATH+"POSTBOX",.F.,,"POSTBOX")
   if ! validntx(SYS_DATAPATH+"POSTBOX",;
      "if(POSTBOX->been_read,[N],[Y])"+;
      "str(POSTBOX->for_user,12)",.T.)
        Alert("Couldn't index the central mailbox!")
        cls
        quit
   else
      set index to (SYS_DATAPATH+"POSTBOX")
   endif
else
   Alert("Central mailbox is unavailable...")
   cls
   quit
endif


****************************************
* Does the user's mailbox exist?       *
****************************************

if !file( SYS_DATAPATH+alltrim(str(nId))+;
```

```
      "\MAILBOX.DBF" )
      MkFile("MAILBOX",SYS_DATAPATH+;
      alltrim(str(nId))+"\")
   endif

   if Net_Use(SYS_DATAPATH+alltrim(str(nId))+;
            "\MAILBOX",.T.,,"MAILBOX")
      if ! validntx(SYS_DATAPATH+alltrim(str(nId))+;
         "\MAILBOX",;
         "descend(MAILBOX->date)*100000+"+;
         "descend(MAILBOX->time)",.T.)
         Alert("Couldn't index your mailbox!")
         cls
         quit
      else
         set index to (SYS_DATAPATH+;
            alltrim(str(nId))+"\MAILBOX")
      endif
   else
      Alert("Your mailbox is unavailable...")
      cls
      quit
   endif

   ////////////////////////////////////////////
   // Paint the main screen                  //
   ////////////////////////////////////////////
   set scoreboard off
   set deleted on
   MainScreen()


   ////////////////////////////////////////////
   // Main loop
   ////////////////////////////////////////////

   do while !empty(nOption)
      @ 03,01 clear to maxrow()-1,10
      @ 03,01 prompt "Read...   "
      @ 04,01 prompt "Send...   "
      @ 05,01 prompt "Erase...  "
      @ 06,01 prompt "Options.. "
      @ 07,01 prompt "Pack/Index"
      menu to nOption
      if nOption <> 0
         @ 03,01 clear to 07,10
         do case
```

```
   case nOption == 1
      @ 03,01 say "Reading"                  ;
             color SYS_BOLD
      @ 04,01 say "your mail"                ;
             color SYS_BOLD
      @ 05,01 say replicate(chr(196),10)     ;
             color SYS_BOLD
      ReadMail()
   case nOption == 2
      @ 03,01 say "Sending"                  ;
             color SYS_BOLD
      @ 04,01 say "new mail"                 ;
             color SYS_BOLD
      @ 05,01 say replicate(chr(196),10)     ;
             color SYS_BOLD
      SendMail()
   case nOption == 3
      @ 03,01 say "Erasing"                  ;
             color SYS_BOLD
      @ 04,01 say "old mail"                 ;
             color SYS_BOLD
      @ 05,01 say replicate(chr(196),10)     ;
             color SYS_BOLD
      @ 06,01 say "Space to"                 ;
             color SYS_HIGHLIGHT
      @ 07,01 say "tag <ESC>"                ;
             color SYS_HIGHLIGHT
      @ 08,01 say "when done"                ;
             color SYS_HIGHLIGHT
      PurgeMail()
   case nOption == 4
      cSave := savescreen(6,10,20,60)
      setcolor( SYS_FOOTER )
      DispBegin()
      DispBox(6,12,20,62,2)
      @ 7,13 clear to 19,61
      DispEnd()
      cTemp := memoread("MAIL.INI")
      @ 7,13,19,61 get memo cTemp color SYS_FOOTER
      read
      if lastkey() <> K_ESC
         memowrit("MAIL.INI",cTemp)
      endif
      ReadConfig("MAIL.INI")
      restscreen(6,10,20,60,cSave)
      setcolor( SYS_COLOR )
```

```
            MainScreen()
        case nOption == 5
            select MAILBOX
            pack
            index on descend(MAILBOX->date)*100000+;
                     descend(MAILBOX->time) to mailbox

        endcase
    endif
enddo
cls
close databases
return
*****************************

//
//    Function:  MainScreen()
//     Purpose:  Displays the main mail screen
//      Syntax:  MainScreen()
//     Returns:  NIL
//
/////////////////////////////
STATIC function MainScreen()
dispbegin()
setcolor( SYS_COLOR )
-> SCROLL()
dispbox(0,0,maxrow(),maxcol(),SYS_BOXSTYLE,SYS_BOLD)
@ 01,01 say padr(" Electronic MAIL",;
        maxcol()-10)+dtoc(date())+" " color SYS_HEADER
@ 02,00 say chr(204)+replicate(chr(205),;
        maxcol()-1)+chr(185)            color SYS_BOLD
@ 02,11 say chr(209) color SYS_BOLD
Dispbox(3,11,maxrow()-1,11,replicate(chr(179),9),SYS_BOLD)
@ maxrow(),11 say chr(207) color SYS_BOLD
dispbox(3,12,maxrow()-1,78,replicate(SYS_FILLCHAR,9))
dispend()
return NIL


****************************************************
```

Reading mail The READMAIL section of the program creates a TBROWSE loop for the user's MAILBOX file. Each option available for this section is handled in this group of functions. The loop uses some of the TBROWSE concepts we discussed in Chapter 6, as well as the N_WHOAMI() function from Chapter 9 and the printing functions from Chapter 10.

```
//
//
//
////////////////////////////
STATIC function ReadMail()

LOCAL getlist    := {}
LOCAL lSort1     := .F.
LOCAL lSort2     := .F.
LOCAL lSort3     := .F.
LOCAL lSort4     := .F.
LOCAL cSender    := space(15)
LOCAL cSubject   := space(25)
LOCAL cUser      := N_WhoAmI()
LOCAL x
LOCAL col
LOCAL b       := TBrowseDB(5,12,maxrow()-1,maxcol()-1)
LOCAL cSave := savescreen(3,11,maxrow()-1,maxcol()-1)
LOCAL cTextSave
LOCAL nKey

b:colorSpec := SYS_COLOR+",N/W,"+;
               SYS_BOLD+",N/W,"+SYS_HIGHLIGHT

select MAILBOX
ChkMail()

if MAILBOX->( lastrec() ) > 0
   col := TBColumnNew(, { || ShowMail() } )
   col:colorBlock := { |xx| if(MAILBOX->read,;
                     {1,2},{3,4}) }
   b:AddColumn( col )

   DispBegin()
   @ 3,12 say padr("   Date    "+chr(179)+;
          "   Time    "+chr(179)+;
          "    Sender     "+chr(179)+;
          "         Subject",maxcol()-12)
   @ 4,12 say replicate( chr(196),maxcol()-12)

   ReadOptions()
   DispEnd()
```

```
***************************************************
** Open the mail file in a TBROWSE window,       **
** and allow user to select the mail and         **
** display it using MEMOEDIT                     **
***************************************************

do while nKey <> K_ESC
  //
  // Check for mail while BROWSING
  //
  if ChkMail()
     b:RefreshAll()
  endif
  dispbegin()
  do while ( nKey := inkey() ) == 0 .and. ;
     ! b:stabilize()
  enddo
  dispend()
  do case
  case nKey == K_UP
     b:up()
  case nKey == K_DOWN
     b:down()
  case nKey == K_PGUP
     b:pageUp()
  case nKey == K_PGDN
     b:pageDown()
  case nKey == K_CTRL_PGUP .or. nKey == K_HOME
     b:goTop()
  case nKey == K_CTRL_PGDN .or. nKey == K_END
     b:goBottom()
  case chr(nKey) $ "Ss" .or. nKey == K_ALT_S
     @ 5,12 clear to maxrow()-1,maxcol()-1
     @ 5,14 get lSort1    picture "Y"
     @ 5,23 get lSort2    picture "Y"
     @ 5,35 get lSort3    picture "Y"
     @ 5,55 get lSort4    picture "Y"
     read
     if lastkey() <> K_ESC
        do case
        case lSort1
           index on str(descend(MAILBOX->date),10)+;
                    str(MAILBOX->time,5) to MAILBOX
        case lSort2
           index on str(MAILBOX->time,5)+;
                    str(descend(MAILBOX->date),10) ;
                 to MAILBOX
```

```
            case lSort3
                index on upper(MAILBOX->sender) to MAILBOX
            case lSort4
                index on upper(substr(MAILBOX->subject,1,16)) ;
                    to MAILBOX
            endcase
        endif
        b:ReFreshall()
    case chr(nKey) $ "Ff" .or. nKey == K_ALT_F
        @ 5,12 clear to maxrow()-1,maxcol()-1
        @ 5,31 get cSender
        @ 5,49 get cSubject
        read
        if lastkey() <> K_ESC
            if !empty(cSubject)
                locate all for ;
                upper(MAILBOX->sender) = alltrim(upper(cSender)) ;
                .and. alltrim(upper(cSubject)) $ upper(MAILBOX->subject)
            else
                locate all for upper(MAILBOX->sender) = alltrim(upper(cSender))
            endif
            if eof()
                go top
            endif
        endif
        b:ReFreshall()
    case nKey == K_ENTER .or. nKey == K_SPACE
        // Display message text
        cTextSave  := savescreen(3,12,maxrow()-1,maxcol()-1)
        DispBegin()
        @ 6,01 clear to 10,10
        @ 6,03 say "iscard"            color SYS_BOLD
        @ 7,03 say "orward"            color SYS_BOLD
        @ 8,03 say "eply"              color SYS_BOLD
        @ 9,03 say "rint"              color SYS_BOLD
        @ 6,02 say "D"                 color SYS_HIGHLIGHT
        @ 7,02 say "F"                 color SYS_HIGHLIGHT
        @ 8,02 say "R"                 color SYS_HIGHLIGHT
        @ 9,02 say "P"                 color SYS_HIGHLIGHT

        @ 3,12 clear to maxrow()-1,maxcol()-1

        @ 3,12 say " FROM: "           color SYS_BOLD
        @ 4,12 say " DATE: "           color SYS_BOLD
        @ 5,12 say "   RE: "           color SYS_BOLD
        @ 3,19 say MAILBOX->sender     color SYS_COLOR
        @ 4,19 say MAILBOX->date       color SYS_COLOR
```

```
@ 4,29 say Sec2Time(MAILBOX->time)   color SYS_COLOR
@ 5,19 say MAILBOX->subject          color SYS_COLOR
DispEnd()
cLastOption := ""
memoedit(MAILBOX->text,7,12,maxrow()-1,maxcol()-1,,.F.,"MEMO_KEY")
replace MAILBOX->read with .T.
commit
if !empty(cLastOption)
   do case
   case cLastOption == "D"
      delete
      b:RefreshAll()
   case cLastOption == "F"
      set key K_F4 to PickUsers
      @ 3,45 say "TO:"   color  SYS_BOLD
      @ 3,49 get cSender picture "@!";
      valid !empty(N_ObjectId(alltrim(cSender),1)) ;
      .or. !empty(N_ObjectId(alltrim(cSender),2))
      read
if lastkey() <> K_ESC
   WriteMail(cSender,MAILBOX->subject,,;
     "FORWARDED FROM "+alltrim(cUser)+chr(13)+chr(10)+;
               alltrim(MAILBOX->text) )
      endif
      set key K_F4 to

   case cLastOption == "R"
      SendMail(MAILBOX->sender,"RE: "+MAILBOX->subject,MAILBOX->text)
   case cLastOption == "P"
      if P_Where()         // select where to print
        if P_start()       // Able to start printing
          ? " FROM: "+MAILBOX->sender
          ? " DATE: "+dtoc(MAILBOX->date)
          ? " TIME: "+Sec2Time(MAILBOX->time)
          ? "   RE: "+MAILBOX->subject
          ? replicate( "-",70)
          for x := 1 to mlcount(MAILBOX->text,70)
             ? memoline(MAILBOX->text,70,x)
             if ! P_Cancel()
                exit
             endif
          next
          ?
          ?
          P_end()
        endif
      endif
```

```
            endcase
         endif
         restscreen(3,12,maxrow()-1,maxcol()-1,cTextSave)
         @ 6,01 clear to 10,10
         ReadOptions()
         b:RefreshAll()
         cTextSave := ""
      endcase
      if lastrec() < 1
         exit
      endif
   enddo
else
   @ 07,20 say "You have no mail in your mailbox..."
   inkey(12)
endif
restscreen(3,11,maxrow()-1,maxcol()-1,cSave)
return NIL
****************************
function Memo_Key(nMode,nLine,nCol)
LOCAL nAction := 0
LOCAL nKey    := lastkey()
if upper(chr(nKey))$"DFRP"
   nAction       := 27
   cLastOption := upper(chr(nkey))
   keyboard chr(K_ESC)
endif
return nAction
****************************
STATIC function ReadOptions()
@ 06,01 say " "+chr(24)+" Prior"        color SYS_BOLD
@ 07,01 say " "+chr(25)+" Next"         color SYS_BOLD
@ 08,01 say chr(17)+chr(217)+" Select"  color SYS_BOLD
@ 09,05 say "ort"                color SYS_BOLD
@ 10,05 say "ind"                color SYS_BOLD
@ 09,04 say "S"                  color SYS_HIGHLIGHT
@ 10,04 say "F"                  color SYS_HIGHLIGHT
return NIL
**************************
STATIC function ShowMail()
return padr(dtoc(MAILBOX->date)+" "+Sec2Time(MAILBOX->time)+"  "+;
            MAILBOX->sender+"  "+MAILBOX->subject,maxcol()-12)
```

Selecting users to receive mail The PICKUSERS() function reads the bindery files to make a list of users and/or groups to whom mail can be sent.

```
STATIC function PickUsers()
LOCAL aUsers       := USER_LIST
LOCAL aGroups      := GROUP_LIST
LOCAL cSave        := savescreen(6,25,18,45)
LOCAL cOld         := setcolor(SYS_FOOTER)
LOCAL aToggle      := {}
LOCAL x            := 0
LOCAL nGroupSize   := len(aGroups)
LOCAL nUsersCount  := len(aUsers)

DispBox(6,25,18,45,2)
Asort(aUsers)
if !empty(aGroups)
   Asort(aGroups)
   Aadd(aUsers,"--- Groups ---------")
   for x := 1 to nGroupSize
      Aadd(aUsers,aGroups[x])
   next
   x := nUsersCounts-nGroupSize
endif
aToggle := array(len(aUsers))
afill(aToggle,.T.)
if x > 0
   aToggle[x] := .F.
endif

x := achoice(7,26,17,44,aUsers,aToggle)
if x > 0
   keyboard chr(K_CTRL_Y)+alltrim(aUsers[x])
endif
setcolor(cOld)
restscreen(6,25,18,45,cSave)
return NIL
```

Checking mail The CHKMAIL function looks to see if any unread mail for this user id is in the POSTBOX file. The N_OBJECTID() function from Chapter 9 provides the object number that is part of the POSTBOX lookup key. If mail is found, it is flagged as received in the POSTBOX file and is transferred into the user's MAILBOX file.

```
**********************************************
STATIC function ChkMail()
LOCAL nId      := N_ObjectID(N_WhoAmI(),1)
LOCAL aGroups := {nId}
LOCAL any_mail := .F.
LOCAL x, arr_
arr_ := N_UserGroups( N_WhoAmI() )
for x := 1 to len(arr_)
   aadd(aGroups,N_ObjectId(arr_[x],2) )
next
***********************************************************
** Open the master file and seek mail for this         **
** user or group.  If OK, copy the mail into MAILBOX.  **
***********************************************************
for x := 1 to len(aGroups)
   select POSTBOX
   seek "Y"+str(aGroups[x],12)
   if found()
      if x == 1 .and. N_RecLock()
         replace POSTBOX->been_read with .T.
         unlock
         commit
      endif
      select MAILBOX
      append blank
      replace MAILBOX->date    with POSTBOX->date_sent,;
              MAILBOX->time    with POSTBOX->time_sent,;
              MAILBOX->sender  with POSTBOX->from_user,;
              MAILBOX->subject with POSTBOX->subject,;
              MAILBOX->read    with .F.,;
              MAILBOX->text    with POSTBOX->message
      commit
      any_mail := .T.
   endif
next
select MAILBOX
return any_mail
**********************************************
```

Sending mail   The SENDMAIL function is used to enter a message into another user's MAILBOX file. This function can be called from the menu or it can be called from the REPLY option during the READMAIL function.

When the mail has been edited, the function passes the information to WRITEMAIL(), which places the mail in the central POSTBOX file.

```
STATIC function SendMail(cSendTo,cSubject,cText)
LOCAL getlist  := {}

if cSendTo == NIL
   cSendTo  := space(15)
   cSubject := space(25)
   cText    := space(TEXT_SIZE)
endif

set key K_F4 to PickUsers
@ 3,12 clear to maxrow()-1,maxcol()-1

@ 3,12 say "   TO: "              color SYS_BOLD
@ 4,12 say " DATE: "              color SYS_BOLD
@ 5,12 say "   RE: "              color SYS_BOLD

@ 3,19 get cSendTo     picture "@!"
@ 4,19 say dtoc(date())+"   "+sec2time(seconds())
@ 5,19 get cSubject
@ 7,12,maxrow()-1,78 get memo cText color SYS_COLOR

read
if lastkey() <> K_ESC
   //
   // Confirm mail should be sent
   //
   WriteMail(cSendTo,cSubject,cText)
endif
@ 3,12 clear to maxrow()-1,maxcol()-1
set key K_F4 to
return NIL
*************************
STATIC function WriteMail(cSendTo,cSubject,cText)
LOCAL was_sent := .F.
LOCAL nObjectId
// Check if this is a user
nObjectId := N_ObjectId(alltrim(cSendTo),1)
if nObjectId == 0
   // Else a group id
   nObjectId := N_ObjectId(alltrim(cSendTo),2)
endif
//
// Add a record
```

```
//
select POSTBOX
if N_Addrec()
   replace POSTBOX->for_user   with nObjectId,;
           POSTBOX->been_read  with .F.,;
           POSTBOX->date_sent  with date(),;
           POSTBOX->time_sent  with seconds(),;
           POSTBOX->from_user  with N_WhoAmI(),;
           POSTBOX->discard    with date()+7,;
           POSTBOX->receipt    with .F.,;
           POSTBOX->subject    with cSubject,;
           POSTBOX->message    with alltrim(cText)
   unlock
   commit
   was_sent := .T.
endif
return was_sent
*****************************
```

Erasing mail Mail can accumulate over time, so users need some way of discarding old messages. The PURGEMAIL() function is used to tag mail for deletion. The option is a TBROWSE screen in which the user uses the Spacebar or Tag key to mark unwanted mail. The Pack/Index option from the main menu is used to physically remove the marked mail from the .DBF file.

```
//
//   Function:  PurgeMail()
//    Purpose:  A TBROWSE() screen to delete mail
//
////////////////////////////////////
STATIC function PurgeMail()
LOCAL col
LOCAL b          := TBrowseDB(5,12,maxrow()-1,maxcol()-1)
LOCAL cSave      := savescreen(3,11,maxrow()-1,maxcol()-1)
LOCAL cTextSave
LOCAL nKey

set deleted off
b:colorSpec := SYS_COLOR+",N/W,"+;
               SYS_BOLD+",N/W,"+SYS_HIGHLIGHT

select MAILBOX

if MAILBOX->( lastrec() ) > 0
   col := TBColumnNew(, { || MarkMail() } )
   col:colorBlock := { |xx| if(MAILBOX->read,{1,2},{3,4}) }
```

```
      b:AddColumn( col )
      DispBegin()
      @ 3,12 say padr("    Date       Time       Sender           Subject",maxcol()-12)
      @ 4,12 say replicate( chr(196),maxcol()-12)
      DispEnd()
      do while nKey <> K_ESC
         //
         // Check for mail while BROWSING
         //
         dispbegin()
         do while ( nKey := inkey() ) == 0 .and. ! b:stabilize()
         enddo
         dispend()
         do case
         case nKey == K_UP
            b:up()
         case nKey == K_DOWN
            b:down()
         case nKey == K_PGUP
            b:pageUp()
         case nKey == K_PGDN
            b:pageDown()
         case nKey == K_CTRL_PGUP .or. nKey == K_HOME
            b:goTop()
         case nKey == K_CTRL_PGDN .or. nKey == K_END
            b:goBottom()
            case chr(nKey) $ "Tt" .or. nKey == K_SPACE
            if deleted()
               recall
            else
               delete
            endif
            b:down()
            b:ReFreshall()
         endcase
         if lastrec() < 1
            exit
         endif
      enddo
else
   @ 07,20 say "You have no mail in your mailbox..."
   inkey(12)
endif
restscreen(3,11,maxrow()-1,maxcol()-1,cSave)
set deleted on
```

```
return NIL
***************************

//
//    Function:  MarkMail()
//     Purpose:  Tags or untags mail for deletion
//
///////////////////////////////////////
STATIC function MarkMail()
return padr( if(deleted(),chr(251),chr(32) )+" "+;
        dtoc(MAILBOX->date)+" "+Sec2Time(MAILBOX->time)+"  "+;
        MAILBOX->sender+"  "+MAILBOX->subject,maxcol()-12)
*****************************************
```

Creating the files The MKFILE() function creates the MAILBOX and POSTBOX .DBF files if they do not exist. It is called at the beginning of the program to ensure that the files are available.

```
//
//    Function:  MkFile()
//     Purpose:  Creates database files if they don't exist yet
//
///////////////////////////////////////
function MkFile(cName,cPath)
LOCAL lReturn := .F.
//
DEFAULT cPath TO ""
do case
case cName == "MAILBOX"
   DbCreate(cPath+"MAILBOX", { {"DATE"        ,"D", 8,0},;
           {"TIME"      ,"N", 5,0},;
           {"SENDER"    ,"C",15,0},;
           {"SUBJECT"   ,"C",25,0},;
           {"READ"      ,"L", 1,0},;
           {"TEXT"      ,"M",10,0} } )
case cName == "POSTBOX"
   DbCreate(cPath+"POSTBOX", { {"FOR_USER"   ,"N",12,0},;
           {"BEEN_READ" ,"L", 1,0},;
           {"DATE_SENT" ,"D", 8,0},;
           {"TIME_SENT" ,"N", 5,0},;
           {"FROM_USER" ,"C",15,0},;
           {"DISCARD"   ,"D", 8,0},;
           {"RECEIPT"   ,"L", 1,0},;
```

```
                    {"SUBJECT"   ,"C",25,0},.;
                    {"MESSAGE"   ,"M",10,0} } )
endcase
return lReturn
***********************************
```

Some miscellaneous functions The following two functions are needed to create a directory for the mail files and to convert seconds into a more familiar format of hours and minutes.

```
//
//   Function:   Mkdir()
//   Purpose:    To create a new directory
////////////////////////////////////////////
function Mkdir(cName)
* 39h - Make a directory
LOCAL aRegs := { 0,0,0,0,0,0,0,0,0,0 }
aRegs[ AX ] := 57 * 256
aRegs[ DS ] := cName          // Directory name
aRegs[ DX ] := .T.            // Using a string
Ft_int86(33,aRegs)            // Execute interrupt
return aRegs[FLAGS] % 2 == 0   // Check carry flag
****************************************************

//
//   Function:   Sec2Time()
//   Purpose:    Converts an integer seconds into a time string
//
//////////////////////////////////////

STATIC function Sec2Time(nTime)
LOCAL hh    := int(nTime / 3600)
LOCAL mm    := (nTime % 3600 ) / 60
LOCAL cAmPm := if( nTime>43200,"PM","AM" )
hh := if(hh=0,12,if(hh>12,hh-12,hh))
return str(hh,2)+":"+;
       if(mm<10,"0"+str(mm,1),str(mm,2))+" "+cAmPm
*************************************************
```

Memo reader The following two functions are used to allow the user to enter text into a memo field. Since MEMOEDIT() normally does not exit with the same keys that the GET system uses, the MEMO_KEY user-defined function handles the keystrokes and emulates the behavior of the GET system.

```
//
//    Function:  MemoReader()
//     Purpose:  A function for reading memo GETs
//
/////////////////////////////////////

function MemoReader(oGet,nTop,nLeft,nBottom,nRight,lReadWrite,cColor)
LOCAL oldColor := SETCOLOR(cColor)
LOCAL cMemo

if lReadwrite == NIL
   lReadwrite := .T.
endif
if cColor == NIL
   cColor   := SYS_COLOR
endif

cMemo := eval(oGet:Block) // Retrieve initial value...
keyboard chr(K_HOME)
cMemo := MemoEdit(cMemo,nTop,nLeft,nBottom,nRight,;
                  lReadwrite,"MemoUDF")
Eval(oGet:Block,cMemo)
setcolor(oldColor)
return ( NIL )

************************************************************************

//
//    Function:  MemoUdf()
//     Purpose:  A function for handling memo-field keystrokes
//
/////////////////////////////////////
function MemoUDF(nMode,nLine,nCol)
LOCAL nKey    := lastkey()
LOCAL nRetVal := 0

STATIC nLastLine := 0

  do case
  case nKey == K_UP

    if nLine == 1 .and. nLastLine == 1
       keyboard chr(K_CTRL_W)
       // Set Exitstate so we will go up one field to previous Get
       GetActive():ExitState := GE_UP
    endif
```

```
   case nKey == K_SH_TAB .and. nMode <> ME_INIT
        keyboard chr(K_CTRL_W)
        GetActive():ExitState := GE_UP

   case (nKey == K_TAB .or. nKey == K_ENTER) .and. nMode <> ME_INIT
        keyboard chr(K_CTRL_W)
        GetActive():ExitState := GE_WRITE

   case nKey == K_ESC
      Getactive():ExitState := GE_ESCAPE
   endcase
   nLastLine := nLine
return ( nRetVal )
```

Summary

In this chapter, we've presented a usable e-mail system to illustrate how you can program on a network. This code makes use of several of the library functions. We hope it whets your appetite for your next networking program.

Appendix A: Function Reference

In this appendix, we list in alphabetical order all the functions we've discussed throughout the book. This should serve as a quick reference when you are using the library functions while programming. The material in this appendix was extracted from source-code headers and formatted by a Clipper application known as TechWriter™. TechWriter allows you to control how the output is created by using a template translation file. By modifying the translation file, you could format the comments from the source code in any fashion necessary. The Norton Guide reader file that is included on the disk accompanying this book was also generated via TechWriter.

TechWriter is a systems analysis and documentation tool that supports all versions of xBase. More importantly, TechWriter fully supports Clipper 5.2 and the object-oriented extensions of Class(Y) and SuperClass. It produces documents in Norton Guide/Expert Help, WordPerfect, or ASCII text format. By the time you read this, many new features will be added to the product, as a new release is imminent. For further information, contact

    John F. Kaster
    Interface Technologies, Inc.
    2314 Mary Baldwin Drive
    Alexandria, VA 22307-1508
    (703) 765-0805 (Voice)
    (703) 765-1836 (Fax/BBS)
    71510,3321 (CompuServe)

APPT_CFG()

Purpose Updates system appointment fields in a real-time mode

Syntax `<logical> := Appt_Cfg()`

Parameters None

Returns TRUE if fields were updated, FALSE if error occured

Examples
```
if ! Appt_Cfg()
   Alert("Couldn't update configuration")
endif
```

Notes This function is used to update the configuration rules for an appointment database. The SETAPPT program uses the .DBF file to control when appointments are allowed, and so on. It assumes a file called SYSTEM exists and has the following structure:

Field	Type	Size
LASTDATE	Date	8
GOODDAYS	Char	7
START1	Numeric	4
END1	Numeric	4
START2	Numeric	4
END2	Numeric	4
START3	Numeric	4
END3	Numeric	4
START4	Numeric	4
END4	Numeric	4
START5	Numeric	4
END5	Numeric	4
START6	Numeric	4
END6	Numeric	4
START7	Numeric	4
END7	Numeric	4

Program File CFGAPPT.PRG

CLEANSTR()

Purpose   Translates strings between NetWare & Clipper. Removes all characters following the NULL character, including the NULL itself

Syntax   `<cString> := CleanStr(cNovellString)`

Parameters cNovellString   String returned from Novell API function

Returns   cString   String with all NULL characters removed

Notes   Strings returned from Novell's API calls are usually filled with NULL bytes. Clipper doesn't like these bytes; this function removes them. This function is primarily for internal use, but can be used if you develop any of your own API functions.

Program File XLATE.PRG

CLIP2INT()

Purpose   Converts a Clipper numeric to an integer string value

Syntax   `<Cinteger> := Clip2Int( numeric )`

Parameters numeric   Value of integer

Returns   cInteger   Binary integer for Novell

Notes   Novell's API calls store integers as two-byte strings in high-low order. Intel microprocessors usually store integers in low-high order. Clipper's I2BIN() function converts numerics to Intel format binary integers. This function essentially does the same for Novell integers. It is primarily for internal use, but can be used if you develop any of your own API functions.

Program File XLATE.PRG

CLIP2LONG()

Purpose Converts a Clipper numeric to a long string value

Syntax `<cLong> := Clip2Int( numeric )`

Parameters numeric   Value of number

Returns cLong   Binary long number for Novell

Notes Novell's API calls store integers as four-byte strings in high-low order. Intel microprocessors usually store longs in low-high order. Clipper's L2BIN() function converts numerics to Intel-format binary longs. This function essentially does the same for Novell longs. It is primarily for internal use, but can be used if you develop any of your own API functions.

Program File XLATE.PRG

CLOSESEMAPH()

Purpose Closes a semaphore in a .DBF file

Syntax `<nValue> := CloseSemaph( cName )`

Parameters cName   Name of semaphore to close

Returns nValue   0 if closed, -99 if problem occurred

Examples
```
if OpenSemaPh("CD_ROM",5) <> -99
   ? QuerySemaPh("CD_ROM")
   CloseSemaPh("CD_ROM")
endif
```

Notes This function resets the specified semaphore to zero.

Program File SEM.PRG

FIXEM()

Purpose Fixes problems detected while opening files

Syntax `<logical> := FixEm( {aErrors} )`

Parameters aErrors   Array of errors

Returns TRUE if all files were fixed, FALSE otherwise

Notes This function takes a list of errors returned from OPENEM() and attempts to fix any problems detected.

Program File FIXEM.PRG

FREE_SEMA()

Purpose Frees a semaphore after a process is complete

Syntax `<logical> := Free_Sema( cName )`

Parameters cName   Name of semaphore

Returns TRUE if semaphore was freed, FALSE if semaphore is not in use or not released

Examples
```
if Wait_Sema( "CD_ROM",5 )
   Alert("CD ROM player is not available...")
else
   RunCDProg()
   Free_Sema("CD_ROM")
endif
```

Notes This function releases a semaphore flag after your program is done with it. You can use semaphores to control access to a wide variety of network resources.

Program File WAITSEMA.PRG

FSDATETIME()

Purpose   Gets the file server date and time

Syntax   `<array> := FSDateTime()`

Parameters   None

Returns   Two element array; element one is server date and element two is server time string

Examples
```
LOCAL aDt := FSDateTime()
if date() <> aDt[1]
   Alert("Your station's and the server's"+;
        "date are not syncrhonized." )
endif
```

Notes   This function reads the date and time from the file server. If a problem occurs, the array will be empty when the function returns.

Program File   SERVDT.PRG

GETAMSG()

Purpose Retrieves a message from the message file

Syntax GetaMsg()

Parameters None

Returns NIL

Examples
```
do while inkey(5) <> K_ESC
   GetaMsg()
   do case
   //
   // Process the keystrokes
   //
   endcase
enddo
```

Notes This function checks to see if any messages are pending for the user. If so, the message is shown on the screen.

Program File GETAMSG.PRG

GETFATTR()

Purpose Determines a file's directory attributes

Syntax `<cList> := GetFattr( cFileName )`

Parameters cFileName   Name of file to check

Returns cList   String of attributes

Examples
```
LOCAL cAttr := GetFattr("REPORT.TXT")
if "R" $ cAttr
   Alert("File cannot be overwritten...")
endif
```

Notes This function returns a string with each set attribute in it. The attributes flags are

A	Archive bit
D	Directory
V	Volume label
S	System file
H	Hidden file
R	Read-only file

Program File GETFATTR.PRG

INDEXCORRUPT()

Purpose Spot-checks an index file's header

Syntax <logical> := IndexCorrupt(cFile [,cExtension])

Parameters
cFile   Name of index file to check

cExtension   Version of index file this is supposed to be (NTX, NDX, MDX, IDX, or CDX)

Examples
```
if IndexCorrupt( "CUST1","IDX" )
   Alert("Recreate the customer index files...")
endif
```

Notes This function makes a guess as to whether the file name specified is a valid index file. Clipper 5.2 supports the following index-file formats:

NTX	Clipper's indexing scheme
NDX	dBASE III+/IV indexes
MDX	dBASE multiple tag indexes
IDX	FoxPro indexes
CDX	FoxPro compound indexes

Program File NTXCHK.PRG

INT2CLIP()

Purpose Converts an integer string to a Clipper numeric value

Syntax `<numeric> := Int2Clip( cInteger )`

Parameters cInteger   Binary integer from Novell

Returns numeric   Value of integer

Notes Novell's API calls store integers as two-byte strings in high-low order. Intel microprocessors usually store integers in low-high order. Clipper's BIN2I() function converts Intel-format binary integers to numbers. This function essentially does the same for Novell integers. It is primarily for internal use, but can be used if you develop any of your own API functions.

Program File XLATE.PRG

LETS_CHAT()

Purpose Interactive chat between two stations

Syntax `<logical> := Lets_Chat( nStation )`

Parameters nStation   Workstation to chat with

Returns TRUE if chat enabled, FALSE otherwise

Notes This function uses the message pipe system to chat between two workstations.

Program File LETSCHAT.PRG

LONG2CLIP()

Purpose	Converts a long integer string to a Clipper numeric value
Syntax	`<numeric> := Long2Clip( cInteger )`
Parameters	cInteger Binary long number from Novell
Returns	numeric Value of long
Notes	Novell's API calls store longs as four-byte strings in high-low order. Intel microprocessors usually store numbers in low-high order. Clipper's BIN2L() function converts Intel-format binary longs to numbers. This function essentially does the same for Novell longs. It is primarily for internal use, but can be used if you develop any of your own API functions.
Program File	XLATE.PRG

LSTRING()

Purpose	Pads a string with NULL characters
Syntax	`<cLstring> := Lstring(cString,nSize)`
Parameters	cString Any string value
	nSize Size of string to create
Returns	cLstring A string with the size as the first byte and padded out with NULL characters
Notes	Strings passed to Novell's API calls need to be passed with the first byte as the size and NULL filled. This function converts Clipper strings into Novell-formatted strings. This function is primarily for internal use, but can be used if you develop any of your own API functions.
Program File	XLATE.PRG

MISCINFO()

Purpose Gets an array of miscellaneous server information

Syntax `<array> := N_MiscInfo()`

Parameters None

Returns An array of server information or an empty array if a problem occurs. The array contains the following information:

Element	Type	Contents
1	Char	File-server name
2	Numeric	NetWare major version number
3	Numeric	NetWare minor version number
4	Numeric	Maximum connections allowed
5	Numeric	Connections currently in use
6	Numeric	Maximum connected volumes
7	Numeric	OS revision number
8	Numeric	SFT level
9	Numeric	TTS level
10	Numeric	Peak connections used
11	Numeric	Accounting version number
12	Numeric	VAP version number
13	Numeric	Queuing version number
14	Numeric	Print-server version number
15	Numeric	Virtual-console version number
16	Numeric	Security-restrictions Level
17	Numeric	Internetwork-bridge version number

Examples
```
LOCAL arr_ := MiscInfo()
if !empty(arr_)
  ? "Server.: ",arr_[1]
  ? "Version: ",arr_[2],arr_[3]," "
  ?? arr_[4]," user version"
endif
```

Program File MISCINFO.PRG

MSGMODE()

Purpose Toggles whether messages will be accepted

Syntax `<logical> := MsgMode( <lAccept> )`

Parameters lAccept   Should broadcast messages be accepted?

Returns TRUE if setting updated, FALSE otherwise

Examples
```
MsgMode( .F. )       // Disable messages
index on soundex(CUSTOMER->name) to CUST_SDX
MsgMode( .T. )       // Enable messages
```

Notes This function allows the user to control whether broadcast messages are accepted. Since a broadcast message waits for a keystroke to continue, you might want to disable messages before a critical process gets started.

Program File MSGMODE.PRG

N_ACCTEXPIRE()

Purpose Gets the date this account expires

Syntax `<dExpire> := N_AcctExpire( cUser )`

Parameters cUser   User bindery name

Returns dExpire   Expiration date of user's account

Examples `LOCAL dExpire := N_AcctExpire( N_WhoAmI() )`

Notes This function returns the user's expiration date, which can be used for scheduling purposes to prevent future activities from being scheduled after the user's access date.

Program File USERBIND.PRG

N_ADD2SET()

Purpose   Adds an object to a set

Syntax
```
<logical> := N_Add2Set( cOwner,nOwnType,;
                    cObject,nType,cProperty)
```

Parameters
- cOwner   Bindery object that owns set
- nOwnType   Owner's object type
- cObject   Object to be added to owner's set
- nType   Type of object being added
- cProperty   Set property to add cObject to

Returns   TRUE if added, FALSE otherwise

Examples
```
if ! N_Add2Set( "FINANCE",2,;
                "JOEB",1,"BELONGS_TO" )
   Alert("Couldn't add JOEB ")
endif
```

Notes   This function is used to add an object to a group owned by another object. For example, you can use this function to place a user bindery object into a group.

Program File   ADD2SET.PRG

N_ADDOBJECT()

Purpose Adds an object into the bindery

Syntax
```
<logical> := N_AddObject(cObject,;
                        nType,;
                        cFlag,;
                        cRead,;
                        cWrite )
```

Parameters
cObject	Object to be added to bindery
nType	Type of object being added
cFlag	Static/Dynamic
cRead	Read security
cWrite	Write security

Returns TRUE if added, FALSE otherwise

Examples
```
if ! N_AddObject( "FINANCE",2,"S","L","S" )
   Alert("Couldn't add the FINANCE group!!")
endif
```

Notes This function is used to add a new object into the bindery. You must specify the object name, type, flag, and security for any item added.

Program File ADDOBJ.PRG

N_ADDPROPERTY()

Purpose Adds a property to a bindery object

Syntax
```
<logical> := N_AddProperty( cObject,;
                            nType,;
                            cProperty,;
                            cFlag,;
                            cItemSet,;
                            cRead,;
                            cWrite )
```

Parameters

cObject	Object to add property to
nType	Type of object
cProperty	Set property to add to object
cFlag	Property flag, Static or Dynamic
cItemSet	(I)tem or (S)et property
cRead	Property read security
cWrite	Property write security

Returns TRUE if added, FALSE otherwise

Examples
```
if ! N_AddProperty( "JOEB",1,"FAX_NUMBER",;
                    "S","I","0","0" )
   Alert("Couldn't add FAX_NUMBER!")
endif
```

Notes This function is used to add a property to an existing bindery object. For example, you can use this function to add a fax-number property to a user bindery object. Keep in mind that this function only adds the property, it does not assign a value to it.

Program File ADDPROP.PRG

N_ADDREC()

Purpose Adds a record to a locked file

Syntax <logical> := N_AddRec(nWait)

Parameters nWait   How long to wait before adding the record

Returns TRUE if added, FALSE otherwise

Examples
```
if !N_AddRec()
   Alert("Couldn't add a record to the file!!")
endif
```

Notes This function replaces the ADDREC() function from LOCKS.PRG. The NETWORK.INI file controls how this version of appending a blank record behaves.

Program File N_LOCKS.PRG

N_ATTACH()

Purpose Attempts to connect to a server

Syntax <logical> := N_Attach(cServer)

Parameters cServer   Server name to attempt to attach to

Returns TRUE if attached to specified server, FALSE if cannot attach for some reason

Examples
```
LOCAL aServers := N_ScanBindery( 4 )
LOCAL x
for x := 1 to len(aServers)
   N_Attach(aServers[x])
next
```

Notes Attaching to a server is not the same as logging in to the server. After you successfully attach to the server, you still need to call the login function to be able to use the server's resources.

Program File ATTACH.PRG

N_BALANCE()

Purpose Gets the current account balance for a user

Syntax `<nBalance> := N_Balance( cUser )`

Parameters cUser   User bindery name

Returns nBalance   User's balance if accounting is installed

Examples `LOCAL nBalance := N_Balance( N_WhoAmI() )`

Notes This function returns the current balance for the specified user. If accounting is not installed, zero will be returned. You can use this function to restrict certain program operations to users with sufficient funds.

Program File USERBIND.PRG

N_BINDLEVEL()

Purpose Gets workstation's access level to the bindery

Syntax `aInfo := N_BindLevel()`

Parameters None

Returns An array with three elements: the object's read security, write security, and bindery id. An empty array will be returned if no object is attached to the network.

Examples
```
LOCAL arr_ := N_BindLevel()
LOCAL cWho
if !empty(arr_)
   cWho := N_ObjectName( arr_[3],1 )
   ? "Hello "+alltrim(cWho)
else
   Alert("Not attached to the network...")
endif
```

Notes This function is used to query the workstation to determine the current bindery object attached to it. You can use the object's bindery id with some other bindery functions to determine the user id of the current object.

Program File BNDLEVEL.PRG

N_CANCELCAP()

Purpose   Cancels a capture and returns control to the local printer. The file is not printed.

Syntax   `<logical> := N_CANCELCAP( [<nPrinter>] )`

Parameters   nPrinter   Optional captured printer to cancel

Returns   TRUE if canceled, FALSE otherwise

Examples
```
if N_CancelCap( 1 )
    Alert("All output to printer LPT1 is canceled!")
endif
```

Notes   This function is used to cancel a capture being run on a printer. No output will be set to the network printer; it will all be discarded if the function returns TRUE.

Program File   CANCLCAP.PRG

N_CAPFLAGS()

Purpose Sets the network capture flags

Syntax `<aOldFlags> := N_CapFlags( [<aNewFlags>] )`

Parameters aNewFlags   Optional array of new capture flags to set

Returns aOldFlags   Current capture flags

Examples
```
LOCAL arr_ := N_CapFlags()   // Get current flags
arr_[ 6] := 2                // Make two copies
N_CapFlags( arr_ )           // Reset the capture flags
N_StartCap()                 // Start a CAPTURE process
```

Notes This function is a get/set block to set the capture flags for the default printer. The array consists of the following 12 elements:

Element	Type	Contents
1	Logical	Should banners be printed?
2	Char	Text of banner
3	Numeric	Which local printer is captured?
4	Numeric	Which network printer is serving it?
5	Numeric	Bindery print-queue object id
6	Numeric	Number of copies to print
7	Numeric	Form number
8	Char	Name of form to load in printer
9	Numeric	Job number
10	Numeric	Maximum lines down
11	Numeric	Maximum characters across
12	Numeric	Time-out value, in seconds

Program File CAPFLAGS.PRG

N_CHGVALUE()

Purpose Changes a property's value

Syntax `<logical> := N_ChgValue( cObject,nType,cProperty,xValue )`

Parameters
- cObject — Object name to be updated
- nType — Type of object being updated
- cProperty — Property to change
- xValue — New value for property

Returns TRUE if property value changed, FALSE otherwise

Examples
```
if ! N_ChgValue( "JOEB",1,;
   "FAX_NUMBER","(000) 555-5309")
   Alert("Couldn't update JOEB's fax number")
endif
```

Notes This function is used to change the value for a given property. For example, after adding a property called FAX_NUMBER to a user object, you would use this function to write the person's fax number in.

Program File CHGVALUE.PRG

N_CLEARCON()

Purpose Clears an individual connection

Syntax `<logical> := N_ClearCon( nConnect )`

Parameters nConnect — Workstation you wish to clear connection from

Returns TRUE if connection is cleared, FALSE otherwise

Program File NCLEAR.PRG

N_CLOSECAP()

Purpose	Closes a capture and returns control to the local printer
Syntax	`<nJob> := N_CLOSECAP( [<nPrinter>] )`
Parameters	nPrinter Optional captured printer to close
Returns	Job number for print queue handling printing, or 0 if a problem occurs

Examples	``if N_CloseCap( 1 ) <> 0``
	   ``Alert("Output redirected to your local printer!")``
	``endif``

Notes	This function is used to close a capture being run on a printer. The output will be sent to the network printer.
Program File	CLOSECAP.PRG

N_CLOSEPIPE()

Purpose Closes a message pipe between stations

Syntax `<logical> := N_ClosePipe()`

Parameters None

Returns logical   Was pipe connection closed?

Examples
```
if ! N_OpenPipe( 2 )
   Alert("Couldn't chat with station two")
else
   N_SendPipe( "Where is the budget file")
   do while empty( cMsg := N_GetPipe() )
      if inkey(2) == K_ESC
         exit
      endif
    enddo
    if !empty(cMsg)
       @ 24,00 say cMsg
    endif
    N_ClosePipe()
endif
```

Notes This function closes a pipe connection that was previously established between two workstations.

Program File MSGPIPE.PRG

N_CLOSESEM()

Purpose Closes a semaphore handle

Syntax `logical := N_CloseSem( nHandle )`

Parameters nHandle   Semaphore

Returns TRUE if the semaphore was closed, FALSE otherwise

Examples
```
LOCAL nSemHandle := N_OpenSem("CD_ROM",5)
N_CloseSem(nSemHandle)
```

Notes This function closes a semaphore created from an early semaphore call. You need to save the handle and pass it to this function to close the semaphore.

Program File CLOSSEMA.PRG

N_CONINFO()

Purpose Gets an array of connection information

Syntax <aInfo> := N_ConInfo(cServer|nConnection)

Parameters
- cServer — Server name to report on
- nConnection — Connection number to report

Returns aInfo — Five-element array with structure shown below or empty array if problem occurred

Examples
```
LOCAL arr_ := N_ConInfo( 1 )
if !empty(arr_)
   ? "You've been logged in since ",arr_[4]," at ",arr_[5]
endif
```

Notes This function is used to determine information about the current connection to the server. It returns an array with the following information:

Element	Contents
1	Bindery id
2	Connection number
3	Object name
4	Date logged in
5	Time logged in

Program File CONINFO.PRG

N_CONSOLE()

Purpose   Sends a message to the file server conole

Syntax   `<logical> := N_Console( cMessage )`

Parameters   cMessage   Text of message, up to 55 characters

Returns   TRUE if message sent, FALSE otherwise

Examples   `N_Console("Please LOAD the PC-Atlas CD...")`

Notes   This function is used to send a message to the file console. The message should be under 55 characters. The message is a one-way message, with no feedback; the function merely indicates that the message was sent, not whether it was received.

Program File NCONSOLE.PRG

N_CONSPRIV()

Purpose   Determines if user has console privileges

Syntax   `<logical> := N_ConsPriv()`

Parameters   None

Returns   TRUE if user has console rights, FALSE otherwise

Program File HASCONS.PRG

N_CONTABLE()

Purpose Retrieves an array of connection information

Syntax `arr_ := N_Contable()`

Parameters None

Returns An array of connection information or an empty array if the user is not connected to a file server

Examples
```
LOCAL aConnect := N_ConTable()
LOCAL x
LOCAL nSize := len(aConnect)
? "You are connected to the following servers..."
for x := 1 to nSize
   ? aConnect[x,1]
next
```

Notes The connection table is a two-dimensional array. There are eight connections, each of which has the following pieces of information associated with it:

Element	Type	Contents
1	Char	File-server name
2	Logical	Attached to a server?
3	Numeric	Connection number
4	Numeric	Network node number
5	Numeric	Server network address
6	Numeric	Server node address
7	Numeric	Socket number
8	Numeric	Receive time-out, in seconds
9	Numeric	Bridge node address
10	Numeric	Packet sequence number
11	Numeric	Connection number at server
12	Logical	Is connection active?
13	Numeric	Maximum time-out, in seconds

Program File NCTABLE.PRG

N_CREDLIMIT()

Purpose   Gets the current credit limit for a user

Syntax   `<nCredLimit> := N_CredLimit( cUser )`

Parameters   cUser   User bindery name

Returns   nBalance   User's credit limit if accounting is installed

Examples   `LOCAL nCredLimit := N_CredLimit( N_WhoAmI() )`

Notes   This function returns the current credit limit for the specified user. If accounting is not installed, zero will be returned. You can use this function to restrict certain program operations to users with sufficient funds.

Program File USERBIND.PRG

N_DEFEXPIRE()

Purpose   Checks the default expiration date for new user ids

Syntax   `<dExpire> := N_DefExpire( cServer )`

Parameters   cServer   Server to check

Returns   Date value, or empty date if problem occurred

Examples
```
LOCAL dExpire := N_DefExpire(N_Contable()[1,1])
if date()+7 < dExpire
   Alert("New user-ids will expire "+;
         "in less than a week")
endif
```

Notes   This function is used to see what date the user id could expire on. You might use this date to limit future scheduling to a date before expiration.

Program File FILESERV.PRG

N_DEFSERVER()

Purpose Gets the default server

Syntax `<cServer> := N_DefServer()`

Parameters None

Returns Name of default server

Program File SERVERS.PRG

N_DELFROMSET()

Purpose Removes an object from a set

Syntax
```
<logical> := N_DelFromSet( cOwner,nOwnType,;
                     cObject,nType,cProperty )
```

Parameters
cOwner	Bindery object that owns set
nOwnType	Owner's object type
cObject	Object to be removed to owner's set
nType	Type of object being removed
cProperty	Set property to remove cObject from

Returns TRUE if removed, FALSE otherwise

Examples
```
if ! N_DelFromSet( "FINANCE",2,;
               "JOEB",1,"GROUP_MEMBERS")
   Alert("JOEB cannot be removed")
endif
```

Notes This function is used to remove an object from a group owned by another object.

Program File REMOVSET.PRG

N_DELOBJECT()

Purpose Removes an object from the bindery

Syntax `<logical> := N_DelObject( cObject,nType )`

Parameters
cObject   Object to be removed from bindery
nType   Type of object to be removed

Returns TRUE if removed, FALSE otherwise

Examples
```
if ! N_DelObject( "FINANCE",2 )
   Alert("Couldn't remove the FINANCE group")
endif
```

Notes This function is used to remove a bindery object. Keep in mind that NetWare's security will probably restrict you from removing objects unless the id has supervisory rights.

Program File REMOBJ.PRG

N_DELPROPERTY()

Purpose Removes a property from a bindery object

Syntax `<logical> := N_DelProperty( cObject,nType,cProperty )`

Parameters
- cObject — Object to be updated
- nType — Type of object being updated
- cProperty — Property to remove from object

Returns TRUE if removed, FALSE otherwise

Examples
```
if ! N_DelProperty( "JOEB",1,"FAX_NUMBER" )
   Alert("Couldn't update JOEB")
endif
```

Notes This function is used to remove a property from a bindery object. For example, you can use this function to remove the FAX_NUMBER property from a user id object.

Program File DELPROP.PRG

N_DETACH()

Purpose Attempts to disconnect from a server

Syntax `<logical> := N_Detach(cServer|nConnection)`

Parameters
cServer — Server name to detach from
nConnection — Connection number to detach from

Returns TRUE if connection was detached, FALSE if problem occurred

Examples
```
if N_Detach( 1 )
    ? "Detached from the first server you connected to"
endif
```

Notes This function is used to detach from a server or a connection. Keep in mind that if you detach from a server, you will have to reattach and log in again to be able to do any work on that server.

Program File DETACH.PRG

N_DOWN()

Purpose Brings down the file server

Syntax `N_Down( lForceDown )`

Parameters lForceDown — Force server down regardless of open files

Returns `<logical>` — TRUE if server is down, FALSE if server couldn't be brought down

Examples Do you really need an example of downing the file server?

Program File DOWN.PRG

N_EXAMSEM()

Purpose Examines a semaphore handle and returns the semaphore value

Syntax nValue := N_ExamSem(nHandle)

Parameters nHandle   Semaphore handle returned from N_OPENSEMA()

Returns Numeric value associated with this semaphore, -99 if semaphore does not exist or problem occurred

Examples
```
LOCAL nSemHandle := N_OpenSem("CD_ROM",5)

if N_ExamSem(nSemHandle) < 2
   Alert("Too many people waiting,"+;
       " try later!!")
endif

N_CloseSem(nSemHandle)
```

Notes This function is used to determine the current value for a semaphore. This allows you to control your program's operation based on NetWare semaphores.

Program File EXAMSEMA.PRG

N_FILLOCK()

Purpose Locks the file in the current work area

Syntax `<logical> := N_FilLock( nWait )`

Parameters nWait   How long to wait to lock current work area

Returns TRUE if locked, FALSE otherwise

Examples
```
if !N_FilLock()
   Alert("Couldn't update the entire file!!")
else
   replace all TAX_RATE with .08
endif
```

Notes This function replaces the FILLOCK() function from LOCKS.PRG. The NETWORK.INI file controls how this version of locking a work area operates.

Program File N_LOCKS.PRG

N_FLUSHCAP()

Purpose Forces the network to print the current capture file

Syntax `<nJob> := N_FlushCap( [<nPrinter>] )`

Parameters nPrinter   Optional captured printer to flush

Returns Job number for print queue handling printing, or 0 if problem occurred

Examples
```
if N_FlushCap( 1 ) <> 0
   //
endif
```

Notes This function is used to send a capture file to the network printer. The capture will not be stopped and all subsequent output will be redirected, as well.

Program File FLUSHCAP.PRG

N_FULLNAME()

Purpose Gets the user's full name

Syntax `<cFullName> := N_FullName( cUser )`

Parameters cUser   User bindery name

Returns cFullName   Full name of this user

Examples `LOCAL cName := N_FullName( N_WhoAmI() )`

Notes This function returns the user's identification string—usually his or her full name.

Program File USERBIND.PRG

N_GETMSG()

Purpose Gets the next pending message

Syntax `<cMessage> := N_GetMsg()`

Parameters None

Returns cMessage   Message text, or "" if no message was received

Examples
```
LOCAL cMsg := N_GetMsg()
if !empty(cMsg)
   @ 24,00 say padr(cMsg,80) color "I"
endif
```

Notes This function returns any pending broadcast messages for the current workstation.

Program File NGETMSG.PRG

N_GETPIPE()

Purpose Gets the messages from the pipe

Syntax `<cMessage> := N_GetPipe()`

Parameters None

Returns cMessage   Text of message from other workstation

Examples
```
if ! N_OpenPipe( 2 )
   Alert("Couldn't chat with station two")
else
   N_SendPipe( "Where is the budget file?")
   do while empty( cMsg := N_GetPipe() )
      if inkey(2) == K_ESC
         exit
      endif
   enddo
   if !empty(cMsg)
      @ 24,00 say cMsg
   endif
endif
```

Notes This function receives a message from the workstation you are connected to.

Program File MSGPIPE.PRG

N_INIT()

Purpose Initializes file-wide settings from NETWORK.INI

Syntax `N_Init(cFile)`

Parameters cFile   Optional file of network parameters

Returns NIL

Examples `N_Init()`

Notes This function allows you to use an .INI-type text file to control message text and timing for the network locking features. The file name defaults to NETWORK.INI if not supplied.

Program File N_LOCKS.PRG

N_ISINSET()

Purpose Determines if an object is within another object's set property

Syntax
```
<logical> := N_IsInSet( cObject1,nType1,;
                       cObject2,nType2,cProperty)
```

Parameters
cObject1	Object to be tested for ownership
nType1	Type of owner object
cObject2	Object to be tested for membership
nType2	Type of member object
cProperty	Set property to test

Returns TRUE if in group, FALSE otherwise

Examples
```
if IsInSet( "FINANCE",2,;
            "JOEB",1,"GROUP_MEMBERS" )
   FinReports()    // Financial report
else
   Alert("Cannot perform this menu option")
endif
```

Notes This function is used to determine if one object is a member of the specified property for another object. For example, you can use this function to determine if a user should be allowed to perform a menu option.

Program File ISINSET.PRG

N_ISMANAGER()

Purpose Checks if user is the manager of a group

Syntax <logical> := N_IsManager(cObject,cGroup)

Parameters
cObject   Object to be tested
cGroup   Group to test

Returns TRUE if object is a manager, FALSE otherwise

Examples
```
LOCAL aMenu := {}
Aadd(aMenu,"Enter Customer")
Aadd(aMenu,"Create Invoice")
if N_IsMember( N_WhoAmI(),"FINANCE")
   Aadd(aMenu,"Issue Credit Memo")
endif
if N_IsManager( N_WhoAmI(),"FINANCE")
   Aadd(aMenu,"Write off charges")
endif
```

Notes This function is used to see if an object is a manager of a group. It can be used to restrict menu choices to only managers of a department.

Program File INGROUP.PRG

N_ISMEMBER()

Purpose Checks for group membership

Syntax `<logical> := N_IsMember( cObject,cGroup )`

Parameters
cObject Object to be tested
cGroup Group to test

Returns TRUE if object is a member, FALSE otherwise

Examples
```
LOCAL aMenu := {}
Aadd(aMenu,"Enter Customer")
Aadd(aMenu,"Create Invoice")
if N_IsMember( N_WhoAmI(),"FINANCE")
   Aadd(aMenu,"Issue Credit Memo")
endif
if N_IsManager( N_WhoAmI(),"FINANCE")
   Aadd(aMenu,"Write off charges")
endif
```

Notes This function is used to see if an object is a member of a group. It can be used to restrict menu choices to only members of a department.

Program File INGROUP.PRG

N_ISOPERATOR()

Purpose Checks if the user has operator rights to the server

Syntax `<logical> := N_IsOperator( cUser,cServer )`

Parameters
cUser   User id to test
cServer   Server to check

Returns TRUE if user has rights, FALSE otherwise

Examples
```
if !N_IsOperator(N_WhoAmi(),N_Contable()[1,1])
   Alert("Don't have sufficient rights")
endif
```

Notes This function is used to see if the user id has operator rights on a server. You could use this function to control access to parts of your Clipper application.

Program File FILESERV.PRG

N_LOGIN()

Purpose Attempts to log in to a server

Syntax `<logical> := N_Login(cUser,cPassword)`

Parameters
cUser   User bindery object name
cPassword   User password

Returns TRUE if successfully logged in, FALSE if not logged in

Program File LOGIN.PRG

N_LOGOUT()

Purpose Attempts to log out from one or more servers

Syntax `<logical> := N_Logout(cServer|nConnection)`

Parameters
cServer Server name to log out from
nConnection Entry from connection table (1–8) to log out

Returns TRUE if logged out successfully, FALSE if not logged out

Program File LOGOUT.PRG

N_MANAGERS()

Purpose Returns a list of managers of a group

Syntax `<aUsers> := N_Managers( cGroup )`

Parameters cGroup Bindery group name to check

Returns aUsers Array of managers within the group

Examples `LOCAL aBosses := N_Managers( "FINANCE" )`

Notes This function returns an array of user ids who are managers of a particular group.

Program File GRPUSERS.PRG

N_MEMBERS()

Purpose	Returns a list of members in a group
Syntax	`<aUsers> := N_Members( cGroup )`
Parameters	cGroup Bindery group name to check
Returns	aUsers Array of users within group
Examples	`LOCAL aMembers := N_Members( "FINANCE" )`
Notes	This function returns an array of user ids who are members of a particular group.
Program File	GRPUSERS.PRG

N_OBJECTID()

Purpose	Returns the object id for a given object
Syntax	`nIdCode := N_ObjectId( <cObject>,<nObjType> )`
Parameters	cObject Object name
	nObjType Type of object
Returns	nIdCode Bindery id number
Examples	`LOCAL nId := N_ObjectID( N_WhoAmi(),1 )`
Notes	Every object in the bindery has a unique number to identify it. This function can be used to determine the number for any object.
Program File	OBJID.PRG

N_OBJECTNAME()

Purpose   Returns the object name for a given object

Syntax   `cObject := N_ObjectName( <nObjectId> )`

Parameters nIdCode   Bindery id number

Returns   cObject   Object name

Examples   `LOCAL cWho := N_ObjectName( 1 ) // Should be SUPERVISOR`

Notes   Every object in the bindery has a unique number to identify it. This function can be used to determine the object's name from a given id number.

Program File OBJNAME.PRG

N_OPENPIPE()

Purpose   Opens a message pipe between stations

Syntax   `<logical> := N_OpenPipe( nStation )`

Parameters nStation   Workstation with which to attempt to connect

Returns   TRUE if connection established, FALSE otherwise

Examples
```
if ! N_OpenPipe( 2 )
   Alert("Couldn't chat with station two")
endif
```

Notes   This function attempts to open pipe communication between two workstations. If both stations connect, the message-piping functions can be used to chat between workstations.

Program File MSGPIPE.PRG

N_OPENSEM()

Purpose	Opens a semaphore object and returns its handle
Syntax	`nHandle := N_OpenSem( cLabel,nInitial )`
Parameters	cLabel Semaphore label name
	nInitial Initial value to set semaphore to
Returns	nHandle Handle for future references to this semaphore, 0 if error occurred
Examples	`LOCAL nHandle := N_OpenSem( "CD_ROM_DRIVE",10 )`
Notes	This function opens or creates a semaphore with the specified maximum value. This is a NetWare semaphore that other programs can recognize as well.
Program File	OPENSEMA.PRG

N_PREFSERVER()

Purpose	Get/set block for the preferred server
Syntax	`<cServer> := N_PrefServer(cServer|nConnection)`
Parameters	cServer Server name to make preferred server
	nConnection Connection number (1–8) to make preferred server
Returns	Original preferred server
Program File	SERVERS.PRG

N_PRIMSERVER()

Purpose Get/set block for the primary server

Syntax `<cServer> := N_PrimServer(cServer|nConnection)`

Parameters
cServer   Server name to make primary server
nConnection   Connection number (1–8) to make primary server

Returns Original primary server

Program File SERVERS.PRG

N_PROPERTIES()

Purpose Scans the bindery object for properties

Syntax `aProperties := N_Properties( cObject,nType )`

Parameters
cObject   Object to determine properties for
nType   Type of object being checked

Returns aProperties   Array of properties associated with this object

Examples
```
LOCAL arr_ := N_Properties("JOEB",1 )
LOCAL x
if !empty(arr_)
    for x := 1 to len(arr_)
        ? x,arr_[x]
    next
endif
```

Notes This function is used to determine what properties are associated with this object. You can also use the N_PROPVAL() function to determine the value for any of the properties.

Program File PROPERTY.PRG

N_PROPVAL()

Purpose Returns the value of a specified property

Syntax
```
xValue := N_PropVal( cObject,;
                     ntype,;
                     cProperty,;
                     lClean )
```

Parameters

	cObject	Object to be queried
	nType	Type of object being queried
	cProperty	Property value to extract
	lClean	Should NULLS be removed?

Returns xValue Varies depending upon object and property

Examples
```
LOCAL cUser := N_WhoAmI()
if !empty(cUser)
   ? "Hello "
   ?? N_PropVal(cUser,1,"IDENTIFICATION",.T.)
endif
```

Notes This function is used to determine the value for a property from another object. For example, you can use this function to determine the full name of a bindery object.

Program File PROPVAL.PRG

N_QJOBLIST()

Purpose Gets the list of jobs within the queue

Syntax <aJobs> := N_QjobList(nQueue)

Parameters nQueue   Bindery id for queue to check

Returns Array of jobs within specified queue

Examples
```
LOCAL aQueues   := N_PrintQs()
LOCAL aAllJobs  := {}
LOCAL nSize     := len(aQueues)
LOCAL x
for x := 1 to nSize
   Aadd(aAlljobs,;
      N_QjobList(N_OjectId(aQueues[x],3)) )
next
```

Notes This function returns a list of jobs in the specified printer queue.

Program File QJOBLIST.PRG

N_QPOSITION()

Purpose Queries/changes a job's print position

Syntax `<logical> := N_Qposition(nQueue,nJob,nSpot)`

Parameters
nQueue   Bindery print-queue id
nJob   Job number in queue
nSpot   Requested new position

Returns TRUE if changed, FALSE otherwise

Examples
```
if N_Qposition( nQueue,nJob,2 )
   Alert("Couldn't change job's spot")
endif
```

Notes This function attempts to assign a new position to the specified job. For example, you can use the function to place a high-priority job near the top of the print queue.

Program File QPOSIT.PRG

N_QREMOVE()

Purpose   Removes a job from the print queue

Syntax   `<logical> := N_Qremove(nQueue,nJob)`

Parameters   nQueue   Bindery id of queue to be updated
                  nJob   Job number to remove from queue

Returns   TRUE if job removed, FALSE otherwise

Examples
```
LOCAL arr_ := N_PrintQs()
Q_Remove( N_ObjectId(arr_[1],3),nJob )
```

Notes   This function is used to remove a job from a NetWare print queue.

Program File QREMOVE.PRG

N_RECLOCK()

Purpose   Attempts to lock a record

Syntax   `<logical> := N_RecLock( nWait )`

Parameters   nWait   How long to wait to lock current record

Returns   TRUE if locked, FALSE otherwise

Examples
```
if !N_RecLock()
   Alert("Couldn't update the record!!")
else
   replace BALANCE with BALANCE + nTransAmt
   unlock
endif
```

Notes   This function replaces the RECLOCK() function from LOCKS.PRG. The NETWORK.INI file controls how this version of record locking operates.

Program File N_LOCKS.PRG

N_RENOBJECT()

Purpose Renames a bindery object

Syntax `<logical> := N_RenObject( cOld,nType,cNew )`

Parameters
cOld   Original name of object
nType   Type of object being renamed
cNew   New name of bindery object

Returns TRUE if changed, FALSE otherwise

Examples
```
if ! N_RenObject( "SARAHL",1,"SARAHB" )
   Alert("Couldn't change the object name")
endif
```

Notes This function is used to rename an object in the bindery.

Program File RENOBJ.PRG

N_SCANBINDERY()

Purpose Scans the bindery for a given object type

Syntax `aObjects := N_scanBindery( nType )`

Parameters nType   Type of objects to be returned

Returns aObjects   List of all objects of specified type

Examples
```
LOCAL aGroups := N_ScanBindery(2)
LOCAL aUsers  := N_ScanBindery(1)
```

Notes This function is used to get a list of all objects in a bindery type. For example, servers are group 4, so N_SCANBINDERY(4) would return all servers within the bindery.

Program File SCANBIND.PRG

N_SENDMSG()

Purpose Sends a message to another workstation

Syntax `<logical> := N_SendMsg( cMessage,nStation )`

Parameters
cMessage   Text of message to send
nStation   Station to send message to

Returns TRUE if message was sent, FALSE otherwise

Examples `N_SendMsg( "PIZZA for lunch",15 )`

Notes This function sends a broadcast message to the requested station. There is no feedback as to whether the station received it, just that the network sent the message.

Program File NMESSAGE.PRG

N_SENDPIPE()

Purpose Sends a text message between stations

Syntax `<logical> := N_SendPipe( cMessage )`

Parameters cMessage   Text message to send to connected station

Returns TRUE if message sent, FALSE otherwise

Examples
```
if ! N_OpenPipe( 2 )
   Alert("Couldn't chat with station two")
else
   N_SendPipe( "Where is the budget file?")
endif
```

Notes This function sends a message between two previously connected workstations.

Program File MSGPIPE.PRG

N_SERVLOGIN()

Purpose	Get/set block for those server logins that are allowed
Syntax	`<logical> := N_ServLogin( [lSetting] )`
Parameters	lSetting Optional TRUE allows login, FALSE disables
Returns	logical Previous setting of logins allowed
Program File	SERVER.PRG

N_SETDATE()

Purpose	Sets the server's date and time
Syntax	`N_SetDate( dDate,cTime )`
Parameters	dDate Date to set server to cTime Time to set server to
Returns	TRUE if date and time are set, FALSE otherwise
Program File	NSETDT.PRG

N_SHELLVER()

Purpose   Retrieves network shell information

Syntax   `cVersion := N_ShellVer()`

Parameters   None

Returns   cVersion   Character representing NETX shell version

Examples
```
? "Running "+N_shellver()+" of the NETx shell..."
```

Notes   This function is used to determine which version of the shell software is currently loaded.

Program File   SHELLVER.PRG

N_SIGNALSEM()

Purpose   Signal semaphore that we are done

Syntax   `logical := N_SignalSem( nHandle )`

Parameters   nHandle   Sempahore handle from N_OPENSEMA()

Returns   TRUE if semaphore released, FALSE otherwise

Examples
```
if N_WaitSem("CD_ROM_DEVICE",10 )
   // CD_ROM()
   N_SignalSem("CD_ROM_DEVICE")
else
   Alert("CD ROM player is not available...")
endif
```

Notes   This function releases a semaphore after the process is complete. Once a semaphore's count reaches zero, the semaphore will be removed.

Program File   NETSEMA.PRG

N_STARTCAP()

Purpose Allows capture of local printers from within a Clipper program

Syntax `<logical> := N_StartCap( [nPrinter] )`

Parameters nPrinter   Local printer number to capture. If not specified, will be default printer.

Returns TRUE if capture started, FALSE otherwise

Examples
```
N_StartCap(1)             // Open a spool file
set printer to lpt1       // Open the local printer
set print on              //
set console off           //
// Print commands
N_EndCap()
```

Notes This function redirects all output from the designated printer to a network spool file. When N_FLUSHCAP() or N_ENDCAP() is called, the spool file is then printed.

Program File STARTCAP.PRG

N_UNIQUE()

Purpose Returns a unique file name

Syntax `<cFileName> := N_Unique( [cExtension] )`

Parameters cExtension   Extension file name should have; defaults to TXT

Returns cFileName   Name of unique file

Examples
```
if "" == ( cName := N_Unique(IndexExt()) )
   Alert("Couldn't create an index...")
else
   index on CUST->zip_code to (cName)
endif
```

Notes This function is used to create a unique file name. It does this simply by incrementing a counter until a file not in use is found. Remember to have your program erase any file it creates.

Program File UNIQUE.PRG

N_USERGROUPS()

Purpose Gets a list of groups of which a user is a member

Syntax `<aGroups> := N_UserGroups( cUser )`

Parameters cUser   User bindery name

Returns aGroups   List of group names, or empty if problem occurred

Examples `LOCAL aGroups := N_UserGroups( N_WhoAmI() )`

Notes This function returns a list of groups of which the specified user is a member.

Program File USERBIND.PRG

N_WAITSEM()

Purpose Waits for semaphore resource

Syntax `logical := N_WaitSem( nHandle,nTimeOut )`

Parameters
nHandle   Sempahore handle from N_OPENSEMA()
nTimeOut   Number of seconds to wait for semaphore

Returns TRUE if semaphore is available, FALSE otherwise

Examples
```
if N_WaitSem("CD_ROM_DEVICE",10 )
   // CD_ROM()
   N_SignalSem("CD_ROM_DEVICE")
else
    Alert("CD ROM player is not ready...")
endif
```

Notes This function waits a specified number of seconds for a semaphore to become available. Semaphores can be used to control access to network resources and data.

Program File NETSEMA.PRG

N_WHATNET()

Purpose Determines which network, if any, is loaded

Syntax <cNetwork> := N_WhatNet()

Parameters None

Returns
- "N"   Novell NetWare
- "L"   LANtastic
- ""   Unknown or not attached to network

Examples
```
LOCAL cWhere := N_WhatNet()
if cWhere <> "N"
   Alert("This program only runs on NetWare...")
   cls
   quit
endif
```

Notes This function is used to determine what network software the user is running.

Program File WHATNET.PRG

N_WHO2BLAME()

Purpose Gets the file-server installation array

Syntax `<array> := N_Who2Blame()`

Parameters None

Returns Array of installation information

Examples
```
LOCAL arr_ := N_Who2Blame()
if !empty(arr_)
   Alert("Call "+alltrim(arr_[1])+" for support")
endif
```

Notes This function is used to extract the installation and network revision information from the server. The returned array contains the following four elements:

Element	Contents
1	Company that installed NetWare
2	Revision number
3	Revision date
4	Copyright information

Program File WHOBLAME.PRG

N_WHOAMI()

Purpose Gets workstation's user id

Syntax cUser := N_WhoAmI()

Parameters None

Returns cUser   Bindery object name for current connection

Examples
```
LOCAL cUser := N_WhoAmi()
if !empty(cUser)
   Alert("Must be on a network to run...")
else
   LogStart(cUser,"MAIN MENU")
   MainMenu(cUser)
   LogEnd(cUser,"MAIN MENU")
endif
```

Notes This function is used to determine the bindery object name for the current connection. You could use this function to determine a user's id code for logging purposes.

Program File WHOAMI.PRG

NET_USE()

Purpose More robust file-opening routine for network programming for use with Clipper

Syntax
```
<logical> := Net_Use(cFile,lExclusive,nWait,;
            cAlias,lNewArea,lReadOnly,cDriver)
```

Parameters

cFile	.DBF file to attempt to open
lExclusive	Opening file for exclusive use?
nWait	Amount of time to wait for opening
cAlias	Optional alias to use
lNewArea	Should file be opened in new work area?
lReadOnly	Is file being opened for read-only?
cDriver	Which data driver should be used?

Returns TRUE if file opened, FALSE otherwise

Examples
```
if ! Net_use( "CUSTOMER",.F.,10,,.T.,.F.,"DBFNTX")
   Alert("Couldn't open the customer file")
endif
```

Notes This function is used open a database file for use. Additional checks are done to ensure you are trying to open a valid .DBF file.

Program File N_OPEN.PRG

NETWARE()

Purpose Shell for calling NetWare interrupts

Syntax
```
<nResult> := NetWare( nService,;
                      cRequest,@cReply )
```

Parameters
- nService — DOS service to call
- cRequest — Request packet
- cReply — Reply packet, passed by reference

Returns <nResult> — Result from AX register

Program File NETWARE.PRG

OPENSEMAPH()

Purpose Opens a sempahore .DBF file

Syntax <nValue> := OpenSemaph(cName,nValue)

Parameters
- cName — Name of semaphore to open
- nValue — Initial value to set sempahore to

Returns nValue — Semaphore value, or -99 if problem occurred

Examples
```
if OpenSemaPh("CD_ROM",5) <> -99
   ? QuerySemaPh("CD_ROM")
   CloseSemaPh("CD_ROM")
endif
```

Notes This function opens the requested semaphore name.

Program File SEM.PRG

P_CANCEL()

Purpose Checks to see if the Escape key was pressed

Syntax `<logical> := P_Cancel()`

Parameters None

Returns FALSE to continue printing, TRUE if Escape key was pressed

Examples
```
if P_Where()                        // Select where to print
   if P_Start()                     // Start the printout
      go top
      do while !eof() .and. !P_Cancel()
         ? CUSTOMER->name,CUSTOMER->balance
         skip +1
      enddo
      P_End()                       // Finish the printout
   endif
endif
```

Notes This function checks the keyboard buffer to see if the Escape key was pressed. If it was, the function sets a variable instructing the P_END() function call to cancel printing.

Program File PSTUFF.PRG

P_END()

Purpose   Finishes the report and prints it

Syntax   `<logical> := P_End()`

Parameters   None

Returns   NIL

Examples
```
if P_Where()                    // Select where to print
   if P_Start()                 // Start the printout
      go top
      do while !eof() .and. !P_Cancel()
         ? CUSTOMER->name,CUSTOMER->balance
         skip +1
      enddo
      P_End()                   // Finish the printout
   endif
endif
```

Notes   This function starts the printer or displays the report to the screen, depending upon the option selected during the P_WHERE() function. If the P_CANCEL() function returned TRUE, then the P_END() function attempts to abort the printing.

Program File PSTUFF.PRG

P_START()

Purpose Sets up the environment for printing

Syntax `<logical> := P_Start()`

Parameters None

Returns TRUE if everything set up OK, FALSE if problem occurred

Examples
```
if P_Where()                    // Select where to print
   if P_Start()                 // Start the printout
      go top
      do while !eof() .and. !P_Cancel()
         ? CUSTOMER->name,CUSTOMER->balance
         skip +1
      enddo
      P_End()                   // Finish the printout
   endif
endif
```

Notes This function is used to set the printer or start a network capture, depending upon what the user picked when P_WHERE() was called.

Program File PSTUFF.PRG

P_WHERE()

Purpose Selects where to print a report

Syntax <logical> := P_Where()

Parameters None

Returns TRUE if printer selected, FALSE if Escape key pressed

Examples
```
if P_Where()                  // Select where to print
   if P_Start()                // Start the printout
      go top
      do while !eof() .and. !P_Cancel()
         ? CUSTOMER->name,CUSTOMER->balance
         skip +1
      enddo
      P_End()                  // Finish the printout
   endif
endif
```

Notes This function is used to select where a report or file should be printed. It checks the bindery to get the name of the network printers and presents them in a picklist for the user.

Program File PSTUFF.PRG

PUTAMSG()

Purpose Places a message into the message file

Syntax `<logical> := PutaMsg( cToUser,cMessage )`

Parameters
- cToUser   Who message is written to
- cMessage   Short text of message

Returns TRUE if message added, FALSE otherwise

Examples `PutAMsg( "GREGL","Pizza for Lunch?")`

Notes This function is used to add a message to a common message file. When the designated user next checks his or her message file, the message will appear on screen.

Program File PUTAMSG.PRG

Q_ADD()

Purpose Adds a file to the print queue

Syntax `<lSuccess> := Q_add( cFilename )`

Parameters cFilename Name of file to add to print queue

Returns lSuccess TRUE if file added, FALSE otherwise

Examples
```
if !Q_Add( "REPORT.TXT" )    // Couldn't add to the
   set printer to LPT        // printer queue, so we
   set console off           // can print it directly
   set print on
   tmp := memoread( "REPORT.TXT" )
   ?? memoline( tmp,78,1 )
   for x := 2 to mlcount( tmp,78 )
      ? memoline( tmp,78,x )
   next
   set print off
   set console on
endif
```

Notes This function is used to add a file to the DOS print queue. If DOS's PRINT command has been installed, you can place a file into the queue for background printing.

Program File QADD.PRG

Q_CANCEL()

Purpose Cancels all jobs in the DOS print queue

Syntax `<logical> := Q_cancel()`

Parameters None

Returns lSuccess TRUE if all jobs were canceled, FALSE otherwise

Program File QCANCEL.PRG

Q_INSTALLED()

Purpose Checks installed state of PRINT.EXE

Syntax `<logical> := Q_installed()`

Parameters None

Returns lInstalled   TRUE if installed, FALSE otherwise

Examples
```
if Q_Installed()                    // If PRINT is installed,
   set printer to temp.txt          // then we print to a file
else                                // for queueing; otherwise,
   set printer to LPT1              // we go directly to the
endif                               // printer
set console off
set print on
```

Notes This function checks if the DOS PRINT program has been loaded.

Program File QINSTALL.PRG

Q_REMOVE()

Purpose Removes a file from the print queue

Syntax `<logical> := Q_remove( cFilename )`

Parameter cFilename

Returns lSuccess   TRUE if removed, FALSE otherwise

Examples
```
if ! Q_Remove( "REPORT.TXT" )
   Alert("Couldn't remove the REPORT.TXT file")
endif
```

Notes This function removes a file from the DOS print queue. It returns TRUE if the file was removed or FALSE if a problem occurs.

Program File QDELETE.PRG

QUERYSEMAPH()

Purpose Queries a semaphore .DBF file

Syntax `<nValue> := QuerySemaph( cName )`

Parameters cName Name of semaphore to query

Returns nValue Semaphore current value, or –99 if problem occurred

Examples
```
if OpenSemaPh("CD_ROM",5) <> -99
   ? QuerySemaPh("CD_ROM")
   CloseSemaPh("CD_ROM")
endif
```

Notes This function returns the value of the requested semaphore.

Program File SEM.PRG

READCONFIG()

Purpose Initializes file-wide settings

Syntax `ReadConfig( cFile )`

Parameters cFile File name containing configuration information. Defaults to USER.INI

Returns NIL

Examples
```
ReadConfig()
? What_Is(1)    // Regular color string
```

Notes This function reads the configuration file and updates the static array values. If the file does not exist, it will be created.

Program File PASSIVE.PRG

SETAPPT()

Purpose Allows an appointment date and time to be set

Syntax `<aApptInfo> = SetAppt()`

Parameters None

Returns Three-element array containing the appointment date in element one and the appointment time in element two. The third element consists of notes about the appointment. If the user pressed Escape, then an empty array will be returned.

Examples
```
LOCAL arr_ := SetAppt()
if !empty(arr_)
   select APPT_LOG
   append blank
   replace APPT_LOG->date   with arr_[1],;
           APPT_LOG->time   with arr_[2],;
           APPT_LOG->notes  with arr_[3]
   unlock
endif
```

Notes This function opens a calendar that allows the user to select a date and time. It will also allow the user to write a note about this appointment.

Program File SETAPPT.PRG

SETFATTR()

Purpose Sets a file's attributes

Syntax `<logical> := setfattr( cFile,cAttr )`

Parameters
cFile   File name to change attributes of
cAttr   New set of file attributes

Returns TRUE if attributes changed, FALSE otherwise

Examples
```
if ("R" $ x:= GetFattr("CUSTOMER.DBF") )
    SetFattr( "CUSTOMER.DBF", strtran(x,"R" )
endif
```

Notes This function changes the specified file's attributes. It is primarily used to remove the read-only flag from a file.

Program File FIXEM.PRG

USESEMA()

Purpose Allows semaphore communication by using a .DBF file

Syntax `<logical> := N_UseSema( cName,nMax )`

Parameters
cName   Name of semaphore
nMax   Maximum entries allowed for semaphore

Returns TRUE if semaphore available, FALSE otherwise

Examples
```
if ! UseSema( "CD_ROM",2 )
    Alert("The CD ROM player is not ready..")
endif
```

Notes This function creates a new semaphore or accesses an existing one. If the semaphore is created or available, TRUE will be returned.

Program File USESEMA.PRG

VALIDDBF()

Purpose Checks that the file specified is a valid dBASE file

Syntax `<numeric> := VALIDDBF( cFile )`

Parameters

cFile	.DBF file name, with no extension

Returns

0	Everything OK
-1	File is corrupt
-2	File does not exist
-3	DBF file is set to read-only
-4	Memo file is missing
>0	DOS error
2	File not found
3	Path not found
4	Too many files open
5	Access denied
6	Invalid handle
8	Insufficient memory
15	Invalid drive specified
19	Attempted to write to write-protected disk
21	Drive not ready
23	Data CRC error
29	Write fault
30	Read fault
32	Sharing violation
33	Lock violation

Examples
```
if ValidDBF("CUSTOMER") <> 0
   Alert("CUSTOMER is not a valid DBF file")
endif
```

Notes This function examines a .DBF file using the low-level file functions and makes a guess as to whether the file is a valid .DBF. If the file should have a corresponding memo file, the function checks if it exists also.

Program File   VALIDDBF.PRG

VALIDNTX()

Purpose Validates that an index appears OK and optionally re-creates it

Syntax `<numeric> := VALIDNTX( cFile,cExpr,lCreate )`

Parameters
cFile	Index file name, with no extension
cExpr	Expression on which file is indexed
lCreate	Can index be created if needed?

Returns
0	Everything OK
-1	File is corrupt
-2	File does not exist and can't be created
-3	Index file is set to read-only
>0	DOS error
2	File not found
3	Path not found
4	Too many files open
5	Access denied
6	Invalid handle
8	Insufficient memory
15	Invalid drive specified
19	Attempted to write to write-protected disk
21	Drive not ready
23	Data CRC error
29	Write fault
30	Read fault
32	Sharing violation
33	Lock violation

Examples
```
if ValidNTX("CUST1","CUST_CODE",.T.) <> 0
   Alert("CUST1 is unavailable...")
endif
```

Notes This function examines an index file using the low-level file functions and makes a guess as to whether the file is a valid .NTX. The expression is stored with the passed expression to see if they match.

Program File VALIDNTX.PRG

WAIT_SEMA()

Purpose Waits for a semaphore before continuing

Syntax `<logical> := Wait_Sema( cName,nWaitTime )`

Parameters
cName — Name of semaphore
nWaitTime — Number of seconds to wait

Returns TRUE if semaphore available, FALSE if not

Examples
```
if Wait_Sema( "CD_ROM",5 )
   Alert("CD ROM player is not available...")
endif
```

Notes This function is used to wait a specified number of seconds for a semaphore flag to become available. You can use semaphores to control access to a wide variety of network resources.

Program File WAITSEMA.PRG

WHAT_IS()

Purpose Returns the selected parameter's value

Syntax `xValue := What_is( nOffset )`

Parameters nOffset   Array element to return

Returns xValue   Value of array element

Examples
```
#define  REGULAR_COLOR   What_Is(1)
#define  HEADER_COLOR    What_Is(2)
#define  FOOTER_COLOR    What_Is(3)

setcolor(REGULAR_COLOR)
scroll()
@ 00,00 say space(80) color HEADER_COLOR
@ 24,00 say space(80) color FOOTER_COLOR
```

Notes This function returns an array element from the static array created by the configuration functions. You would normally create preprocessor #DEFINEs to improve the readability of the function calls.

Program File PASSIVE.PRG

WRITECONFIG()

Purpose Writes configuration information to a disk

Syntax `WriteConfig( cFile )`

Parameters cFile   File name to be written from system global array. Defaults to USER.INI

Returns NIL

Examples `WriteConfig( "MAIL.INI" )`

Notes This function writes the configuration file with the static array values.

Program File PASSIVE.PRG

Appendix B: Sources for Further Information about Clipper and NetWare

In this book, we have covered many aspects of programming Clipper applications to run on a Novell network. In this appendix, we list where you can obtain more information about Clipper and NetWare.

Products

CA-Clipper is published by Computer Associates, located in Islandia, NY. For more information about CA-Clipper and other Computer Associates products, you can contact Computer Associates at (800) 342-5224 or (516) 342-5224.

NetWare is published by Novell, Inc., located in Provo, UT. For more information about NetWare and other Novell products, you can contact Novell at (800) 453-1267 or (801) 429-7000.

Publications

There are two magazines dedicated specifically to Clipper programming and development. There are also several magazines available on NetWare. A few of these are briefly described here.

THE AQUARIUM

The Aquarium is a monthly disk-based technical journal for Clipper. It includes an integrated message center that allows Clipper developers to get fast answers to their questions via the Grumpfish BBS. The magazine is published monthly and contains between 80 and 100 pages of technical Clipper issues and product reviews. Greg Lief and Joe Booth (coauthors of this book) are regular authors for *The Aquarium*.

For more information about *The Aquarium*, contact Grumpfish at:

>Grumpfish, Inc.
>
>2450 Lancaster Drive, NE, Suite 206
>
>Salem, OR 97305
>
>Tel: (800) 367-7613
>
>   (503) 588-1815
>
>Fax: (503) 588-1980
>
>BBS: (503) 588-7572
>
>CIS: 71064,2543 or 70673,355

REFERENCE(CLIPPER): THE INDEPENDENT GUIDE TO CLIPPER EXPERTISE

Reference(Clipper) is a 24-page magazine of technical information and product reviews about Clipper. It is published monthly and does not contain any advertising. Recent issues have covered topics such as array-based table systems, linker reviews, and scatter/gather routines with Clipper 5.01.

For more information, you can contact:

>Pinnacle Publishing
>
>18000 72nd Avenue South
>
>Kent, WA 98032
>
>Tel: (800) 231-1293
>
>   (206) 251-1900

INSIDE NETWARE

Inside NetWare is a technical publication of the Cobb Group. It is aimed toward NetWare administrators and supervisors and contains plain-English tips and techniques to solve network problems. Each monthly issue contains about 20 pages. Past issues have covered topics such as managing server and workstation memory, troubleshooting a network, choosing the best cabling, and using NetWare utility programs.

For more information about *Inside NetWare*, you should contact:

The Cobb Group, Software Journal Publishers

9420 Bunsen Parkway, Suite 300

Louisville, Kentucky 40220

Tel: (800) 223-8720

(502) 491-1900

Fax: (502) 491-8050

NETWARE CONNECTION

NetWare Connection is a technical publication of NetWare Users' International. It is a mixture of basic NetWare management and solutions to thorny network problems. It also lists some questions and answers from Novell tech-support lines. Each monthly issue contains about 24 pages. You can contact NetWare Users' International at:

122 East 1700 South

Provo, UT 84606

Tel: (800) 228-4684

(801) 429-7000

Training

Both Computer Associates and Novell realize the need for technical education about their products. Both companies recognize several authorized training sites.

CLIPPER TRAINING

There are several companies that offer training in Clipper, as listed below. Greg Lief, coauthor of this book, is the president of Grumpfish, which offers training courses as well. All course material has been written by Greg himself.

Grumpfish, Inc.

2450 Lancaster Drive, NE, Suite 206

Salem, OR 97305

Tel: (800) 367-7613

(503) 588-1815

The Amulet Consulting Group
1642 Stanford Avenue
Redondo Beach, CA 90024
Tel: (310) 798-3985

Advanced FI
1500 Skokie Blvd., Suite 8
Northbrook, IL 60062
Tel: (708) 480-8840

DSW Group
1775 The Exchange, Suite 640
Atlanta, GA 30339
Tel: (800) 356-9644
    (404) 953-0393

Financial Dynamics
5201 Leesburg Pike, Suite 701
Falls Church, VA 22041
Tel: (800) 486-5201
    (703) 671-3003

dc Soft Gmbh
Machtlfinger Strasse 26
8000 Munich 70
Germany
Tel: (49) (89) 78 58 910
Fax: (49) (89) 78 58 9111

You can contact these companies for information about their courses and locations. Most of the companies offer on-site training as well as training at their places of business.

NETWARE TRAINING

Novell certifies companies to provide NetWare courses and training. The list of certified trainers is added to frequently, so your best bet is to call Novell and ask for the ones in your area.

Professional developer services

Novell has a program called the Professional Developer's Program (PDP), which gives NetWare-aware application developers streamlined access to NetWare products, development tools, and support services. Through the program you can get discounts on additional copies of NetWare OS and communications products with a one-year renewable license.

Joining the PDP is the only way to get access to some Novell Software Development Kits (SDKs). There is a private forum on CompuServe for PDP members. In addition, through the PDP, Novell offers some marketing support.

This program is available to professional developers of NetWare-aware software products. Contact Novell's PDP in the U.S. and Canada at:

   1-800-RED-WORD

International developers should contact their local Novell office regarding the PDP features in their area. Services vary from country to country.

Appendix C:
Using the Disk Accompanying this Book

The disk provided with this book contains the source code to all the functions listed in Appendix A. In addition, a LIB file has been put together to allow you to plug the functions into your applications quickly.

About the source code

This book was developed while Clipper 5.2 was still in beta. Therefore, due to printing schedules and times, some of the code on the disk might have been updated and may be a little different than the version printed in the text. You should plan on using the code from the disk for your development work. It's a lot easier than typing the programs in yourself, anyway. In addition, please take the time to print and read the README file on the disk. It contains up-to-the-minute information about the function library and EMAIL application.

The disk contains the following five subdirectories for the code from the book:

LIB This directory contains the BLNET.LIB file. This file should be copied into the directory where you keep your Clipper library files. Make sure the LIB environment variable is set to this directory when you link an application using the library.

For example, assuming your libraries are kept in C:\CLIPPER5\LIB and the book's disk is in drive A, you would enter

```
copy A:\LIB\BLNET.LIB c:\clipper5\lib\BLNET.LIB
```

HELP The HELP directory contains an NG-compatible on-line help file. The Clipper package includes an NG reader program that allows you to access pop-up help from within your editor. The BLNET.NG file contains an on-line help file and should be copied to the directory in which you placed the on-line Clipper help files.

For example, assuming your help files are kept in C:\NG\ and the book's disk is in drive A, you would enter

```
copy A:\HELP\BLNET.NG c:\ng\BLNET.NG
```

INCLUDE The INCLUDE directory contains the header files necessary to compile the functions in this book. You should copy the contents of this directory into your INCLUDE directory and be sure to set the INCLUDE environment variable to that directory.

For example, assuming your header files are kept in C:\CLIPPER5\INCLUDE and the book's disk is in drive A, you would enter

```
copy A:\INCLUDE\*.CH c:\clipper5\include\*.CH
```

SOURCE The SOURCE directory contains the source code to all the functions in this book. It also contains the Object files for the non-Clipper components of the library. Finally, it contains a MAKE file and a RESPONSE file to allow you to remake the library.

If you do not want to modify the functions, then you do not need this directory. If you want to add additional functions or make changes to the functions, you should copy all the files to the directory containing your Clipper source code. Be sure the directory exists before you copy the files. For example, if your source code is in C:\CLIPPER5\SOURCE\BLNET\ and the book's disk is in drive A, you would enter

```
copy A:\SOURCE\*.* c:\clipper5\source\blnet
```

EMAIL The EMAIL directory contains the source code to the EMAIL program discussed in Chapters 13 and 14 of this book. It also contain two link files, one for Blinker and one for RTLINK, and a MAKE file to create the program. There is a batch file called DOIT that you can use to compile and link the program. This file assumes that Clipper and RTLINK are in your path. A similar file called DOITB.BAT uses Clipper and Blinker to create the EMAIL program.

You should copy all the files to the directory containing your Clipper source code. The following example assumes that the files are in C:\CLIPPER5\SOURCE\EMAIL and that the book's disk is in drive A. Be sure the directory exists before you copy the files.

```
copy a:\EMAIL\*.* c:\clipper5\source\email
```

There is also a compressed version of the EMAIL executable program on the root directory of the disk. If you wish to install this on your computer, change to the directory in which you want the program stored on your hard disk and enter the following command:

```
A:\UNZIP A:\EMAILEXE
```

This will create a file called EMAIL.EXE that is a working version of the EMAIL program.

Nanforum Toolkit

The disk also contains a copy of the Nanforum Toolkit, which is a public-domain collection of functions that can be used with Clipper. It was put together through the collaborative efforts of many Clipper developers, who all felt that some basic functionality should be added to the Clipper language without having to resort to a third-party library. Glenn Scott is the volunteer coordinator of the project.

The Nanforum Toolkit has gone through several releases and has grown substantially since its beginnings. The library contains over 200 functions broken into the following categories:

Array	Game
Conversions	Keyboard/Mouse
DOS/BIOS	Math
Database	Menu/Prompts
Date and Time	NetWare
Environment	String manipulation
File I/O	Video

HISTORY OF THE TOOLKIT

In October and November of 1990, a discussion on the evolution of third-party products, vendors, and marketing took place on the CompuServe Information Service's Nantucket Forum (NANFORUM). During this discussion, a forum subscriber named Alexander Santic suggested the idea of a user-supported Clipper function library, available to everyone on the CompuServe Information Service. A number of subscribers, including several Clipper third-party developers and some Nantucket employees, expressed their support.

Release 1.0 of the Nanforum Toolkit was made available in April 1991 and had nearly 150 functions. By the time release 2.0 was released in August 1991, release 1.0 had been downloaded nearly 700 times by CompuServe users. By October 1992, release 2.0 had been downloaded over 2100 times, and the source code had been downloaded nearly 1500 times. In addition, release 2.0 was placed on the massive Internet archive site called SIMTEL20, where it was downloaded by Clipper users worldwide. Over the course of the following year, seven patches were issued, each one gathering nearly 1000 downloads.

Computer Associates International, Inc. acquired Nantucket in the summer of 1992 and subsequently changed the name NANFORUM to simply CLIPPER. In addition, the Clipper product itself was renamed CA-CLIPPER. Despite the name changes, forum members decided to keep the toolkit's original name, "Nanforum Toolkit," partly for nostalgia.

The toolkit exists today because of the ongoing efforts of Glenn Scott, the librarian of the toolkit, and Forest Belt and Leo Letendre, who prepare the documentation. The following people have also contributed to the Nanforum library: Dave Adams, Isa Asudeh, Gary Baren, David Barrett, Joseph D. Booth, Sr., Jeff Bryant, Bob Clarke, Brice de Ganahl, Robert A. DiFalco, Paul Ferrara, Jo W. French, Jim Gale, Terry Hackett, David Husnian, John F. Kaster, Steve Kolterman, Joseph LaCour, Steve Larsen, Greg Lief, Brian Loesgen, Ted Means, David Minter, Clayton Neff, Ralph Oliver, Don Opperthauser, James J. Orlowski, M.D., David A. Richardson, Mike Schinkel, John Kaster, Tom Leylan, Alexander B. Spencer, Eric Splaver, Mike Taylor, Paul Tucker, Steven Tyrakowski, Rick Whitt, Keith A. Wire, and James R. Zack.

INSTALLING THE TOOLKIT

The toolkit files are all in a directory called TOOLKIT. Within that directory there are two files, NFLIB.ZIP and NFSRC.ZIP. Due to the size of the source code (over 900K worth of files) and the libraries, the toolkit files are stored in two compressed files.

Installing LIB and the on-line help files The library itself and the Norton Guide help file are both stored in the NFLIB.ZIP file. To install the library and help system, perform the following steps:

1 Create a temporary directory on your hard disk.

    MD C:\TEMP

2 Switch to that directory.

    CD \TEMP

3 Copy the NFLIB.ZIP file from the book's disk. (This example assumes the disk is in drive A.)

    COPY A:\TOOLKIT\NFLIB.ZIP C:\TEMP

4 Decompress the files.

    A:\UNZIP NFLIB

    This process will create two files on drive C, NANFOR.LIB and NANFOR.NG.

5 Copy the NANFOR.LIB file to the directory containing your Clipper libraries. (This example assumes they are in C:\CLIPPER5\LIB.)

    copy NANFOR.LIB c:\clipper5\lib\NANFOR.LIB

6 Copy the NANFOR.NG file to the directory containing your on-line help files. (This example assumes they are in C:\NG.)

    copy NANFOR.NG c:\ng\NANFOR.NG

7 You may now delete the files in the temporary directory and remove the directory from your hard disk.

    del NANFOR.*
    cd\
    rd temp

The library and help files are now installed on your computer.

Installing the source-code files The source-code files are stored in the NFSRC.ZIP file on the disk. The source code is over 900K, so be sure you have enough room on your computer. To install the source code, perform the following steps:

1 Create a temporary directory on your hard disk.

    MD C:\TEMP

2 Switch to that directory.

```
CD \TEMP
```

3 Copy the NFSRC.ZIP file from the book's disk. (This example assumes the disk is in drive A.)

```
COPY A:\TOOLKIT\NFSRC.ZIP C:\TEMP
```

4 Decompress the files.

```
A:\UNZIP NFSRC
```

This process will create tons of files on drive C.

5 Copy all the files to the directory containing your Clipper source code. (This example assumes they are in C:\CLIPPER5\SOURCE\NANFOR.) Be sure the directory exists before you copy the files.

```
copy *.* c:\clipper5\source\nanfor
```

6 You may now delete the files in the temporary directory and remove the directory from your hard disk.

```
del *.*
cd\
rd temp
```

The source-code files are now installed on your computer.

Index

Numbers in boldface designate figures or tables.

A

ACCOUNT_BALANCE property, 192, 195, 198–199
ACCOUNT_HOLDS property, 192, 199
accounting, using TBROWSE in, 131–139
ACCOUNT_LOCKOUT property, 192, 207
ACCOUNT_SERVERS property, 192, 207
ACHOICE() function, 3–4, 250–251
active hubs, 8
ADDREC() function, **57**
API set, NetWare, 66
  accessing via DOS interrupts, 67–69
  calling, 69–70
APPEND BLANK command, **48,** 49–50, 53
APPEND FROM command, 106
applications. *See also particular application*
  controlling with semaphores. *See* semaphores
  loading into high memory, 10–12
  messages between. *See* message files
appointment calendar, functions for, 153–160, 160–163
APPT_CFG() function, 160–163
ArcNet, cabling, 7, 8
ASC() function, 71
AUTOEXEC.BAT file, 12
AVERAGE command, 106

B

banners, 228–229
BEGINAREA command, 14, 15, 16
bindery, 183
  organization of, 184–197
  reasons to use, 183–184
  record formats, 217–218
bindery files, 209, 216–217
bindery objects
  adding, 209–210

components, 185–186
file server as, 206–208
finding, 187–188
group as, 201–204
identifying, 189–190
list of types, **185–186**
print queue as, 205–206
properties. *See* object properties
removing, 210–211
renaming, 211
security levels, 188–189, **218**
user as, 197–201
user ID, 190–191
BINDERY.CH file, 188, 194
black box routines, 3
Blinker, 16–17
BLNET.LIB file, 303
BLOCKS_READ property, 192, 207
BLOCKS_WRITTEN property, 192, 207
broadcast messages, 254–257
browsing databases. *See* TBROWSE object class
buffers, 44–45, 50
bytes, function translation and, 71

C

cables, 7–8
calendar, appointment, 153–160, 160–163
CAPTURE command. *See* capture files
capture files, 221–222
　accessing CAPTURE services, 222
　canceling captures, 226–227
　closing captures, 225–226
　flushing captures, 222, 223–224
　starting captures, 222, 223
cards, network, 6
CD-ROM device, controlling access to, 171
.CDX files, 33–35
CHAT program, 260–261

CHECKLOG program, 299–300
CHKMAIL component, 292, 316
clients, bindery and, 184
Clipper
　compatibility with earlier versions, 32–33
　as compiler, 2
Clipper 5.0 Insights: Object Classes, 125
CLOSE_APP() function, 178
CLOSE_LOCK() function, 179–180
CNR() function, 71
coaxial cable, 7
color in EMAIL system, 297–298
commands, 2–3, 46–48. *See also particular command or subject*
COMMIT command, 45, **48**, 50, 153
communications between workstations. *See* message files
CONFIG.SYS file, 12
configuration files, 145–146
　active, 146–147, 153–163
　CONFIG.SYS file, 12
　passive, 146–152
　reasons to use, 146
　system file, 153–163
connection tables, 266–269
connectors, 7–8
CONNECT_TIME property, 192, 207
console operations, 287–288
console privileges, 281–282
corrupt index files, 37, 41
COUNT command, 106–107
CPU registers, 67

D

database files, 29–30. *See also* files
　browsing. *See* TBROWSE object class
　buffers for, 44–45
　locking. *See* locking files and records
　NETERR() function and, 19
　opening. *See also* files, accessing

determining existence and type of file, 76
file attributes, 80–82
memo files and, 77–80
shared vs. exclusive mode, 82–86
USE command and, 75
semaphores. *See* semaphores
date, file server, 283–284, 288
DBAPPEND() function, 49–50
DBCOMMIT() functions, 50
DBDELETE() function, 51
.DBF files. *See* database files
DBFNDX driver, 99
DBFSIX driver, 99
DBRECALL() function, 53
DBSETINDEX() function, 86
DBSKIP() function, 54
DBUNLOCK() function, 54
DBUSEAREA() function, 55
dedicated servers, 8
default server, 275, 277
DELETE command, **48,** 51
device drivers, using alternate for file opening, 99
DISK_STORAGE property, 192, 207
DOS
  buffers, 45
  Clipper commands and, 2–3, 46–48
  file and record locks and, 110–111
  file attributes, 80–81
  interrupts, 2, 3–5, 59–61
  on networks, 2–5
  printing in, 237–240
drivers (device), using alternate for file opening, 99

E

electronic mail, 291. *See also* EMAIL program
EMAIL program
  checking mail, 292, 316–317

components, 292
configuring color and formats, 297–298
creating files, 321–322
databases required by, 303–304
directory structure, 293
erasing mail, 295, 297, 319–321
forwarding messages, 296
main menu, **294**
managing file size, 298–299
memos, 250–251, 322–324
network and, 292–293
printing messages, 296
reading mail, 292, 293–296, 310–316
replying to messages, 296
selecting users to receive, 316
sending mail, 292, 296–297, 317–319
sorting mail, 294–295
source code, 304–324. *See also particular EMAIL operation*
tips for use, 299–300
ENDAREA command, 14, 16
Erase option, 297
errors
  assumptions regarding, 24–25
  corruption and, 37
  function for repairing, 94–99. *See also* files, accessing
  functions for checking, 19–21, 41–43
  index file locks and, 43–44
  return codes for VALIDDBF() function, **77**
EtherNet cabling, 7, 8
exclusive files
  database files and, 55
  file opening and, 18, 21, 82
  for indexes, 87
  locking and, 104–105
  in OPENEM() program, 91
Extend System interface, 14

F

fiber optic cable, 7
file attributes, database file opening and, 80–82
FILE() function, 76
FILELOCK() function, 22–23
files. *See also particular file type*
    accessing
        alternate device drivers for, 99
        Clipper commands and functions for, 48–55
        .DBF files. *See* database files, opening
        failure, 27
        with FOPEN() function, 2–3, 99–100
        index files, 38, 39–40, 86–90
        with NET_USE() function, 57, 82–86
        with OPENEM() function, 90–94
        repairing errors in, 94–99
        with USE command, 18–21, 46–47
    changing on networks, 21
    locking. *See* locking files and records
file servers, 1, 8
    accessing identification and operating information, 285–286
    as bindery object types, **185,** 206–207
    attaching to, 269–272
    checking console privileges, 281–282
    contacting, 265–266
        accessing information about, 278–280
        clearing connections, 287–288
        connection tables, 266–269
        logging in and out, 273–275
    date and time, 283–284, 288
    detaching from, 272–273
    determining login status, 282–283
    determining network shell version, 280–281
    downing, 287
    functions for, 207–208
    hierarchy, 275–278
    retrieving network installation information, 284–285
FILESERV program, 207–208
FILLOCK() function, **57**
FIXEM() function, 94–99
flags
    Clipper work area, 44–45
    object, 186, 191
    printer, 227–233
FLOCK() function, 22, 23, 51–52, 107
FOPEN() function, 2–3, 46
FREE_SEMA() function, 169–170
FSDATETIME() function, 283–284
FT_DISPFILE() function, 241
FT_INT86() function, 67–69, 222, 237
FT_PEEK() function, 268–269
functions. *See also particular function or subject*
    alphabetical listing of, 327–405
    DOS, Clipper commands and, 2–3, 46–48
    translating between NetWare and Clipper, 71–73
    user-defined, in indexes, 38, 40

G

GETAMSG() function, 248–252
GETFATTR() function, 81–82
GETREADER() function, 117–123
GET system, 251–252, 305–306
GFTIMEOUT() function, 119–121
global settings and parameters. *See* configuration files
GROUP_MEMBERS property, 192, 201
groups
    as bindery object types, **185**, 201
    functions for, 201–204

GROUPS_I'M_IN property, 192, 197
groupware, 291
GT.OBJ file, 8

H

handles, semaphore, 172
hardware, basic network setup, 5–9
headers
    in EMAIL program, 305
    in file structure, 29–30, 31
high memory, loading programs into, 10–12
HOT UPDATE flag, 44
hubs, 8

I

IDENTIFICATION property, 192, 197, 201
IDs, bindery and, 185, 190–191, 197
.IDX files, 33–35
index files, 31–33. *See also* files
    compatibility with earlier Clipper versions, 32–33
    corruption, 37, 41
    dBASE files, 35–37
    FoxPro files, 33–35
    locking, 33, 40, 43–44, 111
    messages and, 248
    opening, 86–90. *See also* files, accessing
    tips for network use, 37–41
    USE command and, 21
INDEX ON command, 38–39, 107
INGROUP program, 202–203
integers, function translation and, 71
interrupts, DOS, 2, 3–5, 59–61
IPX, 9, 254

K

keys. *See* index files
keywords, electronic mail and, 295

L

LET'S_CHAT() function, 260–261
library (.LIB) files, 13–18, 303. *See also* files
linking, memory and, 13–18
LOADHIGH program, 10–12
locking files and records, 21–23, 103
    with APPEND BLANK command, 49
    commands requiring file lock, **106**
    compatibility of earlier Clipper versions and, 32–33
    compatibility with other programs, 110
    DOS function for, 47–48
    failed locks, 27, 112–113
    with FLOCK() function 22, 23, 51–52, 107
    indexes and, 33, 40, 43–44, 111
    levels of, 104–110
    with LOCKS program, 57–58
    mechanism of, 110–111
    multiple records, 113–114, 116–117, 178–180
    multi-user programs and, 117–123
    with N_LOCKS program. *See* N_LOCKS program
    persistency, 112
    with RLOCK() function, 23, **48**, 53–54, 108, 114
    with semaphores, 178–180
    single-record updates, 114–116
    temporary files and multiple-record updates, 113–114
    temporary locking, 117–123
    text and memory files, 117
    unlocking, 54, 114–116

LOCKS program
  enhancing. *See* N_LOCKS program functions, 57
logging in and out
  determining status, 282–283
  functions for, 273–275
LOGIN_CONTROL property, 192, 197–198
long integers, function translation and, 71

M

mail, electronic. *See* EMAIL program
MAILBOX file, 292–293, 298–299, 304
mean number, 106
MEMOEDIT() function, 250–251, 322
memory
  buffers, 44–45
  file servers and, 8
  loading programs into high, 10–12
  locking memory files, 117
memos
  in database files, 77–70
  EMAIL, 322
  internetwork, 250–251
message files. *See also* EMAIL program
  NetWare. *See* NetWare, messages
  placing messages in, 252–253
  retrieving messages from, 248–249
  structure, 247–248
  wait states, 249–252
MKFILE() function, 321
modes
  broadcast, 254–255
  exclusive vs. shared. *See* exclusive files, shared files
MS–DOS Programmer's Reference Manual, 237
MSGMODE() function, 254–255
MULTLOCK program, 116–117

N

N_ADD2SET() function, 215
N_ADDOBJECT() function, 209–210
N_ADDPROPERTY() function, 212–213
Nanforum Toolkit, 67, 241
N_ATTACH() function, 269–272
N_BINDLEVEL() function, 188–189, 190, 306
N_CANCELCAP() function, 226–227
N_CAPFLAGS() function, 229–233, 234
N_CHGVALUE() function, 214
N_CLEARCON() function, 287–288
N_CLOSECAP() function, 225–226, 234
N_CLOSEPIPE() function, 259–260
N_CLOSESEM() function, 174–175
N_CONINFO() function, 278–280
N_CONSOLE() function, 258–259
N_CONSPRIV() function, 281, **282**
N_CONTABLE() function, 266–269
N_DEFSERVER() function, 277
N_DELFROMSET() function, 215–216
N_DELOBJECT() function, 210–211
N_DELPROPERTY() function, 213–214
N_DETACH() function, 272–273
N_DOWN() function, 287
.NDX files, 35–37
NET_ADDRESS property, 192, 206
NETERR() function, 18–19, **40,** 44
NETNAME() function, 53
NET_USE() function, 57, 82–86, 306
NetWare
  API set, 66
    accessing via DOS interrupts, 67–69
    calling, 69–70
  bindery and. *See* bindery

buffers for, 45
getting information about, 284–286
messages
    broadcast, 254–257
    pipe, 254, 257–261
    semaphore services. *See* semaphores, NetWare services
translating functions between Clipper and, 71–73
NETWARE() function, 69–70
network buffers, 45
network cards, 6
NETWORK.INI file, 65–66, 145–146
network operating systems, 9–10, 18–23
networks, 1
    buffers, 45
    cards, 6
    DOS and, 2–5
    file access, 18–21
    file cabinet analogy, 18
    file locking, 21–23
    hardware, 5–8
    index files on. *See also* index files
        creating, 87
        using, 37–41
    installation information, 284–285
    linking and, 13–18
    memory and, 10–17
    printing on. *See* printing
    programming guidelines for, 23–27
    shell programs, 9–10, 280–281
    software, 8–9
    TBROWSE and, 131
NETX, 9–10, 265–266
NEW keyword, 55
N_EXAMSEM() function, 173–174
N_FLUSHCAP() function, 222, 223–224, 234
N_GETMSG() function, 255–256
N_GETPIPE() function, 259

NICs, 6
N_INIT() function, 66
N_ISINSET() function, 204, 281, **282**
N_ISMANAGER() function, 201, 202–203
N_ISMEMBER() function, 201, 202–203
N_LOCKS program, 57–58
    code for, 58–65
    configuration files for, 65–66
N_LOGIN() function, 273–274
N_LOGOUT() function, 274–275
N_MANAGERS() function, 201, 202
N_MEMBERS() function, 201, 202
N_MISCINFO() function, 285–286
N_OBJECTID() function, 190, 316, 233–234
N_OBJECTLIST() function, 234–235
N_OBJECTNAME() function, 189–190
NODE_CONTROL property, 192, 198
nondedicated servers, 8
NONSHARED() function, 91
N_OPENPIPE() function, 257–258
N_OPENSEM() function, 172–173
Novell networks. *See* NetWare
NOVTERM library, 8
N_PREFSERVER() function, 275, 276
N_PRIMESERVER() function, 277–278
N_PRINTQS() function, 233
N_PROPERTIES() function, 193
N_PROPVAL() function, 195–197
N_QPOSITION() function, 235–236
N_QREMOVE() function, 236
N_RENOBJECT() function, 211
N_SCANBINDERY function, 187–188
N_SENDMSG() function, 255
N_SENDPIPE() function, 258–259
N_SERVLOGIN() function, 282–283
N_SETDATE() function, 288
N_SHELLVER() function, 280–281

N_SIGNALSEM() function, 175, 176
N_STARTCAP() function, 222, 223
NTXCHK program, 41–42
.NTX files. *See* index files
NTXLOCK2.OBJ, 32–33
numbers
    finding mean, 106
    summing, 107
N_WAITSEM() function, 175–176
N_WHATNET() function, 67–69
N_WHO2BLAME() function, 284–285
N_WHOAMI() function, 190–191, 311

O

object classes, 125. *See also* TBROWSE object class
object (.OBJ) files, 8, 13–18, 32–33. *See also* files
object properties, 191. *See also particular object type*
    accessing, 193
    adding, 212–213
    deleting, 213–214
    names, 194
    set properties, 215–216
    standard properties, 191–192, 194
    values, 195–197, 214
objects, bindery
    adding, 209–210
    components, 185–186
    file server as, 206–208
    finding, 187–188
    group as, 201–204
    identifying, 189–190
    list of types, **185–186**
    print queue as, 205–206
    properties. *See* object properties
    removing, 210–211
    renaming, 211
    security levels, 188–189, **218**
    user as, 197–201
    user ID, 190–191
OBJ_SUPERVISORS property, 192, 201
OLD_PASSWORD property, 192, 198
OPENEM() function, 90–94
OPEN_EM() function, 19, 21
opening files
    alternate device drivers for, 99
    Clipper commands and functions for, 48–55
    .DBF files. *See* database files, opening
    failure, 27
    with FOPEN() function, 2–3, 99–100
    index files, 38, 39–40, 86–90
    with NET_USE() function, 57, 82–86
    with OPENEM() function, 90–94
    repairing errors in, 94–99
    with USE command, 18–21, 46–47
operating systems
    DOS. *See* DOS
    network. *See* network operating systems
OPERATORS property, 192, 207
overlays, 13–14

P

PACK command, 51, 53, 105
packets, 69
Pack/Index option, 298–299, 319
passive hubs, 8
PASSIVE program, 148–152
passwords, object properties and, 192, 197–198
PASTDUE program, 133–139
P_CANCEL() function, 240, 243–244
P_END() function, 241, 244
phone calls, TBROWSE application for monitoring, 139–143

PICKUSERS() function, 316
pipe messages, 254, 257–261
POSTBOX file, 292–293, 303–304
preferred server, 275, 276
primary server, 277–278
printers. *See* printing
PRINT.EXE program, 237–238
print form names, 228
printing
    accessing network printers, 221–222
        with capture files. *See* capture files
        setting flags, 227–233
    canceling, 226–227, 240, 243–244
    cleaning up print environment, 241, 244
    Clipper on nondedicated server and, 8
    determining place of output, 240, 242–243
    with DOS, 237–240
    electronic-mail messages, 296
    maximum printers on network, 228
    queues. *See* print queues
    starting, 240, 243
print queues, 221, 233–237
    as bindery object types, **185,** 205–206
    DOS, 237–240
    printer flag for, 228
programs. *See also particular program*
    controlling with semaphores. *See* semaphores
    loading into high memory, 10–12
    messages between. *See* message files
properties, object, 191. *See also particluar object type*
    accessing, 193
    adding, 212–213
    deleting, 213–214
    names, 194
    set properties, 215–216
    standard properties, 191–192, 194
    values, 195–197, 214
P_START() function, 240, 243
PURGEMAIL() function, 319
PUTAMSG() function, 253
P_WHERE() function, 240, 242–243

Q

Q_ADD() function, 238–239
Q_CANCEL() function, 240
Q_DIRECTORY property, 192, 205
QEMM, 12
Q_INSTALLED() function, 237–238
Q_OPERATORS property, 192, 205
Q_QPER program, 205–206
QRAM, 10
Q_REMOVE() function, 239
Q_SERVERS property, 192, 205
queues, print, 221, 233–237
    as bindery object types, **185,** 205–206
    DOS, 237–240
    printer flag for, 228
Q_USERS property, 192, 205

R

RAM. *See* memory
Read option, 293–294
READCONFIG() function, 147–149
READMAIL component, 292, 310
RECALL command, **48,** 53
RECLOCK() function, 54, **57,** 58
records
    adding, **48,** 49–50, 53
    bindery, 217–218
    deleting, **48,** 51, 53
    finding next, **48,** 54, 153
    locking. *See* locking files and records
    updating, 52, 54

REFRESHALL() method, 127–131
refreshing screen, 127–131
REINDEX command, avoiding, 21, 38, 105
repeaters, 8
REPLACE commands, 52, 54
Reply packets, 69
report log, program for checking, 299–300
Request packets, 69
REQUESTS_MADE property, 192, 207
RG–58 cable, 7
RG–62 cable, 7
RLOCK() function, 23, **49,** 53–54, 108, 114
root area, 13–14
RTLink, 14–16

S

screen, refreshing, 127–131
security, bindery and levels, 183–184, 186, 188–189, **218**
SECURITY_EQUALS property, 192, 198
semaphores, 165, 171–172, 175–176
    accessing, 168–170
    creating, 166–168
    examples
        controlling access to CD-ROM device, 171
        limiting number of users, 177–178
        record locking, 178–180
    locking, 108–110
    naming, 172
    NetWare services, 171–172
        closing semaphores, 174–175
        examining semaphore value, 173–174
        opening semaphores, 172–173
    reasons to use, 165–166

SENDMAIL component, 292, 317
Send Mail screen, 296
servers
    bindery and, 184
    file servers. *See* file servers
SETAPPT() function, 155–160
SET DEFAULT TO command, 76
SET() function, 76
SET INDEX TO command, 39
SET ORDER TO command, 40
set properties, 215–216
shared files
    database files and, 55
    file opening and, 18, 21, 82
    indexes on, 38–39, 87
    in OPENEM() program, 91
    record locking and, 107
SHARED() function, 91
shell programs, network, 9–10, 280–281
SKIP command, **48,** 54, 153
SPX protocol, 9
START_LOCK() function, 178–179
STATIC arrays, 90
SUM command, 107
SYS.MAIL directory, 209
SYSCON program, 184
system file
    example, 153–163
    reading, 153
    structure, 154
system information
    console operations, 287–288
    file server, 281–286
    workstation, 275–281

T

table, interrupt, 4–5
TBROWSE object class, 125–127
    in EMAIL program, 310–311

examples
   accounting application, 131–139
   with REFRESHALL() method, 127–130
   telephone-call monitoring, 139–143
   networks and, 131
   wait states and, 249–250
telephone monitoring, using TBROWSE in, 139–143
temporary files, locking, 113–114
text files, locking, 117
386Max, 12–13
time, file-server, 283–284, 288
TOTAL command, 107
translating functions between NetWare and Clipper, 71–73
twisted-pair cable, 7

U

UDFs in indexes, 38, 40
UNIQUE program, 113
UNLOCK command, **48,** 54
USE_APP() function, 177
USE command, 3, 18–21, 46, **49,** 55
USER_DEFAULTS property, 192, 207
user-defined functions in indexes, 38, 40
users
   as bindery object types, **185,** 197–201
   EMAIL function to select, 316
   functions for retrieving user information, 199–201
   IDs, bindery and, 190–191
   limiting number of, via semaphores, 177–178
USESEMA() function, 167–168

V

VALIDDBF() function, 77–80
VALIDNTX() function, 87–90, 306
VIA option, 99

W

WAIT_SEMA() function, 169–170
wait states, messages and, 249–252
WarpLink, 17–18
WHAT_IS() function, 147, 149–152
workstations, 1
   accessing information about, 275–281
   accessing name of, 53
   communications between. *See* message files
   connecting to file server. *See* file servers, contacting
WRITEMAIL() function, 318

X

XLATE program, 71–73

Z

ZAP command, 105

■ TO RECEIVE 5¼-INCH DISK(S)

The Ziff-Davis Press software contained on the 3½-inch disk included with this book is also available in 5¼-inch format. If you would like to receive the software in the 5¼-inch format, please return the 3½-inch disk with your name and address to:

Disk Exchange
Ziff-Davis Press
5903 Christie Avenue
Emeryville, CA 94608

■ END-USER LICENSE AGREEMENT

READ THIS AGREEMENT CAREFULLY BEFORE BUYING THIS BOOK. BY BUYING THE BOOK AND USING THE PROGRAM LISTINGS, DISKS, AND PROGRAMS REFERRED TO BELOW, YOU ACCEPT THE TERMS OF THIS AGREEMENT.

The program listings included in this book and the programs included on the diskette(s) contained in the package on the opposite page ("Disks") are proprietary products of Ziff-Davis Press and/or third party suppliers ("Suppliers"). The program listings and programs are hereinafter collectively referred to as the "Programs." Ziff-Davis Press and the Suppliers retain ownership of the Disks and copyright to the Programs, as their respective interests may appear. The Programs and the copy of the Disks provided are licensed (not sold) to you under the conditions set forth herein.

<u>License.</u> You may use the Disks on any compatible computer, provided that the Disks are used on only one computer and by one user at a time.

<u>Restrictions.</u> You may not commercially distribute the Disks or the Programs or otherwise reproduce, publish, or distribute or otherwise use the Disks or the Programs in any manner that may infringe any copyright or other proprietary right of Ziff-Davis Press, the Suppliers, or any other party or assign, sublicense, or otherwise transfer the Disks or this agreement to any other party unless such party agrees to accept the terms and conditions of this agreement. This license and your right to use the Disks and the Programs automatically terminates if you fail to comply with any provision of this agreement.

U.S. GOVERNMENT RESTRICTED RIGHTS. The disks and the programs are provided with **RESTRICTED RIGHTS**. Use, duplication, or disclosure by the Government is subject to restrictions as set forth in subparagraph (c)(1)(ii) of the Rights in Technical Data and Computer Software Clause at DFARS (48 CFR 252.277-7013). The Proprietor of the compilation of the Programs and the Disks is Ziff-Davis Press, 5903 Christie Avenue, Emeryville, CA 94608.

<u>Limited Warranty.</u> Ziff-Davis Press warrants the physical Disks to be free of defects in materials and workmanship under normal use for a period of 30 days from the purchase date. If Ziff-Davis Press receives written notification within the warranty period of defects in materials or workmanship in the physical Disks, and such notification is determined by Ziff-Davis Press to be correct, Ziff-Davis Press will, at its option, replace the defective Disks or refund a prorata portion of the purchase price of the book. **THESE ARE YOUR SOLE REMEDIES FOR ANY BREACH OF WARRANTY.**

EXCEPT AS SPECIFICALLY PROVIDED ABOVE, THE DISKS AND THE PROGRAMS ARE PROVIDED "AS IS" WITHOUT ANY WARRANTY OF ANY KIND. NEITHER ZIFF-DAVIS PRESS NOR THE SUPPLIERS MAKE ANY WARRANTY OF ANY KIND AS TO THE ACCURACY OR COMPLETENESS OF THE DISKS OR THE PROGRAMS OR THE RESULTS TO BE OBTAINED FROM USING THE DISKS OR THE PROGRAMS AND NEITHER ZIFF-DAVIS PRESS NOR THE SUPPLIERS SHALL BE RESPONSIBLE FOR ANY CLAIMS ATTRIBUTABLE TO ERRORS, OMISSIONS, OR OTHER INACCURACIES IN THE DISKS OR THE PROGRAMS. THE ENTIRE RISK AS TO THE RESULTS AND PERFORMANCE OF THE DISKS AND THE PROGRAMS IS ASSUMED BY THE USER. FURTHER, NEITHER ZIFF-DAVIS PRESS NOR THE SUPPLIERS MAKE ANY REPRESENTATIONS OR WARRANTIES, EITHER EXPRESS OR IMPLIED, WITH RESPECT TO THE DISKS OR THE PROGRAMS, INCLUDING BUT NOT LIMITED TO, THE QUALITY, PERFORMANCE, MERCHANTABILITY, OR FITNESS FOR A PARTICULAR PURPOSE OF THE DISKS OR THE PROGRAMS. IN NO EVENT SHALL ZIFF-DAVIS PRESS OR THE SUPPLIERS BE LIABLE FOR DIRECT, INDIRECT, SPECIAL, INCIDENTAL, OR CONSEQUENTIAL DAMAGES ARISING OUT THE USE OF OR INABILITY TO USE THE DISKS OR THE PROGRAMS OR FOR ANY LOSS OR DAMAGE OF ANY NATURE CAUSED TO ANY PERSON OR PROPERTY AS A RESULT OF THE USE OF THE DISKS OR THE PROGRAMS, EVEN IF ZIFF-DAVIS PRESS OR THE SUPPLIERS HAVE BEEN SPECIFICALLY ADVISED OF THE POSSIBILITY OF SUCH DAMAGES. NEITHER ZIFF-DAVIS PRESS NOR THE SUPPLIERS ARE RESPONSIBLE FOR ANY COSTS INCLUDING, BUT NOT LIMITED TO, THOSE INCURRED AS A RESULT OF LOST PROFITS OR REVENUE, LOSS OF USE OF THE DISKS OR THE PROGRAMS, LOSS OF DATA, THE COSTS OF RECOVERING SOFTWARE OR DATA, OR THIRD-PARTY CLAIMS. IN NO EVENT WILL ZIFF-DAVIS PRESS' OR THE SUPPLIERS' LIABILITY FOR ANY DAMAGES TO YOU OR ANY OTHER PARTY EVER EXCEED THE PRICE OF THIS BOOK. NO SALES PERSON OR OTHER REPRESENTATIVE OF ANY PARTY INVOLVED IN THE DISTRIBUTION OF THE DISKS IS AUTHORIZED TO MAKE ANY MODIFICATIONS OR ADDITIONS TO THIS LIMITED WARRANTY.

Some states do not allow the exclusion or limitation of implied warranties or limitation of liability for incidental or consequential damages, so the above limitation or exclusion may not apply to you.

<u>General.</u> Ziff-Davis Press and the Suppliers retain all rights not expressly granted. Nothing in this license constitutes a waiver of the rights of Ziff-Davis Press or the Suppliers under the U.S. Copyright Act or any other Federal or State Law, international treaty, or foreign law.